C000133154

THE COSMIC CONNECTION

Worldwide Crop Formations and ET Contacts

MICHAEL HESEMANN

Gateway Books, Bath, UK

I dedicate this book to my dear
Natalia Zahradnivova
in memory of her first trip to the land of
the circles, and in gratitude for her loving company.

First Published in English in 1996 by
GATEWAY BOOKS
The Hollies, Wellow,
Bath, BA2 8QJ

© Gateway Books, 1996

Translated by Sebastian Folborn

Edited by Palden Jenkins

Distributed in the USA by
ATRIUM PUBLISHERS GROUP,
3356 Coffey Lane,
Santa Rosa, CA 95403

First German publication 1993
as "Botschaft aus dem Kosmos"
by Verlag die Siberschnur of Neuwied

All Rights Reserved. No part of this book
may be reproduced or transmitted in any form
or by any means, electronic or mechanical,
including photocopying or any information
retrieval system, without permission in
writing from the Publishers.

Text set in 10.7 on 12.5pt Bembo
by Character Graphics of Taunton
Printed and bound by
Redwood Books of Trowbridge
Photographs by the author unless stated

British Library Cataloguing in Publication Data:
A catalogue record for this book
is available from the British Library

ISBN 1-85860-017-0

CONTENTS

Foreword 4

1. A Sacred Landscape 7

2. Lords of the Rings 17

3. The Anatomy of a Hoax 28

4. Mandelbrots, Dolphins & the Circle-Makers 33

5. A Global Phenomenon 48

6. The UFO Connection 70

7. A Solution to the Mystery? 77

8. The Mathematical Simulation of Crop
    Circles 86

9. The Ground Component 90

10. The Watchers 95

11. The Return of the Gods 114

12. Messages from the Cosmos 123

13. A Cosmic Message? 139

14. 1992: The First Contact? 144

15. 1993: A New Phase? 151

16. 1994: The Resurrection of Circles 158

Bibliography 164

Index 166

FOREWORD

Two senior citizens, Doug Bower, aged 67 and Dave Chorley, 62, were reputed to have created the unbelievably beautiful patterns in the British crop fields with the help of bits of rope and a plank. Or so the Press would have us believe. We will disprove this myth.

The mystery of the crop circles has been one of the more fascinating subjects of the last decade to cross the pages of the media and engage the public. The phenomenon has been known since the mid-seventies when small aircraft first discovered the unusually beautiful and symmetrical circles in the rich wheatfields of Southern England. Since then the number of the circles has increased dramatically. At first there were just a few, then a few dozen, and eventually hundreds. Finally in 1990 there was a quantum leap; they were no longer simple circles, but complex patterns, 'pictograms' or 'agriglyphs'; and not only in the traditional 'circle country' of Wiltshire and Hampshire, but in other English counties, and indeed, in many countries overseas.

This development continued in 1991 when the first pictograms appeared in Germany. The imperative to find a solution to the origin of the mystery produced in Britain varied ingenious explanations.

There were those who believed that Mother Earth was protesting the every-increasing destruction of her environment. Others were quite convinced that the shapes were caused by UFOs landing in the cornfields. Earth spirits and devas were held to be responsible, along with stationary whirlwinds, morphogenetic fields, the collective unconscious of humanity, the telekinetic powers of the researchers who investigated the circles, clever gangs of pranksters, and geomagnetic energies. Undoubtedly the most hilarious explanation of all was of a band of hedgehogs running around a pair of their copulating brethren!

Let's get the facts straight. Crop circles appear in different crops: wheat, winter barley, rye, oil seed rape, oats, rice, and even in vegetables, groups of trees, or on snow. In grain they form in the summer months (between April and September in the Northern Hemisphere), when the crops reach a certain height and maturity. Their diameter varies, from quite small 'grapeshot' a metre across, to an average size of 45 to 50 metres. Big formations can be up to 180 metres long, covering up to 10,000 square metres.

The stalks are flattened in spiral patterns, often with great precision. The edges of the circles are clean, as if drawn with a compass. The stalks are bent rather than broken, usually continuing to grow. The floor patterns are often complex, with 'layering' or a beautiful 'weaving' effect. Most of the configurations have a slightly ovoid shape, the geometry inexact, their centres not necessarily corresponding with the geometrical centres.

Crop circles are definitely a modern phenomenon, and their increase in numbers in recent years happened before the media coverage they encouraged. There are reports of the odd circle in the 1930s and '40s, but no photographic evidence. Since 1966 crop circles have appeared in Australia, followed by their regular appearance in England from 1972. A report from 1678 of "The Mowing Devil" tells the story of a landowner who refused to pay his workers to reap his field. "May the Devil reap it", swore the farmer. That night the oatfield glowed as if it was on fire, but the following morning the whole field had been cut, as if done by the Devil or an Earth spirit. The mention of fire reminds one of the anomalous phenomena often seen with modern sightings of UFOs. However, 'The Mowing Devil' story sounds to me more like similar tales of vengeance that can be found more prosaically in contemporary Central Europe. They were a popular literary form, and emerged as the first indications for the need for social reform. The text states that the Devil had reaped the entire field, while the illustration shows only a flattened circle.

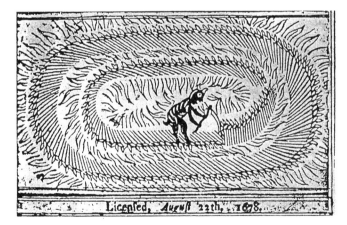

I also doubt the basis of the theories of the meteorologist Dr. Terence Meaden, who believes that the circles were precursors of the prehistoric stone circles of Avebury and Stonehenge. Crop circle researchers have studied hundreds of aerial photographs from the archeological surveys of the 1940s, '50s and '60s without discovering evidence of a circle before 1972. We just have to accept that they are a modern phenomenon.

The last few years have seen the growth of a 'circle subculture', and not a year has passed without half a dozen new books on the subject being released in Britain and Germany, some more useful than others. Most are anthologies, collections of various reports and theories representing the latest research. I have used some of this material in my own book, crediting the authors accordingly.

My intention in this book is to draw down the 'grand design' of the phenomenon, and present a scientifically valid theory of the development and meaning of the crop circles. I will attempt to put together the most significant recent findings to try to bring some light on the mystery. As Michel Eyquem de Montaigne (1533–1592) once said: "Gentlemen, I only picked the flowers and added nothing but the thread that connects them". This thread identifies the crop circles' significance and their possible origin.

As editor of *Magazin 2000*, a German ufological journal I receive daily reports on a variety of subjects, and I travel abroad a great deal on research projects. It is possible that my situation has enabled me to recognise connections that are not apparent to the researchers who are closely involved with the phenomenon itself. It became clear to me that the key to the crop circle mystery lies with another phenomenon – the UFO mystery. They seem both to be preparing us for the return of the extra-terrestrials. The circles are a gentle, aesthetic way of widening our horizons, without submitting us to a traumatic culture shock.

Erich von Däniken (in *Chariots of the Gods*) asks: "How would an extra-terrestrial civilisation effectively communicate with us without being instantly silenced by scientists and national armies?" He finds that Prof. James Deardoff of Oregon State University has the answer: "*Through slow indoctrination, a politics of small measures*".

This indoctrination had to be spread worldwide in a manner that would leave governments and science no opportunity of repression. On the one hand, the message from 'outside' has to be accessible to the public, but it also has to be unacceptable to military institutions and to orthodox science. Something that does not have rational credibility will be ridiculed by the conventional, and will not attract the interest of governments or science (at least not openly). But in this manner, humanity can be helped in small steps, because the realisation of what is really happening around us can only slowly develop. This would allow people to prepare themselves to accept the extraterrestrial message. It makes sense as a clarification of the 'circle-makers' agenda.

The Italian scientist Dr. Roberto Pinotti from Florence also fears that open contact with extra-terrestrials would be a traumatic culture shock. News about extra-terrestrial intelligence could be devastating because of the prevailing lack of direction in our societies. The immediate result of such exposure could be a crisis of world authority which would discredit science, religion and philosophy, but would also threaten socio-economic structures. Fear, panic, mass hysteria, rebellion against authority and widespread chaos would surely develop.

This is why public opinion in the world had to be prepared for the contact before too much information got out. An educational strategy would have to create the natural conditions step by step, so that humanity would not suffer trauma from a confrontation with extra-terrestrial intelligence. I believe that the crop circles are part of such a strategy.

Between 1990 and 1992 I made at least a dozen circle-watching trips to England. I walked through over a hundred circle-studded cornfields, and spent twenty hours in Nick Bailey's two-seater helicopter, photographing the circles and pictograms. I only mention this because many people assume that books are written by chair-bound theorists. The most authentic part of this book are the interviews I made with leading researchers.★

I would particularly like to thank those who have given their time and energy searching for answers to the mystery of the crop circles. My special thanks go to my friends and colleagues who cooperated with me on the preparation of this book: Colin Andrews, Walt Andrus etc; and the staff of the Merlin Hotel in Marlborough for their hospitality; and especially to my co-producer and cameraman Peter Heppa for his professional documentation of our investigations.

★I have made these available in three videos *The Mystery of the Crop Circles*. The first covers the English circles of 1991; the second the German circles, and the third, about the 1992 circles, includes sensational shots of a small flying object above a cornfield.

1. A Sacred Landscape

The birth of a phenomenon

The field-path led the two men past golden yellow ears of the late summer corn covering the gentle ridge of Star Hill. The sun already had set when they got out of the car at the end of the path. Eventually, they reached the top of the hill. At their feet lay Warminster, a sleepy little town which over the years had seen the gradual disappearance of the mysterious lights seen in its night-sky. Opposite, on the other side of the shallow valley, they recognised the terraced outline of Cley Hill. Thousands of years ago, the ancestors of the British shaped it into an enormous, elongated step pyramid. Its ridge became one of their most beautiful cult hills.

It was quiet tonight, too quiet. The only noise audible from time to time was the chirping of a cricket. *"Good that you are here this evening, Bryce"*, the older of the two men muttered, breaking the silence with a quiet voice. *"Do you see the light over there? It seems to be getting closer. This is a good sign"*. Now his companion could identify it, too: a triangular-shaped flying object, surrounded by coloured patterns, crossing the night sky with peculiar manoeuvres. Suddenly, as quickly as it came, it disappeared. *"A UFO"*. Both men were certain. Was it about to repeat its strange display?

It only took a few minutes when a second object appeared in the sky, glaring white, dancing in the air. The elderly Englishman ran to the car looking for his torch. He signalled several times at the mysterious flying object, as if to try to catch its awareness. What happened then was later described by his American companion as follows: *"Suddenly, I heard a noise. It seemed as if something pushed down the wheat. That night, the air was completely still. I looked around. The moon had just appeared, shining brightly. In front of my eyes, I could see a great imprint taking shape. The wheat was forced down in a clockwise direction. 'It' somehow had the shape of a triangle with a diameter of about 23ft (7m). I stood there some minutes, experiencing a tingling feeling going through my whole body. The air surrounding me was warm and smelled sweet."*

The American was a radio journalist named Bryce Bond. His British companion was Arthur Shuttlewood, a major contributor to the study of 'flying saucers', resident in Warminster. He played a central part in one of the greatest waves of UFO sightings in the 45 year-old history of this phenomenon. The date was 15th August 1972 when this episode took place on Star Hill near Warminster. What the two men were not in a position to anticipate at the time was that this was the birth of a phenomenon which to this day and beyond would keep the world in suspense. One of our planet's greater puzzles: the mystery of the Crop Circles.

From this day on, they appeared regularly, year after year, on Southern England's cornfields: firstly single circles, then from 1985 complete groups, then dozens from 1987, and from 1989 hundreds, dotted around the fields across the counties of Wiltshire and Hampshire. Then, in 1990, a quantum jump occurred. Not only were there some 1,200 circles throughout the country: this time complex patterns were added, which multiplied in number and complexity in 1991. And all of this began during that mild summer night in August 1972 when an unknown energy formed an imprint in the wheat after a UFO had been sighted.

Later, Shuttlewood described its forming as follows: *"The corn laid itself down like a lady opening a fan. In this way, a perfect circle formed in less than a minute, while we could hear a very high-pitched sound."* And Bryce Bond explained in still more concrete terms: *"While discussing our sightings, Arthur discovered further imprints: one circle with a diameter of 33ft (10m) and an additional, cigar-shaped imprint. All patterns had the wheat spirally laid on the ground in an anti-clockwise manner."*

The South of England contains some of the more mysterious and beautiful places on our planet. If you drive along one of the narrow country roads through the gentle, green hills and rich, fertile pastures of the counties of Hampshire, Wiltshire, Somerset or Dorset, you will without doubt be influenced by its spell. It is a magic landscape, rich in history, myth and legend, woven into the hills, springs and trees. It was here where King Arthur resided, here his Round Table met, here they searched for the Holy Grail. And it was here the wise Merlin lived, archetype of all magicians, the last shaman, who according to the legend 'spoke with the trees and felt with the stones'.

Many places recall the great magician. Reputedly, he did his work at Cadbury Castle, the legendary 'Camelot'. His grave-mound is located at the town of Marlborough, named after him ('Merlin-barrow' or 'Merlin-town'), and it was he, according to one tradition, who built Stonehenge to be his 'observatory of the seventy doors and windows'. The stones were supposed to have been brought from Ireland by magical forces, from the 'Giant's dancing-ground'.

Today, we know that Stonehenge is much older than the magician. Its oldest part dates back to the time of the pyramids, around 2800BC. Its stones originate from a quarry on the Prescelly mountains near the south-west coast of Wales, 140 miles (220km) as the crow flies, or 240 miles (380km) overland from Stonehenge. And no-one knows how Stone Age people could have mastered this long-distance transport. Expert geomancers consider the structure to be the geomantic 'hub of England': it lies on the crossing of three very ancient 'King's Roads' – the Harroway, the South Downs Ridgeway and the Icknield Way, which interlinked the whole country from west to east and from north to south, long before the Romans arrived.

Archeologists speculate Stonehenge to be one of the country's most important cult centres, similar to Delphi or Eleusis in Greece. They would have used it to celebrate initiations into the Mysteries, directed by a dynasty of high priests or archdruids, of whom Merlin may have been a latter-day one. The British historian Geoffrey of Monmouth, who lived in the 12th century, describes him as the 'prophet of the Demeter', of the Greek goddess of corn. The Mysteries of Eleusis also were devoted to her.

The legendary Abaris, Apollo's high priest, who once travelled on his 'golden arrow' to South Italy to meet Pythagoras, probably also descended from the same lineage. According to the Greek historian Diodorus of Sicily, Abaris worked from a 'circular sun temple' which was located on the green island Hyperborea in the North Sea, and was regularly visited by Apollo on his 'fiery chariot'. More details emerged from Hekatus of Abdera, about 300BC: *"Northwards, offshore in thee adjacent ocean, opposite the land of the Celts (France) lies an island which is not smaller than Sicily. On this island, there is a magnificent grove which is devoted to the sun god, with a strange temple of circular shape. Every twelve years, at the time when sun and moon again reach the same position to each other, Apollo visits the Island."*

It is not difficult to identify this 'circular sun temple' as Stonehenge. When Gerald Hawkins, Professor of Astronomy, investigated the structure for its astronomical orientations, he made an astonishing discovery, which he published in 1966 in his book *Stonehenge Decoded*: the Stonehenge complex is an enormous, prehistoric astronomy-computer which enabled our ancestors to do complicated astronomical calculations – to identify the positions of fixed stars whose positions in the zenith indicate important dates in the course of the year, the changing positions of the Sun and the Moon, and even solar and lunar eclipses could be predicted using an ingenious system of lines, stones and grave-mound positions.

The sacred Geometry of Stonehenge, according to John Michell.

The geomancer and philosopher John Michell goes still further: in his book *A New View Over Atlantis*[1] he shows that Stonehenge was laid out according to a 'sacred geometry' similar to the much later Abbey of Glastonbury. For him it is a 'model of the Universe' and a temple for the Sun and the Moon. As a matter of fact, at the time of the summer solstice, the Sun rises – as seen from the stone circle's centre – over the 'Heel Stone' (from the Celtic 'heol' = sun), a megalith outside the structure, forming the temple's axis. The rising solstice sunlight shines through to the innermost part of the sanctuary. The female opening may once have been roofed. In this way, the Sun consummated the 'holy marriage' of heaven and earth. This gave birth to energies which were conducted to all parts of the country to restore its fertility using 'ley lines', the paths of the earth energies.

Still today, hundreds regularly visit Stonehenge at the time of the Summer Solstice. Until 1990 white robed neo-druids celebrated their rituals there at that time, often with police protection and exclusion of 'vandalising hippies' – or those who were declared as such. However, in 1991 even the druids were refused admittance to the sanctuary, to discourage public disturbance. So on 21st June, England's former principal sanctuary presented itself like a fort, surrounded by road blocks and barbed wire, guarded by police divisions equipped with sticks and guard dogs. So much for sacred landscapes!

Observatory, druid temple or site of the Mysteries, whatever Stonehenge may have been, *"Everyone agrees in one respect"*, held forth the archaeologist Professor Atkinson: *"Stonehenge is predominantly a 'temple', a structure which enabled people to communicate and make contact with otherworldly forces or beings".* However the professor thought this to be understood, it is striking how often mysterious lights and shining discs are observed above the henge.

To the north of Stonehenge lies Avebury, a still older sanctuary from prehistoric times. Following the most recent discoveries, archeologists agree that the stone circle was constructed at least 2,000 years before Stonehenge.

It was the centre of a once-colossal complex with stone avenues and circles, which together formed the shape of a

Stukeley's representation of Avebury's 'sacred landscape'. The monument forms a snake which crosses the sun's disc, a symbol which is also found in the early Egypt.

snake which crossed the Sun's disc. Many of the huge monoliths at Avebury are almost as large as the residential homes in and around the little village of Avebury. Some weigh as much as 60 tons. Phenomenal avenues, built with huge stones which sometimes seem to have faces, lead to the circle.

As peripheral part of the Avebury complex stands Silbury Hill, 135ft (40m) high, Europe's greatest man-made earth mound. Silbury Hill was erected around 2,600BC and once had the shape of a six-stepped round pyramid. Its purpose is unknown, like that of the entire Avebury megalith complex. It could not have been a grave mound – neither archeological excavations nor scanning the Silbury Hill using newest technology found or observed even a trace of a skeleton or of burial objects.

On the other hand, Moses Cotsworth showed, at the beginning of this century, in his work *The Rational Almanac*, that Silbury Hill could possibly be used as a solar observatory – by observing the hill's shadows falling on the north side. As a matter of fact, the monument's meridian aligns with the church at Avebury, erected a mile away, which goes back to a ninth century Saxon chapel. Its font, decorated with an unusual motif, may date back to that time.

A bishop stands there with a crosier and fights two winged dragons. In the Middle Ages, the dragon embodied heathenism, which worshipped it as a symbol of the Earth's energies. Again and again we come upon dragon legends in Wiltshire: we find them as part of local folklore, while Christians dedicated their churches and chapels, erected on many of the old cult places, to St Michael, the mythological dragon-slayer. But local legends also record

Reconstruction of the original Avebury henge – strangely, a pictogram found on 11th July 1992 at Ogbourne near Avebury resembles its fundamental pattern (see opp. page).

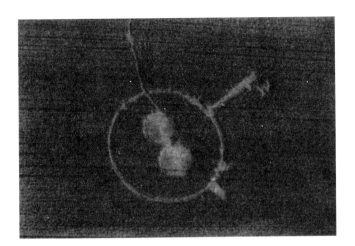

Left: *Ogbourne pictogram, 11th July 1992 (see opp. page).*

Right: *The baptismal font in the church at Avebury shows a bishop who fights two dragons, representing the paganism which worshipped the dragon as the symbol of the energies of earth and cosmos.*

common people who killed the worm, and many village churches in this region keep the relics of such killings – often heavy lances or swords, centuries old. Still today, the ancient energy lines which cross the country are called 'dragon lines', and the massive near-circular ditch at Avebury is also called the 'dragon ditch'. The 'dragon on the wheel' is a common shield symbol, a sign which reminds of the original shape of the site at Avebury, which quite evidently was once a 'dragon temple' or 'serpent temple', a place at which one could link oneself with the Earth's energies to make contact with the cosmos.

One of the early researchers into Avebury was the freemason and archaeologist William Stukeley, a remarkable personality of the 18th century, who was convinced that the original druids had laid out Avebury as a 'sacred landscape': *"The ancients created temples of enormous size with mighty pillars arranged into colonnades similar to a small wood; or domes with wide arches to represent the heavens; they created gigantic colossuses which portrayed their gods; but the honour of a still more comprehensive idea and its execution was reserved to our British druids. They used plains and hills, valleys, springs and rivers to form a temple three miles in length. They embossed a whole country with the stamp of this holy sign, and this in an extremely long-lasting way. The golden Temple of Solomon has disappeared, the proud shape of the Babylonian Belus, the temple of Diana in Ephesus, the one of Vulcanus in Egypt, that of the Capitolian Jupiter are declined and demolished, while Avebury, although older than all of them, as I believe, was left undamaged until a few years ago. And still today, enough traces are left to get a complete impression of the whole."*

Dragon country: The 'green dragon' as a pub sign in Marlborough.

Stukeley's vision of a landscape temple found wide response among the thinkers of his time. The mystic and poet William Blake saw the great spirit of Albion chained up in the hills and valleys of his domain. His kingdom had been seized by a crowd of wretched tyrants and his tremendously large body was hidden from the mortal's eyes by the grey spell's fog. But like Stukeley, Blake also believed in the ending of the unfortunate spell and a glorious resurrection of the holy spirit of Britain through the reconciliation of man with himself and the Earth. He supported his faith with the biblical prophecy of the 'New Jerusalem', the new age, which, as he believed, would dawn in 'Angel-Land' (England), radiating from the 'druid temples' of Stonehenge and Avebury.

Directly connected with Blake's vision of the New Jerusalem is Glastonbury, which the poet-prophet described as Britain's 'most sacred ground'. Glastonbury, like Avebury, lies on an ancient energy line, the St Michael Line, which connects important places from England's prehistory, from Land's End in Cornwall in the West to Hopton in Essex in the East, as the British geomancers Hamish Miller and Paul Broadhurst describe in their ingenious book *The Sun and the Serpent*[2].

Glastonbury: this is the mythological Avalon of the Arthurian Saga, which has enjoyed a high-profile resurrection in recent times in the novels of such authors as Marion Zimmer-Bradley and Mary Stewart. In the Middle Ages, Glastonbury was a popular place of pilgrimage in the British Isles. In its centre lies the famous abbey, which according to legend originated from a church which Joseph of Arimathaea (Jesus' uncle) erected there in 37AD, after he fled to Britain from Roman and Jewish persecution in Palestine. A thorn-tree is still revered as the descendent of the thorn which sprouted from Joseph's staff when he set it into the ground for prayer.

It is agreed by botanists that the Glastonbury Thorn belongs to a species unknown in Europe, but native to Lebanon and Palestine. So, did the legend contain a core of truth? It says that Joseph of Arimathaea, whom the Bible portrayed as a prosperous trader and apparent relative of Jesus – he allowed Jesus to be buried in his family grave – was working in the tin trade. It is well known that the Phoenicians and Jews as early as the second millennium before Christ had a busy trade in tin with Cornwall, the south-western tip of the British Isles.

The legend contains still more. It also says that once upon a time Joseph of Arimathaea had taken his young nephew Jesus with him to Britain, enabling him to visit a druid school at Avalon, which had long been a religious centre for the British. In the 7th century, St Patrick visited the monks at Glastonbury, the descendants of those locals whom Joseph personally introduced to Christ's teachings. He found the grave, which today is still worshipped, and erected a greater church. This church — made largely of wood and elaborately decorated — stood until the 12th century, when it was destroyed by fire.

The local monks decided to reconstruct the Abbey much more magnificently and in stone. During the building work they discovered a grave cross, which carried the Latin inscription "HIC IACET SEPULTUS INCLITUS REX ARTURIUS IN INSULA AVALONIA": "Here lies the famous King Arthur on the Isle of Avalon". While the lead cross disappeared over the course of the centuries, the grave can still be visited today. It survived the destruction of the Abbey by England's blue-bearded King Henry VIII in 1539 – this Catholic place of pilgrimage didn't fit into his Anglican church reform.

Avalon means 'the Isle of Apples'. Something of the Garden of the Hesperides or the biblical paradise may resound here — an area of Glastonbury is indeed called 'Paradise'. The British historian Geoffrey of Monmouth wrote in 1138 in his *History of the Kings in Britain* that King Arthur once had been nursed back to health on Avalon by the sorceress (or fairy) Morgaine (Morgana), who headed the matriarchal sanctuary as high priestess of twelve Sisters; and that after his death in battle, his body was taken to Glastonbury and was buried there by Morgaine.

Glastonbury in old times seemed to have had the function of a 'dimensional gate', an island shrouded in mist, where time seemed to have stood still and the passage to the Beyond seemed to be possible. At that time, Avalon was an island surrounded by the sea and by marshes which later were drained. Passing through the swathes of mist which lay over the water, then seeing the shadowy outline of the 'gate', the Tor hill at Avalon, which would tower above the mists, its summit bathed in sun – we only can suspect what effect this had had on our ancestors.

The 580ft (170m) high 'gate' is like a magic mountain from pre-Celtic times, slightly evocative of a pyramid, elongated in shape and roughly aligned along the St Michael's-Line towards Avebury. It was artificially terraced in Megalithic times, in the shape of what some identify as a Cretan maze. It is orientated towards the sunrise on 1st May, when, some say, a torchlight procession annually followed its maze-path towards the hill's summit to greet the rising sun.

The procession path started at the Chalice Well, a sacred spring, today the site of a fairy-like enchanted garden. It is a place of peace, of meditation. I felt the palpable presence of nature spirits in the bushes of forsythia and the tulips on an afternoon in spring, when I came to Glastonbury for the first time. The water of the Chalice Well contains chalybeate iron and is slightly naturally radioactive. Its reddish colour led to the saga that Joseph of Arimathaea had hidden the Grail here – Christ's cup at the Last Supper. Miraculous healings of illnesses were attributed to the spring during the Middle Ages.

From the Well, the procession path leads circuitously to the Tor summit. At the path's start stand the 'living stones', two rocks which supposedly begin to vibrate at sunrise and sunset. Like mysterious guards, they protect the entrance to the mystery voyage, the entry to the mandala of the Tor hill. According to legend, the top of the Tor – on which was erected a St Michael's Chapel in the Middle Ages, of which today only the tower exists – is at the same time a gate to a different dimension, to the 'underworld' spoken of by ancient Celts. The Grail is supposed to be hidden in underground tunnels under the Tor.

In the 1920s, Katherine Maltwood identified an ancient landscape zodiac around Glastonbury, marked in old field borders, paths and field embankments, which she believed was built ten thousand years ago. Glastonbury itself took the position of Aquarius, represented here by the

Phoenix, with the Tor as the bird's head. The *Glastonbury Prophecies*[3] describe the place as the centre of the 'New Jerusalem', a prophecy which was taken up by William Blake in his hymn "Jerusalem":

And did those feet in ancient time
Walk upon England's mountains green?
And was the Holy Lamb of God
In England's pleasant pastures seen?
Or did that Countenance Divine
Shine forth upon these clouded hills
And was Jerusalem builded here
Among those dark satanic mills?

Bring me my bow of burning gold!
Bring me my arrows of desire!
Bring me my spear! O clouds unfold!
Bring me my Chariot of Fire!
I will not cease from mental fight,
Nor shall my sword sleep in my hand,,
Till I have built Jerusalem
In England's green and pleasant land.

What is more, "Jerusalem" is not just an arcane poem of the 18th century, it is Britain's secret national anthem. It expresses the mystic's conviction that here, in this sacred landscape, within the triangle between the old megalithic/druid temples at Stonehenge and Avebury and the great place of pilgrimage at Glastonbury, the heavenly Jerusalem of the Apocalypse will manifest. There will be a Golden Age, a restoration of the godly order, a reawakening of the old temples and a new observance of the spirit of the Earth. In this way the veil of the materialistic world-view will be lifted and a new perception of paradise will be made possible.

Clearly the flower-power movement of the sixties, the reawakened interest in spirituality and a holistic lifestyle of the seventies, and the New Age movement of the eighties seemed to fulfil Blake's prophecy. Again the searchers after the meaning of life went on pilgrimage to the holy places, studied the knowledge of the Ancients and celebrated ancient rituals and ceremonies in the Ancients' temples, in Stonehenge, Avebury, on Silbury Hill or Glastonbury Tor. As a result, Glastonbury in Somerset gradually has become England's New Age capital. Crystal shops, specialist bookshops, New Age centres, art handicraft shops, picturesque shops with such characteristic names like "The Crystal Cave", "Pendragon", "Avalon", "Merlin's Refuge", "Dragons", "The Glastonbury Experience", "Excalibur" and "Isis" sprang up, catering for a growing demand from visitors.

Quite evidently, this collective awakening to new, yet old values resonated strongly for many. Everything indicates that meditations, rituals and gatherings which were increasingly celebrated at the nodal places of this sacred landscape activated these power-places, set them in renewed vibration – subtle yet still hidden to many. The result was, literally, signs and wonders. People reported mystical experiences and spiritual visions, mediums suddenly received messages from other realms or from long forgotten times. Some who looked attentively at the sky observed strange, coloured lights doing unbelievable manoeuvres, which possibly signalled us that we are not alone in space. And all around the stone circles and mounds built by the megalithic peoples there appeared mysterious signs and symbols on the green or golden cornfields. Truly, signs in the sky and on the Earth seemed to announce great changes!

These signs began to be noticed in the mid-sixties in Warminster, a sleepy town at the feet of the pyramid-like shaped Cley Hill, which so strikingly reminds of a Sumerian Ziggurat. Warminster lies in the middle of the Glastonbury-Avebury-Stonehenge triangle. It is surrounded by six hills which carry such descriptive names as Heaven's Gate, Lord's Hill, Jacob's Ladder, Star Hill or Cradle Hill. *"There are clear indications that Warminster is a window to a different dimension"*, explained Shuttlewood in his classic "The Warminster Mystery,"[4] *"or that some of the local objects attract higher intelligences like beacons"*.

The UFO wave at Warminster (called a 'flap' by sceptics), which was conceivably the overture to the appearance of the crop formations, began at Christmas 1964 when postmaster Roger Rump was rudely awoken in the night. *"I awoke with a start because I thought the tiles were being thrown with raw force from my house's roof into the Hillwood Lane"*, he later reported to the editor of the *Warminster Journal*, Arthur Shuttlewood. A similar shock-

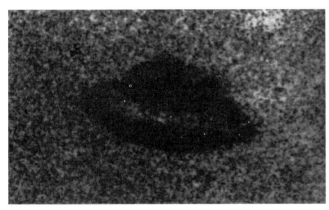

The controversial photograph of the 'thing' in Warminster was taken by Gordon Faulkner, a young factory worker, on 29th August 1965.

wave frightened a housewife while she was walking to the church. And two weeks later, some neighbours woke up because they thought that *"coal rattled down our house wall"*. On the same night, Rachel Attwell, the wife of an air force pilot, was awoken by a *"loud roaring"* and ran to the bedroom window: there, outside in the night sky, hung a shining, cigar-shaped flying object, *"brighter than all the stars"*, as Mrs Attwell recounted to Shuttlewood. Kathleen Penten, who observed it at the same time, described it as *"similar to a flying railway carriage in which all windows were illuminated"*. On 29th August 1965, Gordon Faulkner, a young factory-worker, shot a sensationally clear photograph of a disc-shaped, metallic space vehicle which he handed to the *Warminster Journal*, which later was publicised by the *Daily Mirror*.

Thirty days later, Shuttlewood himself saw from the editorial office a *"large, cigar-shaped object, shining white and amber-coloured, which crossed the sky majestically from right to left"*. With great presence of mind, he grabbed his film camera, when he felt a stabbing pain in his left arm. Despite a temporary paralysis, he managed to catch the eerie UFO for a second on film, before it entered a belt of white clouds. In this way, the journalist was gripped by the UFO-fever. He collected every report of UFOs, and printed them in the local paper. Alone until September 1965, so he found out, over 200 locals had seen the 'thing from Warminster', as they called it.

This photo was taken in 1972 during one of the countless 'sky watches' on the Cley, Cradle and Starr Hills near Warminster.

The more often the UFO sightings in Warminster made headlines in the press, the more the hobby-UFOlogists streamed to their new Mecca in Wiltshire. They came in thousands, and soon regular 'sky watches' were organised on the hills around Warminster, where the mysterious space-vehicles, which could appear and disappear out of nothing and manoeuvre in unbelievable patterns, showed themselves quite regularly.

Amongst the curious onlookers were two Londoners, Steve Evans and Roy Fischer, who regularly came to Warminster from 1971. Among countless UFO sightings, it was a close encounter of quite a special kind which proved unforgettable. It took place when they stared from the top of Cradle Hill into the sky. *"A force-field seemed to pass like a snake through the grass. It rustled loudly, like statics"*, as Evans described his experience. *"It raced straight towards Roy's feet, but then suddenly turned right. The sheep on the pastures went to pieces. At daybreak we found flatly pushed-down grass, as if something had landed"*. But that only was the prelude. It took another year, until Arthur Shuttlewood and Bryce Bond became the witnesses of the creation of the first British crop circle of modern time.

REFERENCES

1. Michell, John, *The New View over Atlantis*, Thames & Hudson, London, 1983.
2. Miller, Hamish, and Broadhurst, Paul, *The Sun and the Serpent*, Pendragon, Launceston, 1989.
3. Blake, W, *Jerusalem*, G A Unwin, London, 1964.
4. Shuttlewood, A, *The Warminster Mystery*, Tandem, London, 1973.

2. THE LORDS OF THE RINGS

Eastward of the 'magical triangle' of Glastonbury-Avebury-Stonehenge lies Winchester, the old Saxon capital of Wessex, the town hall of which still sports a circular wooden object which was reputedly King Arthur's round table. Winchester is overlooked by Telegraph Hill, 550ft (167m) high, which can easily be reached from the A272 road towards Petersfield. Behind the hill stretches a gigantic, natural amphitheatre, the valley of Cheesefoot Head, which people also call the 'Devil's Punchbowl'. Some decades before this area was at the centre of world history, when general Eisenhower spoke here to thousands of Allied soldiers before the D-Day landing in Normandy.

It was a sunny late-summer day in 1983, when Colin Andrews, chief electrical engineer at Test Valley Borough Council, drove in his car along the A272. When he passed the Devil's Punchbowl, he noticed several people had parked their cars at the side of the road and were looking down into the valley. Curious about what was happening, he stopped, looked down and discovered an enormous formation of five circles – a large one in the middle, with four smaller ones around it. Andrews was stirred by what he saw: the pattern's sheer symmetry, and the tidily recumbent position of the wheat, which seemed to form large spirals. All this was so unbelievably fascinating that it drew him in almost magically.

He went down the slope to look at the formation closely. He considered different possibilities by which someone could have made this artwork and dismissed them immediately. What he was seeing – he, a practical engineer, who saw himself as one with two feet squarely on the ground – was going to prove to be the challenge of his life. He felt deep down inside that what had happened there was of utmost importance. But what was it? Did the patterns have a natural cause? Had a UFO, a flying saucer, landed there? Only one thing was clear to him: a human being could not have formed the circle-cross. It was too symmetrical, too accurately

Colin Andrews.

duo was no more dependent on articles in the press and on off-chance calls by farmers and other circle-discoverers.

Busty Taylor.

I asked Busty what impressed him most about the circles, during an interview in August 1991. *"Mostly their beauty"*, was his answer, and then he went into raptures: *"Especially the golden circle's beauty, when the corn is already very ripe. Their patterns – each one seems to have its individual fingerprint – this diversity! You can look at the photos and say at first glance, this is that and that one is that – although gradually it becomes ever more difficult, with over 1,000 photographed circles"*.

When Busty Taylor later examined the quintuplet formation at Clatford on the ground, he discovered traces of a gleaming white jelly-like mass which he had examined by the University of Surrey and by Albury Laboratories Ltd. In its laboratory report, the University came to the conclusion that this 'jelly', although it had some of the characteristics of commercial sugar and honey products, could not have been such a thing – a test using 'Fehling'

solution turned out negative, while the result is positive with customary sweets. A similar jelly-like mass has been found periodically after UFO sightings, and UFO researchers call it 'Angels Hair'.

As Andrews and Delgado found out later, there was indeed a UFO observation in connection with the quintuplet formation at Clatford. The two pensioners Pat and Jack Collins had reported to a police station in Hampshire an 'enormous circular object' which they had seen from the A272 in the evening of 6th July 1985: it seemed to stand upright on its edge like a Ferris wheel and was surrounded by many yellow-white lights.

A good dozen circles were discovered by Taylor, Andrews and Delgado in 1986 – the most beautiful one being in an oil-seed rape field. Rape has a very solid, brittle stem which easily snaps instead of staying bent, and yet the rape plants in this circle weren't broken but had been gently but firmly pressed to the ground. Their flowers were undamaged, and some showed sawtooth-shaped notches 2mm ($^8/_{100}$ inch) apart from each other.

In 1987 there were around 40 circles in Wiltshire and Hampshire: circles, rings, concentric circles, formations of threes and fives. Since the appearance of the first formation of five in 1978, this year saw the phenomenon's second 'quantum jump' towards a greater frequency, diversity and complexity in the patterns. They became increasingly mysterious: dogs which had been taken into the circles got ill and vomited, orange illuminated objects were observed, strange noises heard, large dark flashes seen. Colin Andrews described a "rustling noise of static electricity", when he stood in one of the vortices.

For the first time since 1982, circles were again found in the area around Warminster, mostly at the feet of the White Horse at Westbury – a horse figure cut into the chalk rock in the 9th century in memory of King Alfred's victory over the Danish in 878 – very probably at the place of a very much older, prehistoric landscape figure.

The circles lay opposite the field where circles had appeared in 1982. They appeared in the night, after a wheel-shaped UFO with a ring of many orange-coloured lights had been sighted. Also on the night of 5th August 1987, when a formation of four circles appeared at Upton Scudamore near Warminster, some claimed to have seen UFOs. Two days later, a circle 90ft (27m) in diameter with a double ring was discovered at Bratton near Warminster. It was the first of its kind, a new step towards greater complexity in the circles. Even more so, it became the scene of a mysterious incident.

During an excursion in this picturesque landscape, the Wingfield family noticed the circle from the Bratton slope. The Wingfields had already read about the circles in the newspapers and were eager to examine this strange phenomenon at close quarters. So they climbed down the slope toward the crop circle – the sons and George Wingfield ahead, Gloria Wingfield behind. But then something happened which frightened Gloria so much that at first she refused to walk any further: a dazzling blue ray of light, pulsing and rotating, pointed at them from the

George Wingfield.

ground. Then she saw in front of her blue flashes flickering between the corn ears, which seemed to be a reflection of something invisible. Gloria's experience and the precision of the circles touched George Wingfield deep inside. He felt that he had to do everything possible to get at the root of the mystery. For this he had excellent qualifications.

As a graduate of Eton College and Trinity College in Dublin, he completed his studies in natural sciences in 1966 with a Master's degree. He did his practical work experience at the Royal Observatory at Greenwich, studying stellar spectra and the Earth's magnetism. Later he worked as a systems analyst for the computer giant IBM. The next circle season, 1988, Wingfield used every free minute to get to the bottom of the phenomenon. His temporary conclusion: the circles were *"the product of a non-human intelligence whose nature we still have to investigate, as far as we can do that"*. Their characteristics he described as follows:

- Geometrical form, but imperfect precision of most circles;
- Circular, ring-shaped, elliptical, rectangular and triangular in shape;
- Sharp edge between the flatly-laid and still-upright corn;
- Only in very few cases do the circles cross field boundaries;
- They turn up usually in wheat or barley fields, but sometimes also in rape, rye, oats and high-grown grass;
- They appear mostly between late-May and September (Northern Hemisphere), when the corn has reached a mature height;
- The corn stems are mostly *bent*, not snapped or damaged, when they are found, and usually they go on growing until they are ripe, in this new horizontal position. In a few cases has the strong force at work

during their creation torn individual stems out of the soil and catapulted them out of the circle. Very often, a circle or a pattern has various layers – lower plants pointing in a different direction to the upper ones;

- Furthermore the corn exhibits various 'laying directions': clockwise, counter-clockwise, away from the centre, straight, swastika-shaped, complex, and so on, but always with nearly-geometrical precision;
- 'Changed' or interwoven stems;
- Often (but not always) the circles or formations are formed parallel to ground structures and/or tram-lines;
- They appear overnight and usually without eye-witnesses;
- Fields with circles are often 'visited again' – new circles turn up next to old ones, and previous circles are 'completed';
- Extraordinary diversity of patterns and formations;
- Sizes of the circles between 1.6 and 66 yards (1.5–60m), and lengths between 15 and 220 yards (14–200m);
- Increasing complexity between 1978 and 1992;
- Tendency to appear in immediate vicinity of prehistoric sites and ancient mounds;
- In some cases UFO sightings before a circle's forming;
- Unusual noises in the circles – 5kHz buzz-noise on tape recorders;
- Lasting energy patterns which can be located with dowsing rods;
- Intelligent reaction to the circle researcher's discussions and theories, apparently in an attempt to communicate and to lead us in a certain intended direction.

An example of the last point is the obvious 'game' which the 'circle-makers' played on the meteorologist Dr Terence Meaden. Meaden came across the circles in August of 1980 when the *Wiltshire Times* reported the discovery of an 'inexplicable circular marking' at the feet of the White Horse at Westbury near Warminster. He expressed at that time in the specialist *Journal of Meteorology* the supposition that a "rare kind of vortex wind" could be responsible for the phenomenon – a theory which he modified in 1988 when he made katabatic (freak) winds responsible for the emergence of circle-producing *plasma vortices*. Unfortunately, the bright doctor forgot to ask why these 'katabatic winds' didn't already exist before 1972. As if they wanted to lead Meaden *ad absurdum*, the circles withdrew a year later, sulking, avoided Warminster and shifted their central area of activity to Beckhampton near Avebury. Only in 1990 did they again put in an appearance in the area of the UFO-Mecca, Warminster.

Now the concept of a 'sulking crop circle' may certainly sound odd. However, it is a fact that the 'circle-makers' seem to react intelligently and even seem to answer their critics. When Meaden's more than far-fetched scientific-style theory – though up to today no-one has ever observed a 'plasma vortex', neither has it been scientifically proven to exist – gained greater publicity (not least due to the book *Crop Circles – A Mystery Explained* by Jenny Randles) complete crop formations increasingly turned up for whose origin even Meaden himself could not find any explanation. They appeared in places which had been completely circle-free up to then.

Actually, a 'wandering' of the circles had already taken place in August 1987, when ten circles turned up in a wheat field near Beckhampton. Beckhampton, an area from which crop circles had never before been reported, lies at one end of the Avebury complex, west of the mysterious Silbury Hill. The fields on which they appeared are surrounded by prehistoric mounds and other archeological remains. Stephen Horton, a farmer from Firs Farm at Beckhampton, never suspected what was to happen: from this day on, his fields would become the circles' favoured target.

1988 was distinguished by a yet further evolution of the circles. A formation of five in cross shape, like the five on a dice, turned up on the night of 14th–15th July 1988 at the foot of the Silbury Hill, twenty-four hours after a UFO sighting by Mary Freeman, a housewife from Marlborough. A second quintuplet followed some days later, and five further single circles were added in the following two days – in such a perfect arrangement that one of them lengthened both formations in a way which corresponded to the shaft of a cross, and thus suggested an interpretation as a 'Celtic Cross'. By 4th August, yet another two quintuplets came along. All of them had the corn turned clockwise in the middle circle and in three satellites, but *anti-clockwise* in the case of one of the satellites.

By the end of August there were six quintuplets, mostly in the area around Silbury Hill. Then, once again, the phenomenon developed further. On 10th September, Colin Andrews found, near Charity Downs, next to a 'double-ringer', the most fascinating formation to date: a quintuplet whose four satellite circles were connected by a ring – which gave the structure an even clearer form of a 'Celtic Cross'. Moreover, the stems in the ring were interwoven with each other. *"I would bet my life on it that an unknown intelligence is behind this"*, explained Colin Andrews. *"It is out of question that this formation was created by human hand or by a meteorological phenomenon"*.

1988 was also the first year the formations appeared north of the traditional circle-country of Wessex. On 26th June, a circle with one ring and three satellites was found close to Oadby near Leicester. The night before, a lay preacher and his wife observed how a shining white light hovered over the field in question, only to shoot upwards after a few minutes. At the same time, residents near the field saw a 'bright, white flash'.

When a local person measured the circle and dictated the measurements onto tape recorder, he afterwards noticed high-pitched, repeating sounds on the tape. A BBC television team experienced something similar when it interviewed Colin Andrews inside a circle – a phenomenon which points to magnetic anomalies, since the recording medium of tape is magnetic. In this case, a hollow-sounding knocking noise with about 100 beats per minute was heard, suggestive of heart beats.

Altogether, there were about 120 circles in 1988, far more than in the previous year. Now, Colin Andrews and Pat Delgado had collected enough material to present the phenomenon to the public in a much more comprehensive way than had been possible for previous press reports. In spring 1989 their book *Circular Evidence* appeared, which soon made it to tenth position on the national bestseller list. It became a cult book. The circles' aesthetic qualities were impressive in the large-sized colour prints and in their anecdotal descriptions of the attendant circumstances of their discovery and investigation.

For Andrews and Delgado, it was certain that these *"...objects of great beauty and enormous precision, full of mysterious details..."* were created by an *"...unknown intelligence using an unknown force-field"*. When the Queen put *Circular Evidence* on her summer reading list, the book was guaranteed publicity in the mass media. "A phenomenon of unbelievable fascination" – the press went into raptures and dealt with the crop circles in lengthy reports.

Circle fever had broken out, and the unseen circle-makers seemed to react appropriately to their new publicity. In the area around Silbury Hill, where in 1988 there had been fifteen patterns, forty circles now appeared. Nationwide there now had been some 305 known examples, and their shape and structure was becoming more and more complicated. The quintuplets from the previous year now grew with a sixth circle added, which converted them into long-shafted crosses and took the hypothesised appearance of a landing-place for four-footed spacecraft. A circle with a crooked 'tail' appeared near Cheesefoot Head, after Dr Meaden had announced that he had grabbed the phenomenon "by the tail". The 'double ringers' became more common, and a circle near Beckhampton had the considerable diameter of 114ft (35m).

What's more, they now appeared across the whole country: in Devon and Gloucestershire, Cheshire and Buckinghamshire, Hertfordshire, Essex, Suffolk, Nottinghamshire, Leicestershire, Avon, Kent and even Scotland. The media's increased interest made a coordinated research project, which would get to the root of the circles' origin, an increased possibility. So, Colin Andrews' and Pat Delgado's newly-founded organisation, Circles Phenomenon Research (CPR), initiated 'Operation White Crow'. It got its name from the expression that all crows had to be accepted as black until someone discovered a white crow. A hilltop ridge at Cheesefoot Head, from which one could overlook the entire Punchbowl (in which two circles had already turned up on 27th May) had been chosen as the 'white crow's nest'. For eight days, beginning 10th June, they kept the field under round-the-clock surveillance, with infra-red and night-vision cameras and radar. And everybody who was anybody in the circle scene was involved: Busty Taylor, George Wingfield, even Dr Terence Meaden.

Two respected scientists, Professor Archie Roy from the University of Glasgow and Dr Adrian Lyons, took part at the surveillance project as well, and Dr Meaden specially installed a small weather station next to the 'crow' camp. The excitement of the Operation White Crow team grew when, in the early morning hours of 15th July a shining object was filmed over the Punchbowl. A circle,

however, was not seen after this 'eerie encounter'. And it remained like that until the end of the project.

On the project's last day, 17th June, six participants, among them Wingfield, Andrews, Delgado, Taylor and the medium Rita Goold, decided to try an unusual experiment. In one of the two already-existing circles they attempted to contact with the energy behind the phenomenon. They sat down, relaxed, tuning in to themselves. It was a cool, clear summer night, and an almost-full moon made the landscape radiate a mysterious light.

Then George Wingfield heard a trilling sound. At first he didn't know what had happened. He turned around to his friends, who evidently perceived the same and looked at him as baffled as he himself was. The sound seemed to come from somewhere near the circle, and was completely different to anything which they had ever heard before: it was a rhythmic trilling and buzzing in a very high pitch, not loud, but with a hypnotic effect which went right through those present – more intensive than a cricket's chirping or a rattlesnake's rattling. Then it stopped, and then seemed all at once to come from a group of bushes at the field's edge, maybe 45 yards (40m) away from the circle. Wingfield and the others felt paralysed.

The first who tried to start communicating with the buzzing was Rita, the medium. She asked several questions, and when she said at one instance: *"If you understand us then stop"*, the sound was interrupted for one or two seconds. Then it again came closer to the group in the circle. Whoever or whatever produced it, quite evidently was conscious of the circle researchers' presence. Colin and Rita had the impression that 'something', a kind of light spot, came towards them. Rita sensed it as a small humanoid's head. Whatever it was, so much they all felt: it was something living and intelligent, even if it was invisible or not recognisable.

George Wingfield now turned to this energy-being: *"Please, could you make a circle for us?"* At this moment, a further White Crow collaborator, who had heard the strange noise, entered the field from the camp. When he approached the group, he believed he saw a luminous object in the form of two horns over them. No one among the group had noticed it – which could have been because they all had been very much distracted. When two further project collaborators followed, the noise seemed again to draw back towards the bushes. As a result, the communication was disrupted. Pat and Rita decided to leave it at that for the moment, and so they all returned to the camp.

Some hours later, Colin and George decided to look once again whether something had happened at the 'contact place'. There was nothing to see, but again the mysterious buzzing sounded. This time, Colin Andrews had his tape recorder with him and made some recordings. Later analyses by the University of Sussex revealed that it had a frequency of 5.2kHz. Andrews interpreted it as electrostatic noise and attributed it to magnetic, possibly geomagnetic fields.

Next morning, only 550 yards (500m) away from this place, a circle was found, surrounded by a ring, which must have been created in the night in connection with this strange encounter. George Wingfield's wish had been fulfilled – although the circle lay out of viewing distance from the 'White Crow' camp.

Actually, this wasn't the only case where a buzzing noise had been heard in a crop circle. Colin Andrews already had noticed it in 1987 in two different circles near Andover, and a French UFO group recorded it in June 1989 in a circle near Cheesefoot Head. It came to a spectacular manifestation during bright daylight in a huge 100ft (35m) circle near Beckhampton in the Avebury area, when Pat Delgado was interviewed in July by the BBC television.

The interview was supposed to take place within the circle, and Pat stood, with microphone in hand, ready to answer the reporters' questions. *"Suddenly, I was within a compact, closed energy-field"*, Delgado later told me. *"For me, this energy felt, when I touched it with my fingers, like a thin plastic foil. It had a noticeable edge, and in its innermost a collection of energy, from where the sound emerged"*. The film team's sound engineer, who clearly heard the strange buzzing noise through his headphones, was visibly irritated. It was a rustling and buzzing which was audible on the BBC tape, before the brand-new BBC Betacam SP-camera broke down. The noise was carefully analysed and identified as a 5.0–5.2kHz frequency. All experts, among them Dr Robert Weiss from the Jet Propulsion Laboratory of NASA, USA, who had once analysed the Watergate tapes, came to the conclusion that it was an 'artificial' noise and not, for example, a bird's voice.

A further witness' report which indicated a connection between the circles and the buzzing sound was told to me by George Wingfield: Sandy Reid from Dundee in Scotland often used to wander in the early morning hours to observe foxes and badgers in their natural habitat. One morning around 5.30am at the end of July, he was returning from an excursion along a hill ridge. The day was breaking and the morning chorus had started up to greet him, with a loud chirping. But suddenly, the bird's singing stopped, and in the silence, Reid perceived quite a different noise which came from the hill's foot: a rustling, as if corn was rubbed against itself. There was no wind at all, when in less than ten seconds, down on the field, a perfect circle 30ft (10m) in diameter was formed. When Reid went down to the circle, he felt "a presence", but he didn't know what it was. Some days later, when he again returned to the area, he found a second circle, and when visiting for a third time, he became a witness of a 'trilling', a buzzing noise around the circles – the same noise which the group at Cheesefoot Head had heard.

Stonehenge near Salisbury, according to legend Merlin's observatory, is in reality as old as the Pyramids. The astronomer Professor Gerald Hawkins believes the construction to be a prehistoric astronomical computer, and for John Michell it is a geometric model of the Universe.

Often, mysterious lights and UFOs are seen above Stonehenge – here a photo from 1990.

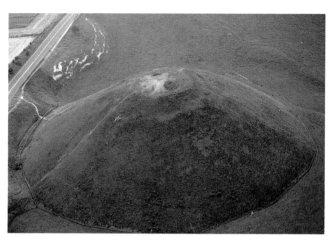

Silbury Hill, Europe's largest man-made ritualistic hill, from the air. It forms the 'navel' of the sacred landscape around Avebury.

View of Cley Hill from the north. Here the crop circle phenomenon began. Cley Hill was a prehistoric stepped pyramid, reminiscent of the Ziggurat of the Sumerians, artificially terraced. At its feet there periodically appear mysterious crop circles.

made. And besides, there were no tracks leading to the circles.

He was the first to tread a way through the dry, bright brown ears of wheat to carry out provisional examinations. The big circle was 48ft (15m) wide, the diameter of the four satellite circles measured 12ft (4m) each. When Colin got back home that evening, his thoughts were still circling around that mysterious 'quintuplet' formation. From then on, he did everything possible to find out more and uncover this mystery. In doing so he met Pat Delgado, a retired electro-mechanical engineer, who had worked as a rocket engineer for the British Air Force and NASA. Delgado had already come across the crop circles two years earlier, in 1981, when they had appeared once before in the Devil's Punchbowl – then only as a group of three.

Pat Delgado.

Delgado had been so deeply impressed that he decided to inform the press. So, for the first time, nine years after the events at Warminster, the crop circles made headlines throughout the world. Their most popular explanation was that they may have been 'landing places' for UFOs –

a theory which soon was refuted due to the ever-increasing diversity in the patterns. Together, Andrews and Delgado began a systematic investigation of the phenomenon.

This included documenting cases of crop circles from the past. There were, for example, rumours going round that even in 1946, two circles had appeared on top of Pepperbox Hill near Salisbury. Then there was a considerable gap until the making of the formation at Warminster in 1972. A single circle was discovered 1975 on a farm near Winchester, which was followed by a second one the next year. The first known *grouping* of circles, the first formation of five, turned up 1978 at Headbourne, some miles north of Winchester. In 1980, the circles preferred Westbury near Warminster, where three circles appeared. In 1981 there were two separate circles and a formation of three. Four circles appeared in 1982, half a dozen single circles and four quintuplets in 1983, and about the same number in 1984.

In 1985, the research duo of Andrews and Delgado were joined by an additional member. On 3rd August 1985, the sports pilot Busty Taylor discovered a formation of five circles around Clatford – a central circle and four satellites, absolutely regular, geometrical and simply perfect. The vortical form of the circles made spirals which reminded Taylor of Katherine wheels. Busty was so fascinated that he couldn't sleep the following night. The next day, he took off again with his aeroplane, found the circles and took photos of them. One of the prints he sent to Andrews and Delgado.

For them, it was the first aerial picture of the circles they had seen, and they were impressed by the formation's precision. Busty also became a victim of the 'circles effect' – the phenomenon wouldn't let him go, and he joined as the third member of the research team. This was a great gain for Andrews and Delgado – not only because Busty was an excellent aerial photographer, but also because he could search the country for circles by plane. The research

Avebury, a stone circle from prehistory, is even older than Stonehenge and originated in its earliest phase around 4500BC.

Glastonbury, the Arthurian legend's Avalon: view towards the Tor, which had prehistoric terraces. On its summit the tower of St Michael's chapel, destroyed by King Henry VIII.

The ruins of the Abbey at Glastonbury, which Henry VIII ordered to be destroyed – though much of the destruction was done by the locals. According to legend, it was built on the site of the first European Christian church, by St Joseph of Arimathaea in 37AD.

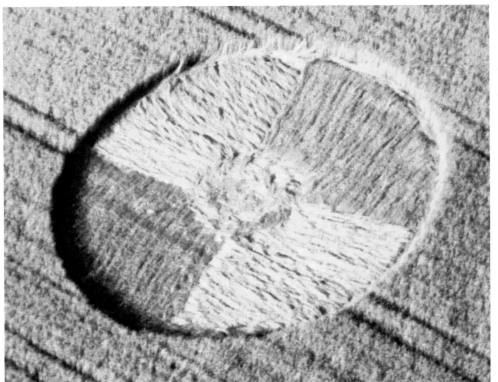

The 'Swastika' at Winterbourne Stoke near Amesbury was discovered on 12th August 1989 and gave a foretaste of what the circle researchers were to encounter the following year. The crop was bent in four directions. This circle gave the death-blow to Dr Terence Meaden's theory that stationary whirlwinds or plasma-vortices had produced the circles – and a fake was also out of the question.
(Photo: Busty Taylor)

The rings in Wiltshire at the beginning of the exciting cereological season of 1990. They appeared on 3rd May 1990 near Bishops Cannings.
(Photo: George Wingfield)

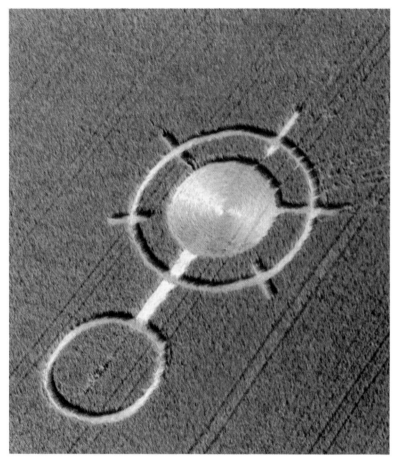

One of the most beautiful pictograms: the 'Sun Logos' at Etchilhampton, 29th July 1990.

The third long pictogram to appear at East Kennett, this one on 27th July 1990. As the picture shows, the pattern isn't orientated to the 'tramlines', but points exactly towards the Silbury Hill (above). In front of it one can see the West Kennett long barrow, a prehistoric mystery chamber.

(Photo: George Wingfield)

The next 'quantum jump' of the phenomenon – the gigantic 184yds (168m) long pictogram at Alton Barnes, Wiltshire, which attracted thousands of visitors after this photo had appeared in newspapers throughout the world.
(Photo: George Wingfield)

A very similar pictogram turned up on the same night at Stanton St Bernard below the Allington 'White Horse'.
(Photo: George Wingfield)

Detailed picture of a pictogram found on 11th August 1990 at Cheesefoot Head, near Winchester.
(Photo: Busty Taylor)

Below: *One of the most beautiful pictograms discovered near Cheesefoot Head on 1st August 1990.*

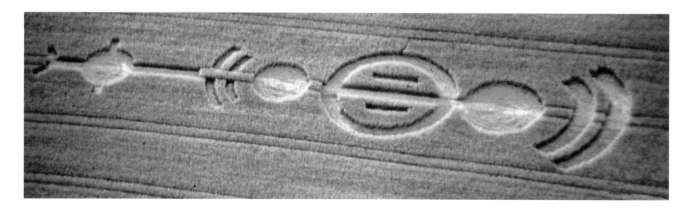

Alton Barnes, 2nd July 1991. This was close to where a large pictogram had appeared the year before. Visitors have made paths from the main shaft to the isolated small circles. (Photo: Paul Greenaway)

On 30th July 1991, this pattern turned up above the 'Avenue' at Avebury. UFOs were suggested in connection with it.

This 'dumb-bell' was formed during thick fog in front of circle researchers' directional microphones and tracking devices in the night of 27th-28th June 1991 near Devizes.

The 'six-pointed star' at Telegraph Hill, discovered on 16th August 1991. The night it appeared, a passer-by claims to have seen a 'light dome' over the place in question. Here, circle researchers had recorded an inexplicable buzzing noise as part of 'Operation White Crow' in 1989.

A small, untouched circle near Milk Hill, above Alton Barnes, not far from Avebury.

East Kennett, 23rd July 1991 – the 'Key' directly points to Silbury Hill, part of the Avebury complex. (Photo: George Wingfield)

The 'insectogram' at Stonehenge, 10th July 1991. The 'ladder' points towards the stone circle. (Photo: George Wingfield)

The 'inscription' at Milk Hill, above Alton Barnes, Wiltshire, middle of August 1991. The archeologist Michael Green reckoned it was a kind of ancient Hebraic, and translated it to be "The Creator, wise and kind".

Detailed picture of the 'insectogram' above.

(Photo: George Wingfield)

East Kennett, 23rd July 1991. The pattern is – with a deviation of only 0.6% – identical in size, shape and proportion with the Alton Barnes formation from the 18th of July, a few miles away.

(Photo: Calyx Photo)

The first 'delphinogram' at Lockeridge, Wiltshire, was 128yds (127m) long and appeared on 30th July 1991.

On the night of 2nd August 1991, when this pattern turned up at Beckhampton, a woman observed a bright disc which hovered over the field. On the next morning, this pictogram was found at the precise place.

The 'Snail' in the Punchbowl at Cheesefoot Head turned up on 30th July 1991. (Photo: Calyx Photo)

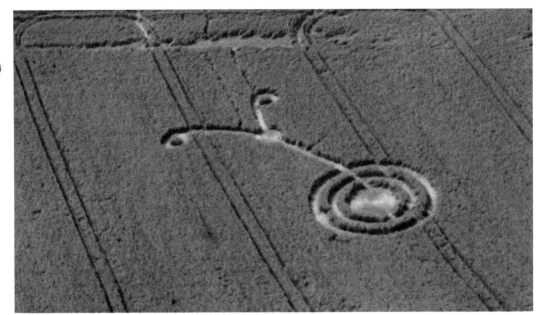

This 78yds (70m) pictogram appeared on 13th August 1991 on the land of the organic farmer Martin Pitt near Marlborough.

The 'ant' at Clatford near Marlborough. Here, the Durckheim brothers filmed a mysterious light-sphere on 18th August 1991. (Photo: R. Wintle, Calyx Photo)

This enormous triangular pictogram of 16th July 1991 formed below the iron age hill fort of Barbury Castle. In the night when it appeared, the custodian of the Castle heard "a thunderous rumbling like a hundred aeroplanes". Other witnesses reported strange lights in the sky. The next morning, the military sealed off the area.

One of the most beautiful circle patterns appeared on 7th August 1991 in Woodford near Kettering, Northamptonshire. The outer one of the six rings had a diameter of 126 yards (115m). Remarkably, this pictogram was a hoax, constructed artistically by some young men, to see if such a thing could successfully be done.
(Photo: G. Wingfield)

While the mysterious buzzing sounds were the circle sensation of the year, the season ended with a surprise which was to give the researchers a foretaste of what awaited them in 1990. On 12th August 1989, the most perfect crop formation the world had yet seen appeared on farmer Mike Bucknell's land at Winterbourne Stoke

near Amesbury in Wiltshire. Its diameter measured 20 yards (18.5m), and its pattern gave Dr Meaden's 'plasma vortex' theory and all other possible 'natural' explanations their final death-blow. The circle at Winterbourne Stoke was a kind of swastika, with a marked quadrature. Its clockwise centre was surrounded by an anti-clockwise ring, which again was followed by a clockwise ring. From the latter, the corn was combed in a cross-shaped manner towards the four points of the compass, right up to a clockwise ring of one yard (1m) width at the edge cleanly bordered the formation.

The circle year of 1990 began early. At the end of April, a group of small circles and some big, ringed circles of up to 60 yards (55m) in diameter turned up north of Devizes in Wiltshire. At the beginning of May, two equally large 'three-ringers' appeared – a formation which had had its premiere in 1989 – surrounded by four satellites within the middle ring. The precise rings were only

6–9 inches (15–22cm) wide and were a phenomenon in itself. No weather phenomenon and no human feet are capable of producing such a fine and precise form. For that reason, Pat Delgado attributed their creation to "pencil lines of energy". In May 1990, George Wingfield detected, during a second plane flight over one of the large 'three-ringers', that a fourth, concentric ring had been formed around it.

Several crop patterns were later extended by 'adding-on'. At the beginning of June, John Haddington and George Wingfield organised a ten day 'circle watch' in the area between Wansdyke and Silbury Hill. It was to become ten days full of mysteries, which reminded Wingfield of Warminster of the late sixties. First, several members of the surveillance group heard strange noises, including a hissing sound. John and a companion shortly later observed a yellow shining object which hovered over one of the fields, out of which came several smaller red lights. Then, George saw mysterious lights which operated slowly and fairly low over the stems of a wheat field. This was repeated a few days later when John and George and a further observer examined a circle formation near Milk Hill. *"The lights moved, faded, met, became brighter and disappeared together. It was not possible to approach them, since then they immediately shot away"*, explained Wingfield, *"but*

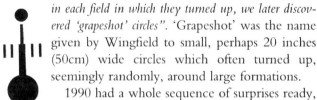

in each field in which they turned up, we later discovered 'grapeshot' circles". 'Grapeshot' was the name given by Wingfield to small, perhaps 20 inches (50cm) wide circles which often turned up, seemingly randomly, around large formations.

1990 had a whole sequence of surprises ready, as well. Not only did the phenomenon develop continually, but also it was to experience a complete quantum jump. 'Crop circles' became *pictograms*, complicated agriglyphs which suddenly presented themselves in an undreamt-of diversity.

The first 'pictogram' turned up on 23rd May on Chilcomb Farm near Cheesefoot Head. It consisted of a smaller circle and a larger one, from which a rectangular path originated, narrowing step-wise towards the smaller circle.

Parallel to the path, there were two rectangular 'boxes' on each side. From then on, the crop circle researchers (who in the meantime had called themselves 'Cereologists', after the Roman corn goddess Ceres), were amazed. *"This has never been seen before..."*, became their standard

comment. And the pictograms varied with each instance: the second pictogram had something Native American about it, like a shield with four beaver's tails, standing on a sphere. And while the first part stood right on a 'tram-line' (the tractor path), this structure, which appeared on 2nd June near Cheesefoot Head, extended right across the field. Number three, found on 16th June on Telegraph Hill near Cheesefoot Head, resembled a dumb-bell, one side of which was surrounded by a threefold semi-circle.

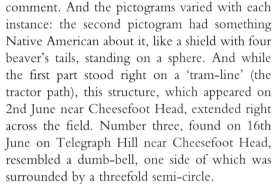

The next formation emerged on 23rd June near Litchfield, Hampshire, stretched a bit longer and lined on both sides of the 'pillar' by two 'boxes' each. The following configuration of 28th June had the dumb-bell's upper circle enclosed by a wide ring, on whose top side the central shaft continued. Lengthwise, it measured an impressive 55 yards (50m). A week later, there was a progression to the 81-yard (74m) pictogram at Crawley Down, where in place of the 'head extension' a new circle with a concentric ring and a new extension was formed.

But the true sensation of the circle year of 1990 was the 201-yard (168m) long Alton Barnes formation, which appeared on 11th July in the Vale of Pewsey, south of Avebury and Marlborough. It consisted of a row of nine circles – five single circles and two successive dumb-bells – which each had a three-finger 'claw' extension. In all of the constituent circles, the corn lay in clockwise rotation. Surprisingly, at the same time, only few miles from Alton Barnes near Stanton St Bernard, at the feet of the White Horse at Allington, a nearly-identical pictogram had appeared. On this memorable night an inhabitant of Alton Barnes heard a strange buzzing sound, which caused all dogs in the village to

bark. According to some reports, none of the farmer's cars were able to start the next morning.

Photos of the Alton Barnes formation went around the world and attracted literally thousands of visitors. With the likelihood that people would trample his crops, the farmer Tim Carson put up an attendant's hut at the field entrance and collected one pound from each visitor – at the end of the season, he had made a hefty £5,000. *"I have never seen so many people who were absolutely high without having taken drugs"*, was how George Wingfield described many visitors' reactions.

When two circle-tourists, the Alexanders from Andover, filmed the Alton Barnes pictogram with their amateur video camera from nearby Milk Hill, they noticed a small, white object which glided slowly over the neighbouring field – just being fertilised by a tractor driven by a farmer's employee. When Colin Andrews later found this employee, he acknowledged he had seen a flashing disc-shaped object that afternoon, *"...as large as a beach ball"*, which crossed the field at corn-ear's height.

And the circles and pictograms continued to turn up throughout the country. Their number can only be estimated, but there must have been around one thousand. There was hardly a day without a newspaper somewhere in the country writing about the phenomenon. England was in a state of circle fever – and this didn't pass unnoticed by the authorities.

In previous years, Colin Andrews and Pat Delgado had observed and even photographed army helicopters over newly-formed circles. The helicopters seemed to take photos of the circles – and on one occasion such an 'official' photo was even leaked by a research team from the army. But now, most days olive green choppers were searching the area for new pictograms around Silbury Hill and Alton Barnes. When Colin Andrews announced the second large circle surveillance project, 'Operation Blackbird', the army also promised to take part.

Sponsored by BBC TV and the Japanese Nippon TV, the Blackbird project was a media circus from the beginning – although quite an effective one. At last, the Cereologists had everything they sought: several 24-hour video cameras, infra-red and night-vision cameras, radar, support and interest. They erected their station in an iron-age hill-fort called Bratton Castle, above the White Horse at Westbury, where they could look over the fields and pastures below – an area which in previous years had repeatedly been a centre for crop circle activities. The project was planned to last three weeks, starting 23rd July 1990. And, to everyone's surprise, on only the second day, it seemed as if a discovery had been made.

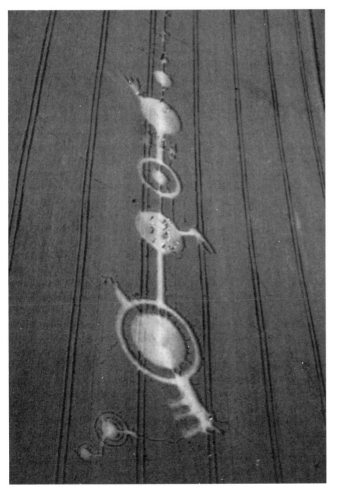

The first double pictogram: at Alton Barnes 11th July 1990.
(Alick Bartholomew)

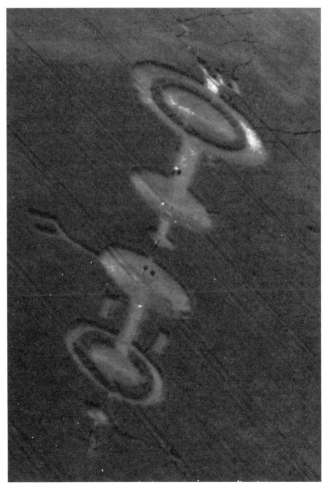

East Kennett double pictogram: 26th July 1990 pointed to Silbury Hill.
(Kate Bartholomew)

3. THE ANATOMY OF A HOAX

It was the morning's news sensation when a euphoric Colin Andrews announced on BBC breakfast television on 25th July that "a major event" taken place during the previous night: *"Yes, we have here an event of greatest importance… are very much excited as you can imagine. We do have two major ground markings which have appeared in front of all the surveillance equipment, performing absolutely to form for us. We had a situation at approximately 3.30am this morning. On the monitor, a number of orange lights taking the form of a triangle… It is a complex situation and we are analysing it at the moment, but there is undoubtedly something here for science."*

Reporter: *"I'm sure you have the nation agog. Are you quite sure you couldn't have been the victim of some elaborate hoax last night?"*

"No, not indeed. We have high quality equipment here, and we have indeed secured on high-quality equipment a major event…. We do have here something of great, great significance… Yes, we have everything on film, and we do have, as I say, a formed object over the field… We are doing nothing more until we have helicopters over the top, to film in detail what we have, before anyone enters the field."

It was really quite a strange pattern which had appeared, just over half a mile (1km) from the circle-researchers' base: two big circles with two small satellites each, in between three lines. Actually, it was asymmetrical, and compared with other formations it was quite primitive, seemed pointless, and lacked the majesty and expressivity of previous pictograms. Following Colin's almost childlike excitement came the wailing and gnashing of teeth.

The "major event" burst like a soap bubble when he and Pat Delgado entered the field. The characteristic vortices of the real formations were missing – the corn appeared broken and trampled down, and right in the circle's middle there was a horoscope game and a wooden cross. The formation at Bratton Castle was a *hoax*, and things were only too obviously arranged to quell any doubt about this. Even a red wire was found, the length of which equalled some of the six circles' radii. Whoever had made the formation must have had the unmistakable intent to humiliate the crop circle researchers thoroughly. And he had achieved his goal: when a chastened Colin Andrews had to admit later that day that he had fallen victim of a crude deception, he became the nation's laughing stock – and one by one the reporters left the 'Blackbird' station at Bratton Castle, amused.

From then on, Cereologists carried out their research more quietly – even excluding the public. But who was behind the hoax? The origin of the 'lights' was soon resolved: it was a hot air balloon, flown by Richard Branson, who emphatically denied any intention of irritating the crop circle researchers. Whoever was behind the pictogram – on closer inspection quite an untidy one – must have had access to insider information, since during the night in question, neither Andrews nor Delgado were at the camp, and neither were the army team (who usually went stalking around in combat uniform, with blackened faces and night-vision equipment) – they had taken a day off on 24th July. Interestingly, Corporal Darren Cummings of the army detachment had explained to the press: *"We are here to prove that the circles were made by man – the scientists here want to prove the opposite"*.

Of course, immediately the army was suspected – a suspicion which George Wingfield shared as well: *"One week after the Bratton hoax, I still struggled with the inconsistencies of this confusing puzzle and specially the illogic of the planks and crosses.*

"Around this time, I received a telephone call from a friend, who shed a completely new light on the whole matter. He had a reliable contact in a high-ranking position in the military – whose name I'm not allowed to mention, for understandable reasons. This man had already supplied sensitive information in the past, which until now always proved extremely valuable.

"Now he disclosed that the Bratton hoax was carried out by a specially-trained unit of the army and that the order came directly from the Ministry of Defence. The operation was carefully planned, prepared in advance and then carried out in complete darkness, quickly and precisely. My informant was even able to speak with an officer who was involved in the planning of the operation, which had the highest secrecy level."

Wingfield thinks it possible that the Ministry had carried out the operation to get 'circle-fever' under control – and to defuse 'Operation Blackbird' before it really observed something explosive. Furthermore, pressure from the public and the press, loudly demanding an official statement, was putting the MoD (Ministry of Defence) on the spot. So to make sure that Pat and Colin wouldn't be tempted to declare the Bratton circles as real, and therefore increase public interest in the phenomenon, the cult items were intentionally placed in the six circles. These false clues were needed to take any possible attention off those responsible.

The BBC immediately took the offending items to be an indication that a 'ritual' had taken place in the circles – and of course hippies and occultists were duly suspected. When Colin Andrews later received a 'letter claiming responsibility', with the logo of the rock group KLF, it seemed as if the perpetrators had been found. Actually, on 2nd August, KLF did make a 'pictogram' featuring their logo – a pyramid and a ghetto-blaster – which was then filmed for a rock video, which later became a world success. According to information given by the farmer on whose land KLF shot the video, four young men needed nearly six hours, in bright daylight, to create the pattern – after they had asked permission and had promised to pay for the damage. Apart from the fact that KLF evidently hadn't been in a position to create the very much larger Bratton pictogram in a much shorter time, in the dark, KLF declared believably that the letter to Colin Andrews wasn't from them – and hence was faked.

Although the army seemed to have achieved their goal of 'proving that the circles were made by man', they remained at Bratton and around Silbury Hill and showed great interest in every new circle formation. A subdued Colin Andrews went on with his circle-watch, with a reduced BBC and NTV crew. It took ten days until he eventually gained the success he deserved. On 5th July, only 440 yards (400m) west of the faked pictogram a real circle appeared straight in front of the lenses of two night-vision cameras. But this time, the 'Blackbird' team avoided public pronouncements.

The film which the cameras had shot was fully analysed using the NASA computer in Basingstoke, Hampshire. It showed a whirl-motion, lasting less than 15 seconds, like a winding snake which ironically formed a question mark, exactly on the spot where the pictogram appeared by the next morning. While this little piece of film was never broadcast, it soon wandered into a BBC archive, a copy of part of the film appears on the video documentary *Crop Circle Communique*[1]. It proved without doubt that there were real circles being made.

The British tabloid press had a good silly-season news topic, thanks to the Bratton hoax. From now, every tabloid presented an obscure personality as 'the man who fooled the world with the circles'. *The Mail on Sunday* even publicised detailed instructions of 'How to make those Corn Circles', and *The Sun* offered a reward of £10,000 to anyone who would solve the crop circle riddle. As a result, *The People* answered by presenting Fred Day (59), who supposedly had produced circles for 47 years. To support this claim they produced an aerial photograph of an irregular crop circle 9 yards (8m) in diameter, which Fred had created with a variant of a rolling-pin – in no more than 32 minutes, according to the paper. While the trained toolmaker announced in *The People* what he wanted to do with the £10,000 offered by *The Sun*, he omitted to explain why he didn't simply collect the reward, instead of receiving a smaller fee from its competitor. Actually, a 'Fred Day' never reported to *The Sun*, and the sum remained unpaid.

In comparison, according to the *Sunday Sport*, George Vernon of Bristol, also known as 'Merlin the Magician', was claimed to be responsible for the circles and to have produced most of them with his 'pure strength of thought'. Since he didn't succeed in the case of the Bratton hoax, he apparently hoaxed this pattern by rolling himself around in the corn. He had discovered his surprising psychic abilities when, a few years earlier, he had slept in a cornfield near Stonehenge, and woke up in the midst of a circle. Anyone still tempted to believe this story will unfortunately have their hopes dashed: he called himself 'Bertie Ollocks' or 'B Ollocks' ('Bollocks!', for the uninitiated, meaning both 'testicles' and 'nonsense'!).

How such an 'exposure story' is created I learned from the landlord of the 'Who'd a Thought It' pub in East Kennett. He told me that, one evening in summer 1989, a film team from ARD (a German TV station) entered the pub. The editor offered £15 to anyone able to produce a crop circle in front of the camera – and 'as much beer as a man can drink in one evening'. Four men volunteered – among them the local undertaker. The circle, which they created using sticks and clothes-lines, was so asymmetrical that everyone knew that it was faked. But the ARD-team was proud to have solved the riddle, and returned to London. The film was presented on *Tagesthemen* (a major German news programme) on 22nd October 1989 to a disillusioned German viewing public.

While this kind of journalism gave the world public the impression that the crop circles were but a silly competitor to the Loch Ness monster, officialdom gave them different treatment. In September 1990, the first of three internal conferences about the crop circle phenomenon took place at the Department of the Environment, at which Members of Parliament, government scientists and civil servants from the Ministries of Defence, Environment and Agriculture were present. Without doubt, an army deputy will have reported the results of the control projects, and also will have shown the film showing an illuminated sphere which an army camera had caught in July, in the area of the Silbury Hill (the film is included in the documentary *Crop Circle Communique*).

According to the London political correspondent for *Die Zeit* (a German newspaper), Jürgen Krönig, the participants of the committee agreed that agriglyphs weren't a meteorological phenomenon. *"The favourite thesis of the sceptics, that the circles were but a large-scale joke, wasn't even considered. The army was instructed to keep the phenomenon under intensive observation and, if necessary, to take 'appropriate steps'. Finally, it was discussed how the topic should be handled in public: in this discussion, the term 'disinformation' was used."* The rejection of the weather theory was at least a sign of progress, and probably due to the phenomenon's 'quantum jump' in 1990.

Also on 11th July 1989, the Minister of Defence answered a parliamentary question about the cause of the circles, put by Teddy Taylor MP, who was told that army helicopters were definitely not responsible for the whorls.

Shortly later, the Ministry of Defence stated that they were *"very probably the result of a combination of wind and local ground-fertility conditions"*. Colin Andrews commented: *"The British government accepted at the time that we were dealing with a real phenomenon, but they chose the wrong explanation. They could equally well have said that everything was a hoax. But they didn't say so – they accepted that the circles are real."*

His colleague, Pat Delgado, told me that he was contacted by Members of Parliament and of the House of Lords and was asked for his cooperation. *"They are more than interested. They want to know, and they have to know, what is happening there on the British fields, just as any other government would be interested. They can't control it, or put up a sign saying 'No crop circles on this field'. It is beyond their power."*

One problem discussed was whether corn from the circles could be contaminated and whether it would be a risk if it came into the food-chain. As a matter of fact, American scientists noticed an increased radioactivity in the circles and suspected that they were irradiated for a short time with a kind of microwave energy. *"Many farmers are worried about this question"*, explained the conservative MP Teddy Taylor. The result was that, from then on, a section of the Ministry of Agriculture in Loughborough took samples of plants and soil from various crop circles.

Furthermore, crop circle researchers experienced more and more strange things in circle country. Chinook helicopters increasingly crossed over the fields of Hampshire and Wiltshire at night with searchlights, and new circles were not infrequently first photographed at daybreak by the army. More and more often, odd strangers appeared at circle-watchers' posts, riddling them with questions. Once, a group on Silbury Hill was photographed person by person with an infra-red camera, allegedly because the stranger wanted to test his new camera.

Jürgen Krönig, German journalist and enthusiastic crop circle researcher, wrote in his excellent German book *Spuren im Korn*[2] ('Clues in the Corn'): *"Repeatedly, I have run into military patrols at night, which had taken up strategically favourable positions. They lie on prehistoric grave-mounds near circle fields, were equipped with infra-red cameras and other pieces of equipment, and had driven to their observation posts in private cars, along the field-tracks. They operated far outside the military's large prohibited areas on Salisbury Plain. One couldn't say that they were pleased about our nightly meetings with them..."* Their official excuses went from 'meteorological exercises' to 'voluntary actions in pursuit of private interests'.

Since private undertakings with official equipment are strictly forbidden in the army and air force, this doesn't sound very convincing. Rather, everything indicates that their orders came 'from the top'. The respected *Wall Street Journal* of 28th August 1989 reported the interest as being at the highest level: *"Employees of the British Ministries of Agriculture and Defence want to know more. Also Queen Elizabeth, from what one hears, recently questioned Margaret Thatcher about the circles. While such discussions are kept secret, a spokesman for Buckingham Palace explained that the Queen will take a recently-published book about the circles to read at her summer residence this month; being England's greatest landowner, she has every reason not to be amused about this."* *Circular Evidence* was on the Queen's official summer reading list, which is publicised yearly by Buckingham Palace.

"Shortly afterwards we received letters from the Court's representatives", Colin Andrews explained to me in autumn 1991. *"Our newsletter was ordered by two members of the royal family, and only a few weeks ago, we again were written to with a request for direct contact."* The sender of the request was Prince Philip, whose interest in the UFO phenomenon was not restricted to specialist circles. The prince requested Lord Zuckerman, a scientific advisor to the British government during the second world war to observe the phenomenon and to keep him up to date.

While there was interest in the circle events in the upper echelons of government, the government, secret services and the military outwardly sought to calm the public. This resembles the official approach of western governments concerning UFOs, which still follows an 'educational program' adopted in 1953 by the 'Robertson Panel' in the Pentagon. According to the protocol, officially released in 1977 under the US Freedom of Information Act, government should *"have two major aims: training and 'debunking'. The 'debunking' aim would result in reduction in public interest in 'flying saucers'... This education could be accomplished by mass media such as television, motion pictures and popular articles. The basis of such education would be actual case histories which had been puzzling at first but later explained."*

Anybody who wishes to understand the reasons for such massive public disinformation as a political strategy should to look into the situation at the beginning of the 1950s. The mass panic which followed the 1938 transmission of H G Wells' radio play *War of the Worlds* was recalled all too clearly – the drama was about the landing of Martians in USA. Since people were unclear about the intentions and origins of extra-terrestrials, it was primarily essential to keep the public calm. This was the time of the Korean conflict, the beginning of the Cold War. The USA had just recovered from the Great Depression of the thirties, won the Second World War, and was about to define its newly-won role as a world power, and their deepest interest was inner political stability.

CIA strategists knew that knowledge of the presence of extra-terrestrials in earthly air-space implied culture shock for too many people – all of a sudden our complete world-view, everything we regarded as certain, could begin to totter. They feared that people would lose trust in our political, religious and economic authorities, if there is a power which is light-years ahead of us, towards which our leaders and protectors would be quite helpless. The result was a political strategy of disinformation, whose aim it was to make the UFO phenomenon appear a meaningless

agglomeration of confusing or fraudulent cases, or to discredit UFO researchers in every conceivable way.

Busty Taylor, the pilot, who rendered outstanding service in discovery and photographic documentation of countless new circles from 1985 on, is convinced that the British government employs similar strategies in the case of crop circles. *"The government wished that this had never happened"*, he explained in his calm matter-of-fact way. *"At best, everything should subside. In my opinion, the government was behind the hoax at Bratton Castle. At the time, the whole world watched this spot, 'Operation Blackbird'. What a wonderful opportunity they had to tie a knot in the crop circles' tail! Manufacture a hoax and prove to the world that everything is but a gigantic joke. I quite clearly think the matter to be engineered – but it is difficult to prove. They have to discredit the phenomenon. For if they told the public the truth, it would probably thoroughly destabilise most governments."*

The CIA also collected information about crop circles and, as a 1990 document proves (by the internal US political commission 'Majestic 12', and leaked to me), they attached great importance to their effect upon the public. The ex-police sergeant and UFO researcher Anthony Dodd from North Yorkshire, who specially investigated some crop circles in the North of England, reported to me that some local farmers had received instructions from the authorities to harvest the fields in question immediately, whether or not the corn was ripe. *"In other words: they wanted to see formations gone from the fields before the public could examine them"*, believes Dodd.

It was not until September 1991 that the 'Section for Disinformation' succeeded in giving crop circles a definitive blow.

REFERENCES

1. *Crop Circle Communique*, directed by John Macnish, Circlevision, 1991.
2. *Spuren im Korn*, Jürgen Krönig, Zweitausendeins, Frankfurt am Main, 1992.

4. Mandelbrots, Dolphins & the Circle-Makers

The bad weather of spring 1991 was presumably to blame for a later than usual start to the circle season. Throughout all of June, formations appeared almost shyly, hesitatingly, in the still-unripe wheat. But nevertheless, the circle-makers let the researchers know quite early that this summer would be full of surprises.

Of all places, it would have to be Glastonbury where the first crop circles appeared, on 14th April, 2 miles (3km) from the Tor, in a field of winter barley at Butleigh Wootton, during daylight and under truly strange attendant circumstances. On that Sunday afternoon, Dave Harris, a young man, riding his bicycle along a country lane, claimed that he had observed a mysterious, bell-shaped, silver-coloured craft, which hovered only 25ft (8m) above a field. The lad said that he fell shocked from his bicycle when he saw a spiral-shaped ray of 'aura-like light' come out of the UFO, pointing down at the field. Then, the mysterious craft disappeared with fast, abrupt manoeuvres and a buzzing noise. The lad rode back home, told his friends what he had experienced, and went back with them to the field in question. The young people found a place on which the corn was spirally laid down on the ground. And although this case caused a controversy later, it clearly marked the beginning of a season full of surprises.

The circle-makers took their time, and let crop circle researchers puzzle about this incident for a while. Apart from a few smaller patterns (such as an ordinary dumb-bell in a rape field), they made their presence felt only at the beginning of June, with a formation at Cheesefoot Head.

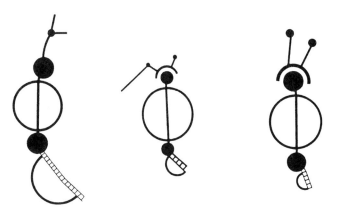

It was the first 'Insectogram', as circle researchers soon were to call it (although it resembled more a snail than an insect), and the first of five, which appeared in the following four weeks (7th June to 7th July) – the most beautiful of which finished off the series but a few hundred yards from the megalith temple of Stonehenge.

The 'Insectograms' gave the phenomenon a new dimension. Until then there had been mostly 'classic' symbols which appeared in the cornfields, but they now appeared almost funny or bizarre, without any initially

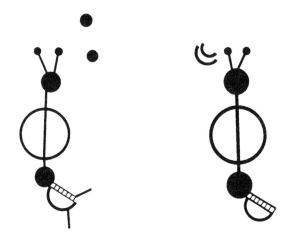

recognisable meaning. But they nevertheless exhibited the same characteristics as other authentic agriglyphs, and so people had to come to terms with the fact that, as George Wingfield formulated it, *"there seems to exist but one rule for crop circles: to break all of our fixed expectations and to surprise us anew almost daily"*.

The insectograms were followed by 'threefold dumb-

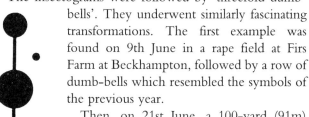

bells'. They underwent similarly fascinating transformations. The first example was found on 9th June in a rape field at Firs Farm at Beckhampton, followed by a row of dumb-bells which resembled the symbols of the previous year.

Then, on 21st June, a 100-yard (91m) dumb-bell appeared at Lockeridge, Wiltshire. The puzzle intensified when an almost identical copy of this formation turned up on 2nd July on the field at Alton Barnes, only 220 yards (200m) away from the place where the gigantic world-famous pictogram had been in the previous year.

The term 'identical copy' should be taken literally. A measurement of both formations by John Langrish showed that the difference in dimensions was no more

than 0.6%. George Wingfield described to me the mysterious attendant circumstances under which the Alton Barnes pictogram appeared: *"It was discovered in the early morning by a travelling salesman. On the night in question, a mist lay over the valley, and in this mist the formation was formed. On this night, a farmer, Malcolm Innery, who lives in the village, was woken up around 1.30am by a rumbling like thunder. He thought at first that it came from a big C-130 Hercules bomber which might have flown close over the roofs, but when he looked out of the window, he saw nothing. Others from this village also heard the noise, and some immediately said: 'My God, the circles are back again!'"* From then on, a whole number of pictograms turned up in pairs, with similarly minuscule differences in size. And they got larger and

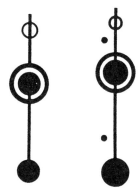

larger: the 'magic key' at Alton Priors, discovered on 11th July on the land of Tim Carson, measured 120 yards (110m), just like its twin of 27th July near West Kennett (difference: 0.9%).

After the 'keys' came the 'delphinograms' or 'whales', which appeared between 30th July and 22nd August, seven in number. The 'dolphins', with their sharp ends and the circles surrounding them appeared rather like cross-sections through a UFO, together with its energy-field. After two six-pointed stars and a mysterious inscription, some scribblings with 'insecto'-character, gigantic

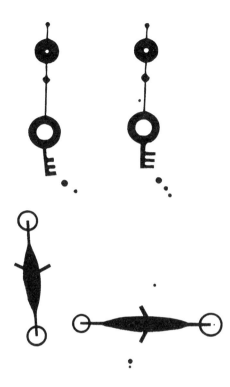

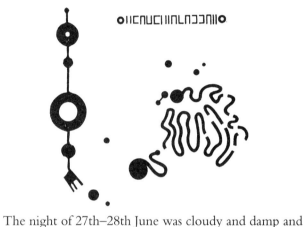

phone which digitally recorded all sounds within the spectrum of 2–40,000 Hertz. A remote-controlled 'Skystalk' TV camera was installed on a 55 yard (50m) long hydraulic grasping arm, to record the motions of everything which would dare to enter the fields at night. Furthermore, a clever alarm system was installed around the observed field which would trigger at the presence of any intruder.

'threefold dumb-bells', a formation 200 yards (180m) in length and a whole number of other strange symbols had turned up, the circle season 1991 ended on 18th August with a totally new symbol which resembled the convolutions of a human brain. Maybe it was advising us to use the same and... think!

As previously in 1990, so also in 1991 there was again a number of coordinated experiments to get on the trail of the 'circle-makers'. The first surveillance project, 'Chameleon', was stationed on Morgan's Hill near Devizes in June, run by John Macnish and David Morgenstern in co-operation with the BBC. A year before, the enormous four-ringed 'Celtic-Crosses' had turned up here. Besides video equipment, the Chameleon project had at its disposal a high-sensitivity directional micro-

The night of 27th–28th June was cloudy and damp and didn't seem very promising. Furthermore, at 3.00am, mist came down, which slowly thickened to fog. Nevertheless, the circle researchers decided to keep the cameras and directional microphones running. Only at daybreak did the fog slowly disperse. When the view of the field was finally clear, a dumb-bell shaped formation lay in front of them: a large and a small circle, the large one 21 yards (19m), the small one 9 yards (8m) in diameter. The vortex turned clockwise in the large circle, opposite in the small one, both being linked with each other by a 6.5yds (6m) long connecting path. The pattern lay only 660 yards (600m) from the Chameleon camp. A thorough examination of the fog-damp field, looking for footprints, led to a negative result: there were no tracks left by human intruders.

Neither the camera nor the directional microphone had recorded anything special. The pictogram must have been formed out of nowhere.

'Operation Blue Hill', headed by Dr Terence Meaden and Professor Ohtsuki of the Tokyo Waseda University, who brought eighteen more Japanese scientists, likewise camped on Morgan's Hill. During one night at the end of June, the research team located an object on radar which overflew the fields, sometimes slowly, at other times with great speed. It was certainly no aeroplane, and Dr Meaden was hoping finally to have tracked down one of his 'plasma vortices'. But although visibility was clear during that night, none of the people involved could make out any object in the sky. It seemed to be simply invisible.

Under still stricter security provisions than those used in 'Project Chameleon' or 'Operation Blue Hill', a complex cross pictogram was formed a few weeks later, close to the Prime Minister's country residence at Chequers, within a maximum-security zone guarded 24 hours a day against

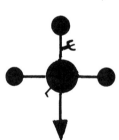

terrorists and infiltrators. Interestingly, the 'Celtic Cross' consisted of three satellite circles connected with each other by beams extending from a central circle, and – in place of the fourth circle – a triangle which, similar to a compass card, pointed directly at the summer residence – obviously a message from the circle-makers to the government! When representatives of the local press enquired of PM John Major's office whether the formation's creators had been tracked down by the safety system, the official answer was that there hadn't been any security risks since the circles were caused by a meteorological phenomenon. While, as always, we were left puzzled about precisely what weather conditions could cause such an orderly symmetrical form

as this pictogram, we at least could breathe a sigh of relief: a hoax was certainly not under consideration.

A further observational station was erected in August on 'Adam's Grave', a prehistoric site above Alton Barnes, where gigantic pictograms were formed in 1990 and 1991 – in 1992 three large formations had even turned up within three weeks. This time, the project was run totally by Japanese from Nippon TV, who, equipped with the most modern instruments, did everything possible to film the creation of a circle. They were supported by Colin Andrews and some of the British circle enthusiasts, who suffered from the Japanese director Mitchihito Ogawa's army discipline – he quickly acquired the nickname 'Crop Circle Napoleon'. He led a strict regime over his army of Japanese technicians and cameramen, five monitors and equally many cameras – among them a newly-constructed ultra-low-light camera with an image-resolution amplifier (which guarantied optimal picture quality if a circle should put in an appearance), ultra-sound instruments, radar, high-sensitivity directional microphones and sensitive instruments for measuring even the smallest temperature changes (to register the body temperature of possible hoaxers). But evidently, the circle-makers avoided Ogawa and his command hill. Only once, the Sony cameras recorded a number of mysterious red lights which manoeuvred over Adam's Grave.

As if the 'yellow invasion' hadn't been enough, circle tourism developed in Merlin's homeland. Local circle researchers feared the worst when in June we announced the coming of a group of 85 Germans who, guided by Johannes von Buttlar and myself, sought to examine some newly-formed circles. In their nightmares circle-researchers feared trampling of any newly-formed pictogram before sufficient examination and documentation were possible. This fear proved unfounded. On the contrary, our group made sure we visited only circles which had already been examined, after consultation with researchers, permission from farmers and clear instructions to participants to enter fields only via the tram-lines.

At the end of July, a group of Americans followed, who held meditations within the formations and became a popular subject for helicopter-flying circle photographers. The much-reviled though well-organised 'circle tourists' probably caused far less devastation than the disorganised crowds of weekend trippers who held picnics inside pictograms, dogs and children in tow, often leaving a trail of garbage and cigarette butts behind – or the curious onlookers, who entered a newly-formed pictogram before researchers could get there and often caused irretrievable damage, even if not intending to do so.

The summer of 1991 certainly wasn't a quiet summer in the circle country, even though the national and international press this time kept quiet about the phenomenon. Over 250 new formations and pictograms and over 600 new circles in all parts of England appeared during the summer of 1991. It brought a new trend in the phenomenon, following from the 'quantum jump' of 1990: fewer single circles, and instead gigantic, complicated agriglyphs.

While in 1990 there had been only twenty-five crop formations in Wiltshire and Hampshire, the number rose eightfold in 1991 – and pictograms turned up for the first time in other parts of the country. But the centre of the events was again the mysterious Silbury Hill at Avebury, in whose immediate area about forty of these mysterious symbols appeared. Twelve of them, and a few dozen 'grapeshot' circles (so named by George Wingfield) were located on Firs Farm, belonging to farmer Stephen Horton – who wasn't greatly amused by the profusion of circle phenomena occurring on his land and disrupting his normal farming routines. *"During the first few years, this was still an interesting phenomenon"*, he confided to me on camera, *"but now, we have so much to do on the farm that they only*

disturb us, because all these people run around on my land, drive up and down the tracks without permission, park cars in the way, and risk fire when they throw their cigarette butts into the dry corn". He had a point.

Because agricultural insurance against cereological activity doesn't exist, he took a £1 entrance charge per visitor – an income which mostly flowed towards his church community. But if he could talk to the circle-makers, he said, he only had one wish: *"Please look for another farm next year!"*.

An example of the effect of the circles on farmers was at Levetts Farm, near Marlborough, farmed by Martin Pitt, a specialising organic farmer. Martin Pitt had always believed that the circles were a gigantic red herring. He had even allowed the 'Wessex Sceptics' to hoax a circle on his land for television, to prove that genuine circles were improbable. But when a 77-yard (70m) pictogram really appeared on 13th August 1991 on one of his fields, he couldn't be held back any more. We heard of Pitt's pictogram on 14th August, and immediately drove to Levett's Farm to film the comparatively new pattern. The talkative bio-farmer just had brought a Channel Four TV team into nearly bird's-eye view with his fork-lift truck, when he gave us his second interview of the day:

"When I came onto the field yesterday morning – I found the formation around 6.30am – I paid special attention to whether there were any indications that humans had been on the field, but I couldn't find anything, no footprints, no wheel tracks. Everything was absolutely smooth, as if each individual cornstalk had been brushed. The stems at the edge stood there upright, absolutely undamaged, and in front of them the smoothly laid-down corn. Not a single stem was broken. At the centre there was a spiral made out of woven corn, from which, leading off, the plants lay in a spiral shape. I can't stress enough how absolutely smooth and flat everything was, with every ear just in the place

it belonged. The path, the connection at each side, which formed a straight line, was so precisely laid out, as if it had been measured, and also the distances between the satellite circles are exactly the same. I have no idea how the formation could have been created."

But the true miracle of the circle season of 1991 was also the greatest, most sophisticated and beautiful of all formations, euphorically named by the press (with a little help from Saddam Hussein) 'the Mother of all Pictograms'.

It was during the night of 16th July that the 110 yards (100m) wide triangle had been formed – on a total area 12,000sq yds (10,000m²)! – at the foot of an Iron Age hill-

fort site at Barbury Castle. Local residents saw mysterious lights and heard a rumble of thunder. The town of Wroughton (near Swindon) had even had a power cut during the night in question.

Fortunately, that morning the circle photographer Richard Wintle went circle-hunting with helicopter pilot Nick Bailey, and discovered the formation around 9am, which he photographed before curious onlookers entered it. Wintle's photos show no footprints in the still-green wheat field and no other indications of a hoax. His photos are especially valuable, because the pictogram was seriously damaged during a heavy thunderstorm a couple of days later, and thousands of trampling visitors finished it off. The triangle at Barbury Castle caused a sensation. *"Now explain this one!"*, hollered the British press, impudently expecting the 'crop circle pundits' to give a simple answer – especially Dr Terence Meaden, who, faced with the complicated pattern, hardly a manifestation of his 'plasma-vortices' and 'mini-tornadoes', was at his wits' end. The military seemed to be

interested in the formation, for the roads all around Barbury Castle were closed in the early morning, allegedly due to an 'exercise'.

But while no one believed that the beauty and harmony of the Barbury Castle pictogram could be surpassed – John Michell even found in it the key proportions of 'sacred geometry' and thought it to be a 'divine revelation' – a symbol appearing at the end of the circle season caused a still greater sensation.

This formation was discovered on 13th August by the pilot Steven Cherry-Downes on a wheat field at Ickleton near Cambridge. Two days later a photo of the unbeliev-

ably aesthetic formation appeared in the local newspaper, the *Cambridge Evening News*. It aroused the attention of mathematicians and scientists at the University of Cambridge, who immediately recognised its symbolism: it was a gigantic 'Mandelbrot Set'. This was the first formation to date which portrayed a symbol unmistakable to humans. The Mandelbrot Set, also called 'Appleman' by mathematicians, is an important element of Chaos Theory, named after its discoverer, the French mathematician Benoit Mandelbrot, who had taught for some years at Cambridge.

While the press, as a result, suspected a student joke, Mandelbrot's colleagues resolutely rejected this possibility, for a Mandelbrot Set cannot simply be drawn and calculated like a normal geometrical pattern – one has to build it up point for point. Even then, it is virtually impossible that it could be constructed as cleanly, accurately and elegantly as this 61-yard (56m) pictogram. Even the science magazine *New Scientist* had to admit that it is actually impossible even to draw such a diagram without a computer, let alone form it in a corn field. *"This is undoubtedly the next step towards a higher complexity of the corn patterns"*, the mathematician John Sayer wrote to Pat Delgado.

*"While the Barbury Castle formation still had a clear geometrical basis, the Mandelbrot Set at Ickleton represents a logical conclusion in the foregoing development of the crop formations. Earlier formations were of an artistic or representative nature. They don't only **look** like something – they **are** something.*

*"The Mandelbrot symbol takes a step forward, a quantum jump away from pure schoolbook geometry. It leads us into the field of Chaos Theory, fractals, computer technology and infinity. The Ickleton formation doesn't only look vaguely like a Mandelbrot – it **is** a Mandelbrot, and if it means something, then it must mean everything a Mandelbrot Set means."*

This meaning implies that there is a hidden order behind apparent chaos, for the 'Appleman', in the world of fractals, is the only island of stability in an ocean of intricate chaos. The Mandelbrot can be found at any level of magnification of the design created by applying the mathematical formulae Mandelbrot developed – it hides microscopically within any larger representation of the black, heart-shaped pattern. It is the trade mark of the transition from chaos to order, of Creation itself, when 'God's spirit' created the universe out of primordial chaos – and it is also a symbol of the end of the world when Creation sinks back into chaos.

Furthermore, the attendant circumstances under which the Mandelbrot at Ickleton appeared were extraordinary enough. Exactly one year before it appeared, on 11th August 1990, the *New Scientist* published a reader's letter by Martyn Hughes from Highworth, Wiltshire: "With each summer, the crop circle formations become more complex. How long will it take until we will see a complete Mandelbrot diagram?". On the night of 11th August 1991, a Mrs Urwin drove with her son along the B1102 near Ickleton. Around 1.15am she noticed that her car was followed by a silver-blue light sphere. The UFO approached the car within less than ten yards, then it disappeared. On 12th August, farmer Hugh Raybone discovered the corn pattern. One day later the pilot Steven Cherry-Downes noticed it.

Not surprisingly, then, cereologists were only too enthusiastic when they met on the second weekend of September in Glastonbury for the first yearly 'Cornference', organised by the magazine *The Cerealogist*. The rented hall proved to be far too small, so great was the interest. Everybody who was anybody in the cereological scene presented the results of their research from the last four months. The season was at its end, the fields practically all harvested. All researchers agreed that neither a hoax nor the weather were behind the circles, and that an unknown, extremely creative intelligence was active, whose spiritual nature they were just beginning to understand. Did the circles indicate the beginning of a new age, or did they warn us of impending catastrophes? Or were they saying something else? Most agreed that it was now more important to decipher what the circle-makers wanted to tell us, than to endlessly discuss theories about the means of their creation.

But then, things started happening quite differently. Only one day after the *Cornference* had ended so confidently in Glastonbury, the world of cereology collapsed.

"The Men who conned the world", read full-size headline of the tabloid paper *Today* on Monday 9th September 1991. *"How we made the circles and fooled the world."* And, one day later: *"Come on, Pat, admit it, we've got you!"*. *"The mysterious crop circles, which baffled scientists all around the world, are a gigantic hoax"*, yelled the paper – which is part of the Murdoch group, News International. It told the story of two unbelievably active pensioners, who declared themselves responsible for the circle events of the last thirteen years. Doug Bower (67) and David Chorley (62) from Southampton claimed to have done it all, equipped with ropes, planks and a baseball cap with a bizarre wire

construction, supposedly used to help them to draw straight lines.

It all had been a hare-brained idea, which they had cooked up one night in a pub, in 1978. Since then, the two claim to have set out night after night to make new circles – altogether over 200 of them, mostly in the area around Cheesefoot Head, but also at Warminster, Westbury and Stonehenge. It had gone on six years, before Doug's wife got suspicious – presumably, he must have 'escaped' her undiscovered, up to that point! Then he had let her in on his secret, and Dave confirmed it. *"It was like being high – we couldn't stop"*, the pensioners admitted to *Today*. They had their greatest fun, they said, when the circle-pope Pat Delgado had suggested in an interview that 'superior intelligences' were behind the circles. *"We could hardly stop ourselves laughing. This was good. We heard it the first time while we were driving along, and we had to stop, for tears ran down our cheeks and we were slapping our thighs roaring with laughter."*

The more active circle researchers became, the more enthusiastically Doug & Dave accepted the challenge, *Today* asserted. The success of Delgado's and Andrews' book *Circular Evidence* made Bower and Chorley get jealous – and their old age played its part in persuading the duo to give up. *"You couldn't imagine how much energy it takes to make the circles on summer nights under the moonlight"*, explained Doug, *"and when we heard that the government wanted to make funds available for further research into the phenomenon, we both had the feeling one could use the money better for artificial kidneys and heart transplants."*

A nice story. It lacked the claim that Doug & Dave were responsible for building Stonehenge, however. But could they prove their adventurous anecdotes? They could not. There were no photos, no records, nothing at all. Only a case of Pat Delgado with the wool pulled over his eyes. On the Friday before the *Cornference*, *Today* had invited Delgado to examine an 'insectogram' to Ightham

near Sevenoaks in Kent. Enthusiastic that it so accurately resembled the 'insectograms' found in June and July near Stonehenge, Delgado let himself get carried away, to make an all-too-confident comment, recorded on tape by *Today*: *"This is by no means a hoax"*, Delgado had explained. *"'This is without doubt a wonderful moment in my research work."*

On Sunday evening, he just had just returned from Glastonbury, and *Today* reporter Graham Brough confronted him with the two pensioners: Doug & Dave were said to have created the pictogram in the presence of Brough, deliberately to test Delgado. It was they who had made all the circles, and who had, for 13 years, played tricks on him. Delgado went white as a sheet, started stuttering, and appeared irritated. He was shattered. It seemed that everything for which he had worked over the previous ten years, for which he had sacrificed everything, in which he had invested all his time, energy and enthusiasm, had suddenly become utterly pointless. Now he felt like a fool, like Don Quixote, caught tilting at windmills. And tomorrow, thanks to *Today*, he would be the world's laughing stock.

Outwardly, Pat Delgado tried to keep his composure. *"You have brought much good into this world"*, he stammered. *"With this here, you have brought millions of people together. Thousands have told me that the crop circles have changed their lives. On the other hand, what will become of it? And do you know how much excitement you caused for the police and the army?"* Then he sat down, and rang Colin Andrews. *"Colin, are you sitting down? I have bad news. We have here 100% bad news..."* On Monday, Doug and Dave's 'disclosure' appeared, followed on Tuesday by a detailed description of Pat Delgado's reaction.

On the same day, a press demonstration for dozens of interested TV stations and reporters from across the world was on TV, with Doug and Dave demonstrating their unbelievable abilities in front of the cameras. The result was more than embarrassing – not for the circle researchers, but for the pensioner duo. After one full hour, they had produced nothing other than a more or less dumbbell-shaped mess, which had about as much in common with the original as Stonehenge had with a garden shed.

Alright, it was a circle in the corn. But the corn was broken, the edges unclean, there were no vortices – not a single characteristic of the real circles was recognisable. A second crop formation made for the press, for which Bower and Chorley took still longer, turned out just as pathetic. The experts withdrew, shaking their heads. Was that supposed to have been the riddle's final solution? By no means! *"I think that we all have been taken in by the press"*, Colin Andrews remarked aptly, *"for there is nothing impressive here, except for two very athletic gentlemen in their sixties."*

In front of a running camera, Andrews then asked *Today* reporter Brough whether the two hoaxers had genuinely claimed that they had made their first circles in 1978. Brough confirmed this. The first circle mentioned in Andrews' and Delgado's bestseller *Circular Evidence* indeed dated from the year in question. But in the meantime, Andrews had photos available which showed some earlier crop patterns. Who then, if Doug and Dave claim to be the 'inventors' of the crop circles, had made these? And if they had faked 200 circles during the last thirteen years, according to their own statements, by whom were the remaining 2,300 or so circles created?

According to their own statements, Doug and Dave had never been active in the Avebury area – which, since 1988, had become the centre for circle activities. Who is supposed to have created these formations? Who made the tetrahedron at Barbury Castle or the Mandelbrot at Cambridge? Who made those in other parts of the country? Since the country was swarming with people, and since there was the danger of being discovered at any time, why had an incomplete formation never been found? Anybody who gave serious thought to the Bower/Chorley story was able to see how it was becoming visibly implausible.

"Okay, we invite them to a confrontation on television", the *Today* reporter explained to Andrews. *"You throw questions, whatever you like, and I can guarantee you that the two can answer everything."* But it was not to come to that. At the next meeting, Andrews asked Doug & Dave whether they were also responsible for the famous 'Celtic Cross' at Longstock, which had decorated the cover of his book *Circular Evidence*. The pensioners explicitly affirmed they had done it. How had they managed to make the corn in the circle be interwoven so well? No answer – deep silence. Then, sheepishly, Dave said: *"That one we didn't make"*. So on it continued, one question after the other. At the end, one had to ask which circles Bower and Chorley really had faked – if any.

The respectable British press reacted similarly. *"I find it easier to believe in little green men than in this story by Bower and Chorley"*, commented a columnist of *The Independent*. Also the BBC reacted reservedly. The reputable Swiss newspaper *Neue Zürcher Zeitung* mentioned a *"little convincing confession by hoaxers"* and postulated: *"the English crop circles remain a mystery."*

The press reaction in Germany was completely different. The *Kölner Stadtanzeiger* made the duo into 'artists' and explained categorically: *"The mysterious circles in the English cornfields are a gigantic deception"*. *Die Welt* even talked of a *"hare-brained idea"* and *"the best joke for the last ten years"*, which they likened to the faked Hitler diaries – with the difference that the crop circles were better *"because they fooled the world for over ten years"*. But that was a bit too simplistic.

All this fuss was made about little or nothing, even though it was as good as ruled out that a hoaxer team could have created the circles unnoticed, night after night. Too often there were circle researchers in the area, and too many fields had been kept under surveillance. While making my own investigations, I came across three circle enthusiasts who had spent the night on a burial mound at

Firs Farm at Beckhampton when, only 110 yards (100m) from them, a 44 yards (40m) long 'delphinogram' turned up. *"We didn't hear anything – and we didn't sleep very deeply"*, asserted one woman from the group. *"All that must have happened very quickly. When we lay down sometime after midnight, nothing was visible. And when we woke up at sunrise, it lay in front of us."*

A group of black-clothed circle hoaxers, the 'Wessex Sceptics', confessed their responsibility for making three formations – which had been recognised as hoaxes by the experts. During one such action, the construction of a ring, they had been discovered. Circle researchers had tracked them down. But there was still more deviousness connected with Doug and Dave. Circle enthusiasts remembered that in the weeks before the 'disclosure' the two were often seen within crop circles, engaging those present in conversation and questioning them. Doug pretended to be a student and collector of bird-calls, and amazed his audience with strange stories. He claimed to have once recorded a bird's call while in a circle. Instead, on the tape, there was a conversation which, according to the contents, had been carried out 30 years before. Then Doug had asked people where further circles were, and what those people present had experienced in this one.

"These men are liars", explained a woman researcher to George Wingfield, a few days after the *Today* report, *"and I can prove that. We met them on 20th August at Cheesefoot Head and told them things which they later included in their* Today *story, where they maintained that they themselves had experienced it"*. Then Julie, the circle enthusiast, went into details. *"I told Doug & Dave of a man I had met in one of the newest formations. He was looking for a jelly-like substance which he had found there on the day on which the circle had turned up. 'I know what that was', said Doug, 'that was the contents of an aeroplane toilet!', and he smirked widely. I told him that it couldn't have been that."* Then, in *Today*, Doug reported that, one day when he was working with Dave

on a circle, he was *"struck unconscious by something which fell from the sky. Somehow, I managed to get back to the car, and I could feel how blood was running down my neck. When it got light, I saw that the stuff on my head was the frozen discharge of an aeroplane toilet."*

The probability that this story is true is about one trillion to one. Apart from the fact that it is improbable and illegal for aeroplanes to discharge the contents of their toilets during flights, Doug would hardly have survived an impact by an ice block, however small, coming from a great height, and at a high speed. Another episode from their repertoire was evidently inspired by Nick Riley from Manchester. Nick had discovered some pieces of brown iron ore within or around a circle, and showed one of them, shaped like a small figure, to Doug and Dave. *"This is a meteorite"*, explained Doug. *"No, this is basic iron ore"*, said Nick. But the two always knew better, and *Today* wrote: *"To keep the experts in a good mood this summer, Doug and Dave got some meteorites and placed them in a circle near Stonehenge"*. Nick Riley still keeps the little stones, and they really are not meteorites, but basic iron ore. But apart from this hotchpotch of curiosities, the lack of proof and the continual climb-downs, the question remains: what or who is behind the two hoaxers? Are they really two funny pub-brothers who wanted to pull the world's leg and be in the public spotlight for a few weeks?

In the beginning, one could believe that Bower and Chorley could really have faked a few patterns, but their miserable press presentations and their stories' absurdities excluded even this possibility. Anybody who wants to test the effectiveness of their 'tools of the trade', please attach a bent wire to a baseball-chain and try to draw straight lines in the corn with it, at night without lighting, under rain, in thick fog, on slopes and on curved hill ridges. After a while, you'd go home. For the means of construction is admittedly media-effective, but it is cereologically useless. And how could Doug and Dave carry out their work for such a long time – Doug six years, Dave all of thirteen years – without their wives noticing anything? However deeply wives may sleep, they will soon have noticed the scratched hands, dirty trousers, boots encrusted with dirt and the sweaty socks.

What remained at the end of the day was much ado about nothing. Whoever it was who wanted to dampen down all circle enthusiasm, he or they had achieved it with style and élan and a minimum of effort. It was a small note in the *Today* report which made circle researchers ask questions. It indicated that there was more behind the story than only the publicity-addiction of two jokers. *"Today has paid no money"*, it was said in an article. Underneath: *"Copyright MBF Services"*. Who was 'MBF Services'?

Initial inquiries at *Today* were met with reluctance on the part of the editors of the tabloid. That MBF was not mentioned a second time indicates that the copyright assertion by the 'service' appeared in the paper only inadvertently. Finally, *Today's* deputy chief editor, Lloyd Turner, explained to George Wingfield that 'MBF Services' was a freelance press agency, which had passed on Doug and Dave to the paper. *"It is only an agency which had checked the details for us, that is all... a totally common press agency, nothing else, a freelance agency"*. They had never worked for *Today* before, *"but they brought us in contact with these people, and hence they have the copyright"*. This was all that one could find out. When Wingfield asked Graham Brough for the address and telephone number of MBF, the telephone was hung up.

Investigations by cereologists among other papers and press agencies revealed that 'MBF' was totally unknown. It seemed as if the mysterious 'press agency' had never before nor thereafter publicised even one single article. There is no telephone and no fax number. And the official British trade index lists only two firms with the short-hand symbols 'MBF': one, 'MBF Ltd' at Paisley, Scotland (Macfarlane Business Forms) manufactures postage stamps and supplies the British Post Office. The other one, 'MBF Consultancy', is a 'research and development laboratory' with an office in Shepton Mallet in Somerset. 'MBF' here stands for 'Maiden Beech Farm', a sealed-off area near West Crewkerne, Somerset, where they work on a number of classified defence projects, among them the development of SDI – 'Star Wars' – technology.

This reminded George Wingfield of a conversation which he had had years before with an ex-member of MI5, the British secret service. *"How would the secret service proceed to spread disinformation?"*, asked Wingfield. *"There you are at the right address"*, replied his contact man, *"for I was involved in it when MI5 circulated disinformation around the world concerning the Northern Ireland conflict. For this purpose we founded a seemingly private press agency, on whose desks our own people sat."* This sounds familiar! And how did MI5 handle it when somebody asked for the telephone number of such a 'press agency'? *"This was to be avoided at all costs. If this proved impossible, a special number was arranged on the end of which one of our men sat. In one case in Belfast, there was a Belfast number which was automatically connected with one of our desks in London, where someone with a Northern Irish accent answered the calls."*

Colin Andrews is also convinced that the fuss about Doug and Dave was engineered. He still remembers what an American CBS reporter, who had shot a film about the circles, told him. A friend of this reporter, a government scientist from France, had warned him to avoid risking his reputation for the crop circles, for shortly the British government would engage two artists and would present them to the press as the crop circle creators, to *"put an end at last to the wearisome fuss"*.

And if *Today* hadn't paid any money, who had? Bower and Chorley had said the motive for their 'disclosure' was that they now wanted to earn some money with 'their work'. Did they really get nothing out of that *Today* campaign, as the tabloid had claimed, even though it had caused a worldwide sensation, with their irreplaceable help?

Pat Delgado had recovered from his setbacks in the meantime, and in spring 1992 he published his newest book *Crop Circles – Conclusive Evidence*, where he discussed the embarrassing Doug and Dave story. On 4th November 1991, Delgado had presented his case in London, on invitation by the well-known Foreign Press Association Club. Among some twenty foreign journalists present, Graham Brough was also there – and a reporter asked about MBF Services. Tactically, Delgado handed the question over to Brough, who started stuttering. *"MBF was a joke, which was cooked up by* Today *at that time. Such an agency never existed."* The consequence of this 'confession' was that a journalist lodged a complaint against *Today* and Brough at the complaints appeal committee of the British Press Council, particularly concerning the deliberate attempt to mislead the public. It remains to be asked whether the *whole* story wasn't just a bad 'joke'.

The twenty farmers must also have thought the matter a 'bad joke', for soon after publication of the *Today* article they reported Bower and Chorley to the police on a charge of wilful damage to property. Out of 'lack of evidence of an actual criminal offence' the court rejected the charge, and the case was taken no further.

And yet, an example had arisen in the summer of 1991 showing how quickly public interest in crop formations could be deflated, simply by presenting a pair of alleged hoaxers. Effective opinion-forming, without even the help of Britain's largest-circulation tabloid, seems surprisingly simple.

CIRCLEGATE

More than a year after 'Doug & Dave', there were substantial indications that their appearance in the media was only one part of a larger-scale operation aiming to discredit the crop circle phenomenon.

All through the summer of 1992, a small group of dubious individuals tried to disturb the work of serious crop circle researchers, through hoaxes and disruptive and sometimes upsetting manipulative activities. Real formations were 'souped up' artificially, and false pictograms were formed right next to research stations, where they seriously distracted researchers' attention from the real circles.

One of the activists in this plot was Robert Irving, also called 'Spiderman' in cereological circles. He was a dubious photographer who up to now had attracted attention by tracking down crop circle researchers during their nightly watches and taking photos of them. Once, when asked who paid him, Irving, a nephew of a high-ranking civil servant in the Home Office, apparently mentioned a 'foundation'. Irving had been a member of the 'Beckhampton Group' of local crop circle researchers, whose dissolution in August 1992 goes back to a great degree to his negative influences.

Among Irving's closest friends was Jim Schnabel, a young American who tried to present the phenomenon in several newspaper articles as a big illusion, and the circle researchers as credulous dreamers – in the quality *Independent*, among other papers. Schnabel originated from a suburb in Washington DC and studied at Duke University, before he continued his studies – financed by an American foundation – first at Lincoln College at Oxford and then at the University of Bath. In July 1992 he won the second prize at a crop circle hoaxing competition sponsored by the German magazine *PM* and the *Cereologist*. Later he admitted to have faked further formations together with Irving.

Were Irving and Schnabel two harmless nutcases – or were their 'actions' backed by brains and possibly finance behind them, possibly from the secret services? To find out, the British UFO researcher Armen Victorian had a lengthy telephone call with Schnabel on 30th August 1992, which he recorded on tape. Victorian pretended to be an African named 'Mr Ntumba', and claimed that Irving had already introduced him to his secret service activities, and that he was now interested in collaborating with that campaign.

In the course of the conversation, Schnabel revealed details of an anti-crop circle plot, which in addition to the British also involved USA, Germany and the Vatican. The aim of the plot was, according to Schnabel, to discredit the crop circle phenomenon so much that it would 'disappear' from the media, and thus public awareness, since it was feared that the circles could bring about a 'change of world consciousness'.

In England, the tapes caused a stir, after their publication at the Quest International UFO Conference at Leeds in mid-September 1992, and soon there was some talk about a 'Circlegate'. However, Schnabel came to explain that the whole conversation had been a joke, saying he had recognised Victorian and had wanted to pull his leg. A nifty excuse.

The fact is that Schnabel said nothing on the tape which wasn't known to insiders long before. And his diverse actions – together with Irving – indicate that he – whether on his own account or on somebody's instructions – quite obviously had an interest in bringing crop circle euphoria to an end and in bringing circle researchers into disrepute. The complete 'Schnabel Tape' was published in *Magazin 2000* in Germany (no 93, April 1993), and here follow the most interesting passages:

AV: You know, there is a story...

JS: *I don't quite know who you are, so I don't want to talk about it in too much detail.*

AV: No, but I've been reading some of these magazines they have issued about groups and these articles about the 7-foot green men... groups put out that there's intelligence in it, *etc, etc,* and now Mr Irving says that to me. You see, I was a bit taken back. Is there any interest from the intelligence part in it as well?

JS: (...) *Are you talking about MI5, or are you talking about UFOs? ...Yes, well, I mean... off the record, I mean I think a number of agencies throughout the world have taken an interest in this.*

AV: Well, that we've heard, haven't we?

JS: *It is potentially a very explosive phenomenon.*

AV: I mean, how can they exploit the phenomenon?

JS: (...) *We believe there is certainly something very sinister about what's going on, er... I don't know whether you are Christian man or not...?*

AV: Yes, I am a Christian, of course I am. ...I'm a Catholic.

JS: *Well, yes, yes, so am I. And some of us feel concerned that, er...*

AV: Some arms of the government are doing something, psychological warfare or psychotronic weaponry, you know.

JS: *We think that sometimes a little bit of intrigue... sometimes is necessary in cases as serious as this, um, and sometimes measures have to be taken. But I think, I mean, overall, I think that the phenomenon is something which we think will disappear very shortly.*

AV: How? I mean, I'm sorry, I'm just curious. It's mind-boggling, what you are saying! But how do you know that will happen?

JS: *Well, we think that people will no longer take notice of it, I mean, it may continue, but, er, it...*

AV: But why do you say 'phenomena'? You proved that this is man-made... how could it be a phenomena? Or am I in the dark, or I've missed something somewhere?

JS: *Well, I think some of them are definitely man-made; I mean definitely.*

AV: But so, we are suggesting that there's also a part of it that is genuine?

JS: *I think there is a part which is entirely sinister and I'm not sure how genuine it is or whether it's made by people, but it's something very sinister...*

AV: Are we talking about magic, dark powers?

JS: *Possibly, yes, and I think that it...*

AV: Now hang on, I'm getting a bit... it's intriguing when we say dark powers... are we talking about... sort of... Satan and that sort of thing...?

JS: *Absolutely!*

AV: I see, so there isn't any sort of military implication or the test of weaponry, or anything of that sort which is sinister?

JS: *Oh, I wouldn't say that.... I think it's a very complex issue though...*

AV: Are we talking about the part of the military wing who's under the brainwashing, or whatever, of the sinister forces who are doing this – you know, making it a bit more complex?

JS: *Well it's very difficult to explain to you – to explain the structure of some of these organisations, but... I can't go into detail, but, er, basically it is something which is concerning people worldwide and various organisations have pooled their resources, worldwide, and are involved...*

AV: How about the British government? Are they also...

JS: *Well, yes. The German government, the American government, the Vatican has some involvement as well.*

AV: But how about Robert (Irving)? Does Robert have anything with any of this to help them along with it, to determine what is going on?

JS: *I wouldn't want to comment on the record or anything like that.*

AV: Of course not. What you're saying makes me worried. He is definitely on the good side...

JS: *He is... he is one of our best people, yes.*

AV: And he is helping the governments to determine which faction is doing this...

JS: *Yes, it's very... extremely sensitive, sensitive work as you can probably imagine...*

AV: It is, er, now, let's see, are we talking about military, or are we talking about intelligence, are we talking about the negative side, you see what I'm trying to say?

JS: *It is not quite a military thing, but there are elements of military intelligence which have loaned resources.*

AV: Ah! We are talking about people who have had a career, they've left their career, they have corporations *etc.* They are developing some kind of weaponry, and these are the testing ground.

JS: *No, no, no. I wouldn't, I wouldn't go into that, it's much more of a spiritual warfare type of angle, I think...*

AV: And are they trying to exploit the populace, I mean, what are they trying to achieve? That's what I'm trying to determine.

JS: *I think they are trying to bring about changes in world consciousness and ... for evil, you know, not for good, and, eh, there are some of us who are concerned about this and would like to see this new trend stopped.*

AV: Is there any positive element in the government who are supporting people like yourself or Robert or anybody else for that matter?

JS: *We have support, yes, we have support at the highest levels.*

AV: That's marvellous. Is it the British government or a....

JS: *It involves several countries and as I say...*

AV: Are we talking NATO allies or are we talking about...?

JS: *NATO? ...It is not at NATO level, but it's Germany involved, and this country (Britain) and the United States... the Vatican as well.*

AV: I see... are we talking about...

JS: *It's actually, it involves a supernational organisation which I will not name.*

AV: Supranational?!

JS: *Supernational organisation.*

AV: Oh, good God! ...This is above my head.

JS: *Which has ties to these countries and organisations*

AV: Are we talking, for example Trilateral, that sort of thing?

JS: *I wouldn't want to get into any specifics. (...)*

AV: And the information that you gather is passed on to the higher-ups in order to be filtered out and deductions have to be taken, obviously; that should be the case?

JS: *Yes, yes... we are not only just feeding information, we are taking active measures.*

5. A Global Phenomenon

Looking around the globe in search of an international dimension to the phenomenon, we begin with our European neighbours. The following list doesn't lay claim to completeness, and anybody who has information available about further formations anywhere in the world is requested to kindly inform us, the Centre for Crop Circle Studies or other well-known researchers.

Ireland

In spite of Ireland's profusion of prehistoric sacred sites, there are but two reliable cases of crop formations on the Emerald Isle. In 1972, near Loughhuile, Co Antrim, a simple, ten yards wide circle appeared on the slope of a field. Two circles appearing together, one 20yds, the other 10yds in diameter, were observed in August 1982 on the Big Isle at Lough Swilly, Co Donegal.

Sweden

The only circle known to have appeared in Scandinavia before 1993 appeared in April 1972 at Hjortkvarn near Örebro, after a brightly-illuminated UFO had crossed the field in which it was found. It consisted of two concentric rings, swirled in different directions, of which the outer one had a diameter of 16yds (15m).

In the event of another crop circle appearing again in Sweden, and in order to monitor and record such an eventuality, the Swedish Defence Institute, the Meteoro-logical Service and the Swedish UFO Organisation held a conference on 5th May 1991 and created 'Project Circle Study' (see *Cereologist* 4/91).

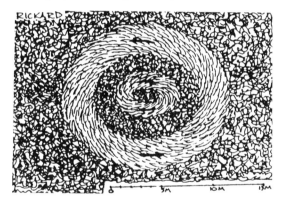

The first real 'circle summer' in Sweden came only in 1993. *"Reports of inexplicable circles in Swedish corn fields now regularly appear in the newspapers"*, wrote Per Nilson in the *Cereologist* (10/93), and *"they can't be ignored any longer"*. The first turned up on 6th July 1993 at Sala in Vastman-land, north-west of Stockholm, after two brothers had observed how the sky had suddenly turned unusually red around 5.00am. Shortly thereafter they discovered two circles in a wheat field, 6½yds and 13yds (6m and 12m) in diameter. A 17½yds circle (16m) was found by a woman during her morning walk with her dog on 19th July at Harplinge in Halland, south Sweden. A circle

The 'Mother of all Pictograms' appeared on 16th June 1991 at Barbury Castle near Swindon, Wiltshire. It was discovered by the circle photographer R. Wintle of Calyx Photo, Swindon, who went searching for crop circles that morning with a helicopter.

The two last 'UFOgrams' appeared on 18th and 22nd August 1991 near Froxfield, Hungerford, Berkshire (photo) and Alton Priors. Inside the latter, a shining object was photographed one day after its formation.

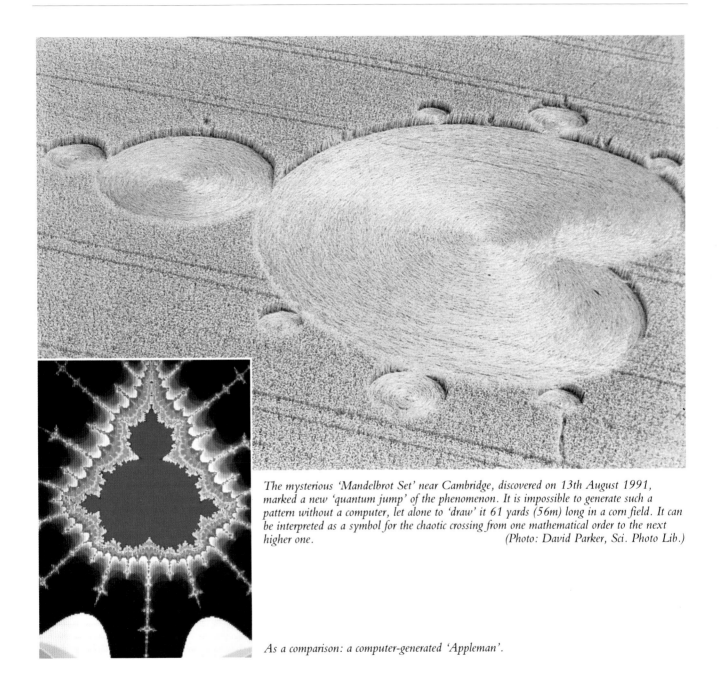

The mysterious 'Mandelbrot Set' near Cambridge, discovered on 13th August 1991, marked a new 'quantum jump' of the phenomenon. It is impossible to generate such a pattern without a computer, let alone to 'draw' it 61 yards (56m) long in a corn field. It can be interpreted as a symbol for the chaotic crossing from one mathematical order to the next higher one.						(Photo: David Parker, Sci. Photo Lib.)

As a comparison: a computer-generated 'Appleman'.

The 'Brain' or 'Serpent' were names given to this maze, appeared at the end of August 1991 at Froxfield near Hungerford, Berkshire. Scientists pointed out that it resembles a DNA chromosome bombarded by ultra-violet light, under an electron microscope.

The 'Curlyman' near Stonehenge, Wiltshire, end of July 1991 – a mixture of a 'little horned man' and Tree of Life.

(Photo: George Wingfield)

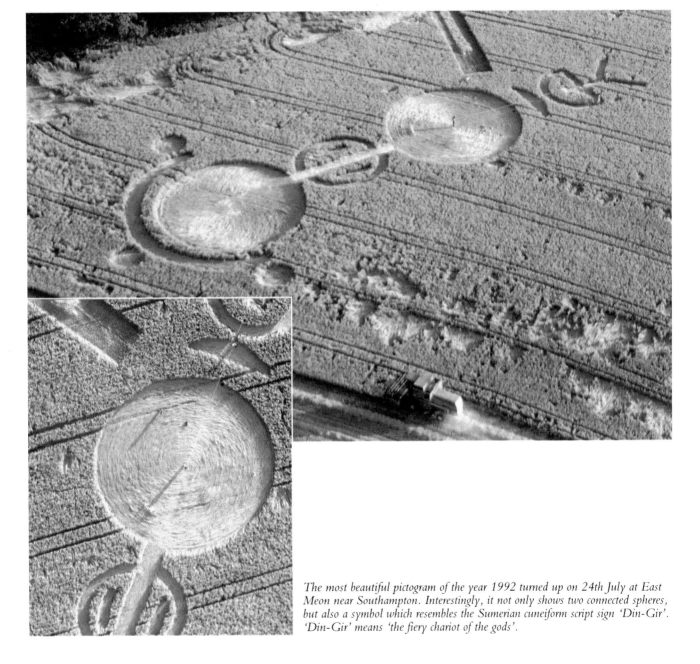

The most beautiful pictogram of the year 1992 turned up on 24th July at East Meon near Southampton. Interestingly, it not only shows two connected spheres, but also a symbol which resembles the Sumerian cuneiform script sign 'Din-Gir'. 'Din-Gir' means 'the fiery chariot of the gods'.

One of the first pictograms in 1992 appeared on 5th June at Old Sarum near Salisbury, Wiltshire. The formation's axis points to the centre of the Iron Age hill-fort, which was extended by the Romans into a fortress, and later accommodated a Saxon town.

Two small, tidy circles at Woodhenge, Wiltshire, end of July 1992.

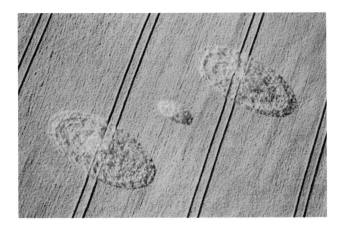

Firs Farm, 18th June 1992.

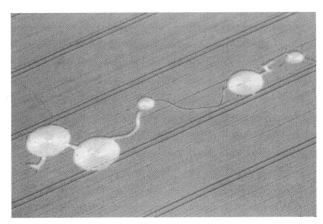

Milk Hill, 16th July 1992.

The 'Snail' at Alton Barnes, 9th July 1992, was 151 yards (138m) long.

Oliver's Castle, 24th July 1992. Beforehand, this pattern had been visualised by Dr Steven Greer's CSETI-Group.

Upton Scudamore near Westminster, Wiltshire, July 1992.

Alton Priors, 12th August 1992.

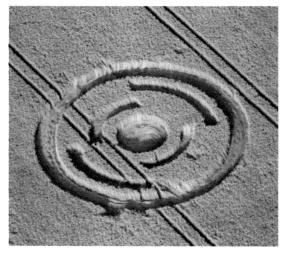

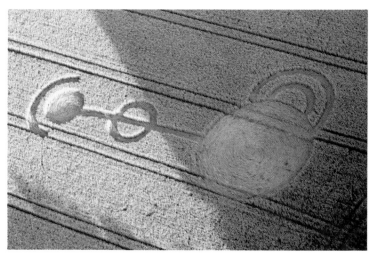

Andover, 18th July 1992, almost identical to one near Winchester on 6th June 1990.

Petersfield, Hampshire, 24th July 1992.

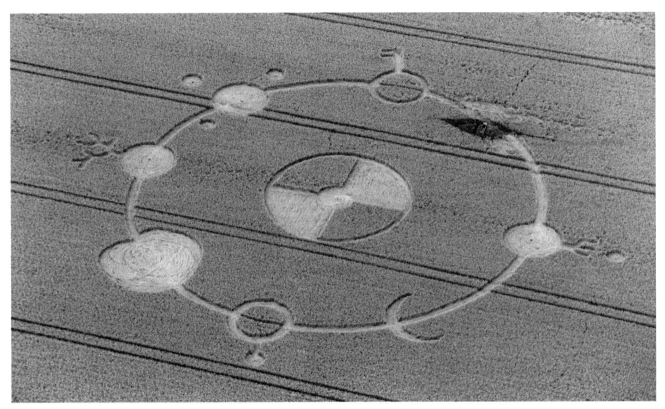

The last pictogram of the year 1992. The 'Dharma-Wheel' appeared on the night of 16th August 1992 at the foot of Silbury Hill and had a diameter of almost 55 yards (50m). It was interpreted as a mandala, with the sun symbol as the Godhead at the centre, and the symbols for the different states of consciousness at the outer ring. "It is interesting that the circle-makers, although they chose the culture-region of the British Islands as the receiver for their message, used here a very ancient Indo-Germanic symbol system… to make a statement for man's spiritual development", wrote Michael Green. He interprets the symbols (beginning at the left, counter-clockwise) as the Horns of Cernunnos (representing animal powers), the heart of Mother Earth, the energy of sexuality, the half-moon of individuation, the trinity of personality, soul and spirit, the – integrated – wellspring of the waters of inspired knowledge, the key to the mysteries, and the task of Initiation (if the triad of personality, soul and spirit merges to the One and merges with the centre, a transformation takes place). This corresponds to the Celtic gods Cernunnos, Modron, Daghda, Sulis, Taranis, Lugh, Mapon, Donn and (at the centre) Bel. Unfortunately, this highly interesting symbol was harvested only two days later.

(Photo: D Christopher)

Near Silbury Hill, 28th June 1992.

Alton Barnes, Wiltshire, August 1992.

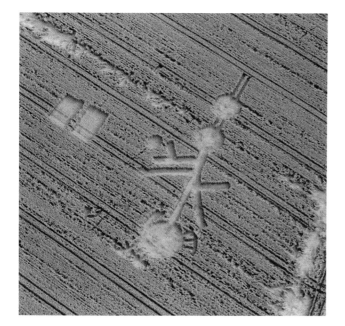

Upton Scudamore, Wiltshire, July 1992.

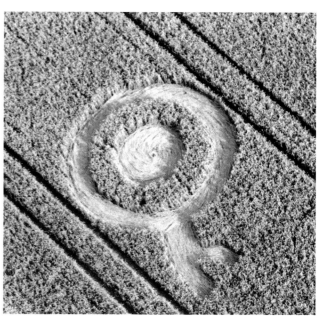

Alton Priors, Wiltshire, August 1992.

The largest and most interesting German pictogram, which was found on 22nd July at Grasdorf, Lower Saxony, extended over 5,000m² (almost 6,000 square yards) and attracted thousands of visitors. It was placed at the foot of the 'Thierberg', an ancient Teutonic Moot site.

One of the visitors to Grasdorf tracked down three heavy metal plates with a metal detector, with which he then mysteriously disappeared. A few days later the finder sent this photo of one of the plates to the owner of the field, which surprisingly bore the pattern of the pictogram.

Two of the three plates from Grasdorf were presented in October 1992 at the 'Dialogue with the Universe' Conference at Dusseldorf.

One of the first German crop circles appeared on 20th July 1992 near Marburg, Hessen. The night before, a couple observed some "balls of light the size of footballs".

(Photo: M. Vogt)

Two pictograms appeared on the night of 26th/27th July 1992, near Ettlingen, Karlsruhe.

(Photo: Dr J. Moller)

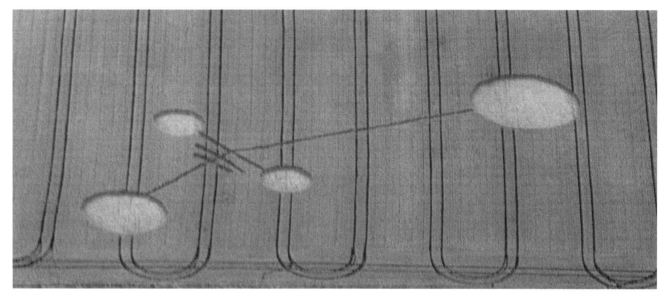

This 88.4m long pictogram appeared in Netze, near Waldeck on the night of 23rd/24th July 1991. People in the neighbourhood did not notice anything.

Close-up shots of the Netze pictogram reveal astonishing details that support its authenticity. Incidentally, the two tracks were made by local visitors.

(Photos: G. Best)

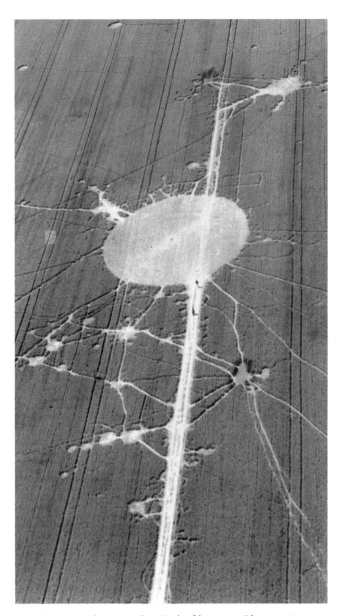

Groups of three grass circles appeared in both 1975 and 1976 in Zurich Canton, Swizerland. Edward 'Billy' Meier claimed that they were impressions made by spacecraft, and that he had been in touch with their occupants.

A circle 70m wide appeared at Szekesfehervar on Plattensee in Hungary on 26th June 1992.

The first Italian crop circle was discovered in a maize field near Modena.

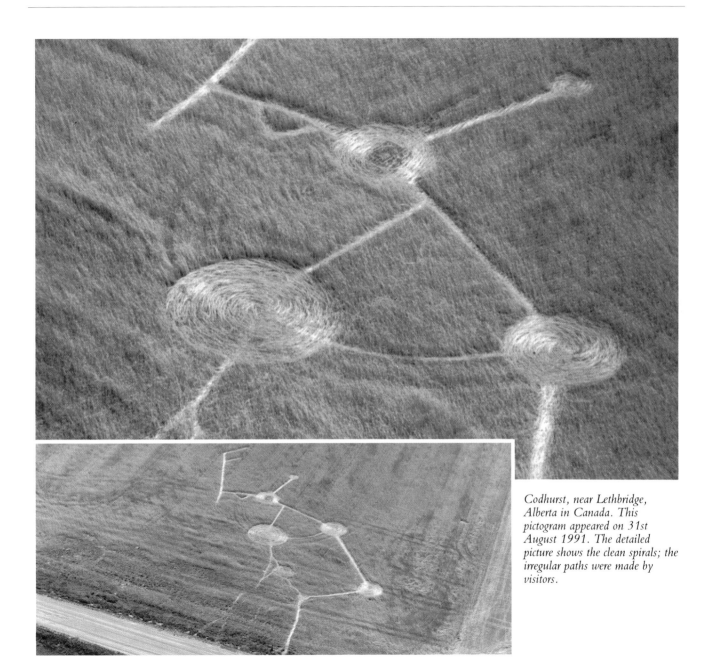

Codhurst, near Lethbridge, Alberta in Canada. This pictogram appeared on 31st August 1991. The detailed picture shows the clean spirals; the irregular paths were made by visitors.

The 'Warner Brothers', 1st September 1991. These beautiful circles appeared on a flat hill in the middle of a golden crop field near Warner, Alberta, in Canada.

A detailed shot from the Warner pictogram shows the complex layering that would be hard to copy. The dry and brittle stalks were not broken.

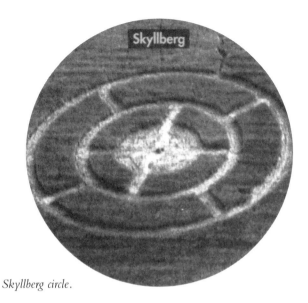

Skyllberg circle.

which turned up on 19th July at Höganäs in Scania (Skåne) in southernmost Sweden was 20yds (18m) in diameter, while two days later an ellipse of 17.7 x 16.2yds (16.2 x 14.8m) was found at Ljungby in Halland.

The most impressive Swedish formation however was the pictogram from Skyllberg in Närke (between Stockholm and Gothenburg), a photo of which appeared on 30th July in the Swedish press: a circle, surrounded by two concentric rings of utmost precision, the outer one with a diameter of 105yds (96.4m), from which emerged an 'F' key-symbol, accompanied by two smaller circles. Only 800yds away was a 40yds (36.6m) wide wheel with diagonal rungs.

In line with the brief of 'Project Circle Study', all the crop patterns were measured up and mapped by the Swedish military.

Netherlands

Under the heading *"Cirkels in het korenveld biolgeren ufologen"* ('Circles in a corn field astonish UFOlogists') the daily paper *Het Parool* on 24th August 1990 reported the appearance of two circles at the beginning of the month in a wheat field belonging to farmer Gert-Jan Petrie at Haarlemermeer, south-west of Amsterdam. The first circle, which Petrie discovered while harvesting, had a diameter of 10yds (9m), and the second, about 1.25 miles (2km) away, was 8yds (7.5m) wide. In both circles, the stems lay in a clockwise direction, the larger one being surrounded by five miniature circles of about 30in (80cm) in width. *"I have never before seen anything like that"*, admitted Petrie. *"The corn ears were largely undamaged. It looks to me as if a hovercraft had landed in the field."* (*Cereologist*, 2/1990).

Seven crop circles appeared in summer 1993, most of them in the province of Limburg in the south of the Netherlands, as David M Summers and Herman J Hegge of Contact Network International told me. The first – near Valkenburg – was reported to them on 20th July, a second one was reported on the next day aside the motorway from Heerlen to Aachen, and a third was discovered in the same region by members of CNI. Two further pictograms turned up in the same period at Roermond/Brabant, not far from Maastricht. One Roermond formation consisted of six circles, arranged in a cross-shape.

The largest circle of the year was just south of Houthern, which turned up during the night of 26th July right next to the motorway, and 34yds (31m) wide. While it had already been visited by hundreds of curious onlookers by the time the CNI-team arrived, they managed to visit two smaller undamaged circles, 11yds and 16yds (10m and 15m) wide, south of Houthern. The corn in these lay cleanly and unbroken in a clockwise direction. The most interesting formation of the year had already appeared on the night of 10th July at Ubachsberg, not far from Heerlen: a central circle, surrounded by two rings and four cross-like arranged satellites, with two circles, a triangle and a circle which was connected via an 'L' pattern with a semi-circle. Now CNI has set up a 'crop circle hot-line', so that further Dutch pictograms can be investigated still quicker.

Heerlen.

Germany

Rumours about crop circles in Germany were already circulating at the first German circle conference, which took place in June 1991 in Hamburg. There was talk about circles 'in the region of the Extern-Stones', and of a pictogram beside the Frankfurt-Cologne motorway near Idstein-Wörsdorf. But there was no concrete information on the Externstein circles, and the Idstein double-circle of 27th May 1991, 27yds (25m) wide and located in a rape field, proved to be an arbitrary joke by local teenagers. The rape, which had been trampled down all over, didn't really allow any other conclusion, even though residents had claimed to have observed strange lights on the night in question.

But the beginning of the German circle-era was, undoubtedly, July 16, 1991. This was when a journalist from Kiel discovered a circular 'thing' in the Rendsburg-Eckenförde district. Her report in the local newspaper started a bushfire – cropcircle fever spread throughout Germany, and never a day passed during the next two weeks without a new circular event being reported.

While the Felm formation was crude and irregular and obviously a hoax – one line had even been corrected – the other patterns had the same harmony, precision and beauty that their British counterparts had displayed. And, while crop circle expert George Wingfield joked that he had "brought some circle-seed to Hamburg", I began to ask myself whether a human-made circle might be understood by the circle-makers as some kind of signal – and answered.

Farmer Hans-Günther Müller was sure that the crude ring, measuring some 210ft in diameter and with a satellite ring and smaller 7.5ft circle in the centre, had been made by hoaxers – he found footprints long before the first visitor entered it. He filed a claim against persons or persons unknown at the local police station, but even this did not protect him from an invasion of thousands of sightseers who literally blitzed his field after the circle had made headlines in the German press.

The reply from the real circle-makers followed on the night of July 17th/18th in Damp on the Baltic Sea, just a few miles from Felm. On that night, a Berlin holidaymaker, Lothar Kräke observed from the balcony of his holiday apartment a "round, black, soundless object" flying in the direction of the field. A housewife also claimed to have seen a "circular, black object with many lights".

Indeed, landowner Christian Detlev Graf in Reventlow discovered three circles in one of his fields near Damp by the Baltic, 43ft (13m), 13ft (4m) and 11ft (3.50m) in diameter, on the morning of 18th July 1991: clean, symmetrical and precise. Some days later the physicist Joachim Koch from Berlin detected *"the presence of an extremely strong electromagnetic energy"*. Meanwhile, local miller Siegfried Waschull (58), on the other hand, was convinced that *"...those were deer. At this time of year, bucks hunt does round in circles – this results in bedlam"*.

Whoever was behind the circles, the 'official' explanation seemed all too unlikely. Four law students from Kiel are supposed to have made them, as NDR (North German Radio) 'revealed' on a radio program on 26th July. They were 22–26 years old, who "were bored during the vacation". It is understandable that they wanted to stay anonymous, to avoid being made liable for compensation by the affected farmers. However, the way the identity of the law students was disguised was odd: joke masks, stilts with which they claimed to have entered the fields unnoticed (despite all the footprints), and with them perfectly-fitting long black check stilt-trousers. Does all this fit in with bored law students? How did they manage to fake five circles in Schleswig-Holstein during the night of 23rd–24th July, as they later explained in public? They had claimed to have needed all of four hours for a primitive ring at Felm. Why were three circles found at Damp, while the students maintained that they had been disturbed during the making of the first circle at Damp by a pair of lovers, who were looking for their own 'corn field nest'? Who made the two other pictograms? Were they supposed to be the work of the lovers?

Actually, I learned from trustworthy sources (from an NDR employee) that it wasn't law students who displayed their tricks in front of the camera, but circus artists, paid for their small spectacle. But still, the announcement of their 'confession' went out in the press, even to England – and fulfilled its purpose. The 'Mystery of the Crop Circles' seemed solved, the nation laughed about the student 'joke', and the innocent trust of those who had fallen for their tricks was betrayed. Quite obviously, someone who had learned from the 'official' hoaxers, Doug and Dave in England, got the idea to deflate circle-mania by means of publishing 'confessions' in the media, with some success.

But, as in the case of Bower and Chorley, the four students of circus-sciences (which, we have to admit, has something in common with studying Law), did not present any evidence for their claim. On the contrary, in the face of the fact that the most beautiful formations turned up in Hessen, Lower Saxony (Niedersachsen) and Westphalia (Nordrhein-Westfalen), the confession by the gang of four becomes ever more improbable. Did they really travel through Germany at night and produce up to nine pictograms in one night (on 24th July)? And if they admit that the ring at Felm failed so badly because they had to 'practise at first' – why then were other hoaxer-gangs so much more successful straight off?

If we mark the twenty-six German crop circles which appeared between 16th July and 15th August 1991 on a map, then it begins to emerge that Schleswig-Holstein (north of Hamburg and south of Denmark) is Germany's 'circle country' – even excluding the (at least) three hoaxed circles. Interestingly, this region, with sea to the east and west, is also the one with the greatest density of prehistoric sites – over two hundred known grave-mounds and stone circles from the Neolithic period and the Bronze Age are there.

It is in the area around Schleswig Bay, where three circles were located, that Thorsberg Moor, the main sanctuary of the Teutonic tribes of the north, is to be found. Next to this sacrificial moor stand ancient tumuli and the Kummerhy stone circle with its runic stone and 6ft high 'watcher stone' containing 45 'cups'. The order of these stones has an astronomical significance similar to that of Stonehenge. Half a mile east of Thor-Moor there is a sacred well which, because of its light radioactivity, is claimed to have therapeutic effects. Ancient Teutonic pilgrim festivals, still celebrated on Jacobi-day (at the beginning of August), provide continuing evidence of a strong, age-old tradition which has parallels with the ancient British sanctuaries found in Wiltshire. But, let's have a look at the most important German crop circle events of 1991.

20th July, Marburg/Hessen:

On the night of Friday/Saturday, Michael Vogt from Marburg and his wife left her parents' house at Marburgs Zuckerberg to drive home to their apartment. Suddenly, on the way to their car, Mrs Vogt spotted "balls of light, about the size of footballs, but not totally round" manoeuvering above the street at altitudes of between 3ft and 15ft. The luminous balls flew "at an amazing speed and totally noiselessly". A few minutes later, they shot away.

To their surprise, the following week the Vogts read about a Marburg pictogram which had been discovered by an amateur pilot on the morning after their strange experience, on the other side of the hill, where their parents live. The pictogram was dumbbell-shaped, comprising a big ring connected to a small circle. "Not a single stalk was broken. The wheat was laid down in a circular pattern," Vogt reported when I interviewed him.

21st July, Heinzenhausen, Rheinland-Pfalz:

On this Sunday morning, a neighbour told farmer Otto Rodrian about a circle, 66ft in diameter, which had appeared in his barley field. The circle consisted of eleven concentric rings, each about 3ft wide. On the night in question, a man from Lauterecken, some three miles away from the circle, reported having seen a reddish, ball-shaped object flying in the direction of Rodrian's field.

22nd July, Grasdorf, near Hildesheim, Lower Saxony:

The largest and most complicated German pictogram was discovered by early-morning joggers on 23rd July. The

roughly 110yds (100m) long and 55yds (50m) wide formation at Grasdorf near Hildesheim, Lower Saxony – it covered an area of 5,000m² (6,000 sq yds)! – consisted of seven symbols and thirteen circles – with a cross within the circle in the middle, suggesting the ancient sun symbol. In general it reminds us of a Scandinavian rock painting, the object in the middle being the 'sun chariot', an ancient sacred symbol of the Scandinavians and North Teutons.

Actually, the location of the pictogram is archaeologically significant: it lies at the foot of the Thieberg, a *Thing* or ancient Teutonic tribal parliament site, possibly on top of a prehistoric processional path.

In the immediate vicinity is the Wuldenberg, an ancient Germanic Wotan sacred site on which a church was erected under Charlemagne, and the Holy Grove (Heilige Holz) of the Teutons, which was fought over right into the Middle Ages. When a feudal lord gave the order to fell this sacred wood in 1273, he was murdered by the people of Grasdorf: a small civil war was the result, and the wood stayed untouched until the 19th century. So this very ancient Saxon heartland, christianised no earlier than the 9th century as a result of the victory of Charlemagne over the Saxons, had been a sacred landscape for at least 4,000 years. Dr Nowothnig, an archaeologist from Hannover, described the neighbourhood as "one of the most significant prehistoric cult areas of Europe".

The discoverer of the pictogram, farmer Werner Harenberg, told me that when he had found it, it was so exactly and cleanly laid down that a hoax was unquestionably ruled out. Also Tim Schunemann, from Goslar, who visited the formation on 24th July, told me that the circles were perfect in form, the longest axis being oriented exactly east-west, the edges and the pathways were exact and the margins between lying and standing corn were abrupt, the spirals in the circles were exactly and perfectly laid, with the spiral centre-points approximately a half metre from the geometrical centres of the circles, and the corn was laid anti-clockwise and unbroken.

Members of the research group EFODON carried out radioactivity measurements with a Geiger-Müller counter. The result: the needle showed peak values of up to 0.737 microsieverts/hour, about 76% more than the radiation limit for work-places in Germany − and dropped back again to a lower reading over time. In normal circumstances this is impossible, since radioactivity normally stays constant. So was the instrument indicating a hitherto unknown energy?

So was this a real pictogram? Much speaks for it. When a person going for a walk passed the field around 11.00pm, nothing unusual was visible, so its creation must have happened later. There are signs of quite unusual causes of this pictogram: that night Christian Fiedler from Grasdorf had seen an orange-coloured, pulsing light, which moved to and fro at great speed in the area in question. Thousands came to visit the formation, and farmer Harenberg started collecting entrance fees at the field's edge, following the example of his British colleagues. For this purpose, he ordered his Turkish farmhand, Kemal Kücück, to watch the field and collect entrance fees. During the following weeks, Kemal started to get more and more interested in the phenomenon and began to record, journalistically, the anomalies and absurdities he observed day by day. Some visitors, he noted, had pendulums and dowsing rods with them, others brought Geiger counters and metal detectors. And one of them was successful on 2nd August, was a man with moustache turned up in blue painter's overalls with a high quality metal detector, and located metal in the three circles accompanied by semi-circles. He marked the locations with paper tissues, and shortly thereafter he returned with pick and shovel and began to dig. From a depth of 18in (46cm) he excavated three 10lb (4.5kg) metal plates, about 10in (27cm) wide, covered with soil and dirt. He promised to bring them to the farmer and drove away, never to be seen again. Instead he sent Harenberg a photo of one of the plates, which bore exactly the same symbols which had appeared on the fields.

Whatever this unexpected (and, in cereology, unique) discovery means, a hoax or deception is improbable. The plates had been found too deep in the ground, and the soil sticking to them had been too firm. Additionally, the 'treasure-hunter' had come at exactly the right time, just after rain had softened the soil. Almost all of July the weather had been sunny, and the soil had been bone-dry when the pictogram turned up, such that it can most probably be ruled out that 'somebody' had buried the plates there − even though this classically 'Fortean' phenomenon raises many eyebrows.

A little later, Kemal told the story of this strange discovery to a group of visitors. "I would pay DM20 just to see these mysterious plates", said one man. "And I would pay DM20,000 to buy them", another man, an industrialist from a nearby city, added.

A little later, the industrialist was confronted by a man in a leather jacket. "Are you serious?", he asked. "Definitely." "Then give me your card. I can put you in contact with the finder." "Really?" "Wait for his phone call."

Two days later the man received, as promised, a call from the finder. They arranged to meet at an autobahn resthouse near the finder's home in Essen in the Ruhr area. The industrialist was allowed to bring a friend of his, a jeweller, with him. At the meeting, the finder brought out three metal plates, each of different size and weight, but all round in shape and about 8ins in diameter. Each bore the same symbol – the Grasdorf pictogram. The finder told his story, identifying himself as a professional treasure hunter who had spent fifteen years searching for Roman and medieval coins and artefacts and selling them to antique dealers and collectors.

He had been watching a TV discussion about the German crop circles at the end of July during which German astrophysicist and bestselling author, Johannes von Buttlar, had discussed the possible connection between crop circles and ancient sites.

"Maybe this could help me to find an undiscovered archaeological site," he thought to himself, "and I might find a hoard of ancient coins or jewellery."

So, after the next rainfall, he went to the most prominent (and, for him, nearest) German crop formation at Grasdorf – and made his discovery! Back at home, he cleaned the crusted plates with chemicals. And now, here they were!

With his heart beating faster, the industrialist touched the mysterious find. The first plate was made of bronze and weighed about 8lbs, the second, of silver, about 11lbs and the third, of gold about 16lbs. He handed them to his jeweller friend. After examining them, the expert was more than amazed.

"This is the finest gold and silver I have ever seen in my 30 years' career," he said.

The finder wanted DM250,000 (about £100,000) for all of them. This, of course, was a lot of money even for a wealthy industrialist. On the other hand, his jeweller friend confirmed that the gold plate alone would have a metal value of not less than DM160,000 (£65,000) or could be cut and sold in parts. At the end of lengthy negotiations, the industrialist finally bought the bronze and silver plates for DM50,000 (£20,000). The finder kept the gold plate which was never seen again. It was not until 1993 that some German crop circle researchers, including myself, received colour photographs of a golden-coloured crescent-shaped Grasdorf plate, cut down the middle. Had the finder sold only one half, keeping the second half for himself? Unfortunately, the researchers were neither offered the plate for investigation nor did they receive any other information.

The bronze and silver plates, now the property of our industrialist, are available for serious investigation. They were shown at my international UFO conference, "Dialogue with the Universe", in Düsseldorf, Germany in October, 1992 and used again when we filmed a piece on the Grasdorf case for the US-TV programme, "Encounters" in April, 1994. In addition, the Tübingen lawyer, Dr Roemer-Blum, arranged a scientific evaluation at the German Federal Institute for Materials Research (Bundesanstalt für Materialprüfung) in Berlin. Their conclusion, after carefully analysing both plates was:

"Plate one (silver colour) consisted mainly of quite pure silver (what an understatement!), with an additional ingredient accounting for less than 0.1%. The weight of the plate was 4.98kg (11lbs). Plate two (bronze colour) consisted of a copper-tin alloy (of which the tin content amounted to 10%-15%), 1% nickel and traces of iron amounting to less than 0.1%."

This meant that the silver plate consisted of 99.9% pure silver, purer than sterling-silver. Furthermore, a spectographic analysis of both plates proved that they had not been made from a cast but from some kind of conglomerate of silver nuggets and natural copper and tin pieces of the type found in Germany's Harz forest, not far from Grasdorf. They had been produced, either by heating up to a degree that partially melted the metals – or in a low-gravity environment. We are left with the question of what hoaxer would go to such expensive lengths, in terms of cost and effort, simply to pull the wool over the eyes of the press and a few crop circle enthusiasts?

24th July, Netze, near Waldeck, Hessen

It happened during the night of July 23/24. At about 11pm, just before she got into bed, Susanne Bieling took one last look through her window at the wheatfield outside. Everything was quiet, bathed in the soft light of a full moon. But, when she got up at 6 o'clock the following morning and looked out of the window again, she saw something mysterious – a giant pattern, consisting of four major circles and some connecting lines, in the wheat. At first, Susanne Bieling believed that what she saw was some sort of hoax. Then she went out and entered the pictogram. The wheat formed a precise alignment, with every stalk lying down, side by side, to form perfect spirals. Nothing looked broken or trampled down. There was nothing to indicate that this was the work of hoaxers.

Her neighbour, Frau Bernhard, had got up at 5am and was, perhaps, the first to see the mysterious pattern. She, too, had heard nothing during the night. An engineering student, Günter Best, took measurements and found that the formation was 88.4 metres long, with the biggest circle measuring 48.8 metres, the circle at the other end, 13 metres and the two smaller ones, 8.20 metres each. His mother-in-law's cat, Speedy, who had previously regularly gone into the field to catch mice, never entered it again. Best's CD system never functioned properly afterwards, either. Another witness reported seeing "a kind of fireball" on the night in question.

3rd August, Bornheim-Hemmerich, Nordrhein-Westphalia:

Gabriele and Heinrich Seebauer were cycling along the country roads around Bornheim, with their British friend, Peter Rosenbaum, when they came across something mysterious. It was a pictogram, measuring 120ft in diameter, with three concentric rings and satellite circles, each measuring 7.5ft in diameter, connected through small 'gangways'. Returning that evening, with a measuring-tape and a tape-recorder to record their observations, the finders discovered that the pictogram had been formed with great precision. When they played their tape-recording back later, they heard a whistling sound, although they were sure that none of them had whistled during the time that they had taken their measurements.

So, to sum up the 1992 crop circle situation in Germany, naming only the most important events, we found: 8 hoaxes, 9 crop circles whose evaluation we leave open – because of lack of data – 9 real circles... and a number of details which we also see in Britain: the connection with prehistoric sacred sites, strange whistling sounds in connection with newly discovered circles, UFO sightings on the 'nights before' and finally some mysterious light spheres which a couple called Vogt had observed in Marburg.

Belgium

In the first half of June 1992 the first Belgian crop circle turned up near the village Saint Sauveur, north-east of Tournai. The phenomenon was preceded by a hefty thunderstorm, and the farmer who owns the field swore that almost at the same place as the formation, one year before, one of his horses had been struck by lightning. Also, on the night in question he had seen a flash come down in the direction of the field, exactly at the place where next morning he discovered the 32ft (9.8m) wide circle of anti-clockwise laid corn. A second circle, an exact copy of its predecessor, turned up in the same wheat field in the first week of July.

When the journalist Simoulin from the newspaper *La Dernière Heure* took a photo of the circle on 11th July, he had several black dots on the pictures which couldn't be traced back to any fault in the film. Furthermore, he discovered two small white lights on the photos which seemingly hovered above the circle.

A little later a neighbour of the farmer found four further circles in his own fields, arranged in a square, each 30ft (9.2m) wide. In contrast to the two first circles, the corn lay in a clockwise direction. Also at the village of Forest, 3.4 miles south-west of Saint Saveur, circles were discovered at harvesting at the end of July, 550yds away from a Romano-Gallic ruin.

France

Unconfirmed reports speak of circles at Aix-en-Provence in 1976 and Avallon, as well as at Figeac in the Dordogne. But only from 1993 did the crop circles really feel at home in France. A whole number of formations appeared, as the press reported, and were thoroughly examined by the local gendarmerie for the tracks of possible jokers. One of them had the shape of a 'giant with antennae': two large circles next to each other, with an extension crowned by a small circle.

Italy

The first documented case is a ring which was sighted and photographed in August 1985 in a maize field near Castions de Zoppoca. There were rumours of a further circle 1990 at Grosetto. Johannes von Buttlar told us of a dumb-bell formation which he saw from his plane in September 1990 in a valley in Sicily.

Spain

A rare example apparently appeared at Aloalo de Guadaira near Seville.

Switzerland

In canton Zürich, some dozens of threefold formations, around 2yds wide each, were found in 1975–76, mostly in forest clearings and on grassland. According to the Swiss farmer Eduard 'Billy' Meier, they were traces of landings by extra-terrestrial craft, with whose pilots – inhabitants of the Pleiades – he claims to be in contact. The similarity to crop circles is noteworthy: here too the stems were gently folded down without being snapped, and they kept on growing horizontally without standing up again, with fresh grass overgrowing the flat-laying stems. According to Meier the anti-gravity propulsion of the Pleiadian 'Beam Ships' – as he calls them – is responsible for the phenomenon.

Months later, American and Japanese researchers who examined Meier's claims were able to detect magnetic anomalies and radioactivity of up to 400% above the norm – this was long before the Chernobyl disaster. On many occasions they obtained 'pulsing' readings on Geiger counters, similar to those detected in German crop circles. Interestingly, during this period Meier also recorded strange 'buzzing noises' with his tape recorder, on the same frequency – 5.2kHz – as their British counterparts. And also there are witnesses for Meier's UFO contacts: a few dozen neighbours and friends had observed how illuminated discs appeared from the forest clearings in which the crop-whorls were found on the next day (Moosbrugger 1991).

Berne crop circle.

Only in 1993 did any formations appear again in Switzerland. On 18th June, 6 miles (9km) west of Berne, below a railway line, a ring of 12.6yds (11.5m) width was found, from whose centre a straight line emerged, which kinked at an angle of 100° and led to a small circle.

Hungary

In the midst of a UFO-sighting wave the first crop formations turned up in summer 1992 in the Puszta area in

Hungary. Overnight on 26th June an enormous, 77yds (70m) wide circle appeared near the town of Szekesfehervar near Lake Balaton, followed by two further, irregular and untidy formations three nights later. While the two significantly smaller circles from 29th June were traced back to two students, who in September were fined 630,000 Forints (around £4,000 or $6,000US), the origin of the initial circles remains unsolved. The Hungarian police paper *Zsaru*, in their 'UFO Dossier' on 16th July, asked whether it had been extra-terrestrials who had left their traces there at Puszta. Either-whichway, the circle became a place of pilgrimage, and parents came and put their children in the middle of the circle to charge them with 'strange and wonderful energy', while residents from Szekesfehervar said they had observed light phenomena and a dome-shaped craft in the night of 25th June.

The pictogram at Ozora, Hungary. (Photo: H Hegge, CNI).

A complete pictogram – a dumb-bell – was discovered in June at Ozora. Finally on 8th July the inhabitants of Tiszaujvaros in the north of Hungary found two circles in a rye field. Both had the corn lying anti-clockwise, both had a diameter of 8yds, one of them being encircled by a 31in (80cm) wide ring.

Maybe the Puszta crop circle was a circle-makers' reaction to Hungary's newest tourist attraction: a 'UFO landing track' in the outskirts of Budapest, a pattern made of white gravel on green grass which the businessman Szandor Ambrus had built in April 1992. It consists of a cross which links two semi-circles with each other – a symbol which allegedly had been observed at the underside of a UFO (a symbol which had also been seen in Spain in the 1970s). The phenomenon repeated in 1993 and 1994.

Romania

On 27 June 1994 the first crop circle appeared in a wheatfield in Rumania, near the village of Arad: It was a small circle, 18ft in diameter, surrounded by a wide ring, 126ft in diameter. At least five eyewitnesses observed, at about 4.00am, how the formation was made.

"I was frightened," Ioan S. reported. "Suddenly, the entire wheatfield was illuminated by a bright light. I heard a frightening hissing sound and saw all the stalks flattened to the ground."

"It was like a nightmare," witness, Catalin P. claimed. "I saw strange lights, but was too frightened to look more closely."

I. Ungar confirmed the story, while his wife, Muela, added, "My husband approached the field and suddenly heard a terrible hissing sound. The entire field trembled, although the weather was totally windless at the time. Then he saw a light flashing and fled into the house."

Further details were observed by a 48-year-old shepherd, Traian Crisan, whose flock was asleep 450ft from the wheatfield. "I do not know what the thing was, it did not land," he said. "It stood in the air, 9ft above the wheatfield. I saw this light gliding towards the field, a light shaped like the moon but much bigger. I ran into my hut. It seemed to hover over the hut while the walls and the roof shook. When I went back outside, a strong wind blew away my hat and rain-cape. The wind was so strong that I couldn't stop myself falling to the ground. The object was round. I saw a small opening with two individuals standing in it, holding a kind of tube. The were no taller than me (1.65 metres) and both bearded. One appeared to be about 40-years-old and had a long beard like that of an orthodox priest. His face was slim and his eyes slanted like the eyes of a Chinaman. Both men wore things like headphones and had instruments in their hands. During the time that the object flew over me it was hissing loudly and the wind was gale-force. My sheep ran to a nearby maize-field and the dog hid himself in the hut, whining. When the thing accellerated, a bluish flame shot out from its underside and continued upwards, like an arrow. The thing itself was a bit bigger than the ring made on the cropfield. It had a dome made of what looked like glass or plastic and there was a white light inside. The rings appeared after it had shot away and I was the first to see them. Since that night, my sheep have refused to enter that meadow again."

Of course, we could identify those two men as Doug & Dave, returning from their latest hoax-tour through Russia, masking themselves with face beards and revelling in the latest result of their circlemania.

Bulgaria

According to the Bulgarian weekly newspaper *Orbita* several pictograms appeared in summer 1990. The most beautiful of them was a configuration of four circles which were connected via a ring.

This formation, which – although lacking a central circle – resembled the basic structure of England's 'Celtic Crosses', was formed on 22nd July 1990 and was 25–25.7yds (23–23.5m) wide, with a diameter of 3.5–4yds for the individual circles.

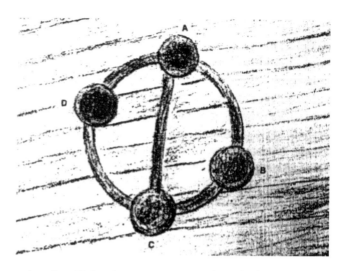

Another Bulgarian paper reported a whole number of spirally-shaped whorls which appeared between 14th and 19th June in the vicinity of the city of Drujba near Sofia.

Czech Republic

During the first days of August, 1994, two concentric circles of wheat, flattened clockwise and measuring 30ft and 36ft in diameter, were found near Zihobce. Each was surrounded by four smaller circles, measuring between 9ft and 12ft in diameter and pointing in four opposite directions. Similar circles had been discovered in Kolinec about a week earlier.

CIS (former USSR)

Twenty-seven circles turned up in the summer of 1991 on the territory of the former USSR, the test pilot Dr Marina Popovich, author of the book *UFO-Glasnost*, told me. According to Dr Aleksei V Arkhipov from the Institute for Radio Astronomy of the Ukrainian Academy of Sciences, dozens of circles, ovals and pictograms with diameters of between 2yds and 44yds (2–40m) were discovered on wheat fields in Ukraine.

But 1991 was by no means the first circle year in the CIS. In June 1990 a circle appeared in a wheat field near Krasnodar in the north-western Caucasus. Fearing that it was the devil's work and that, like the 'Caucasian chalk-circle', one would never be able to leave it, village inhabitants avoided the circle. It was not until one week later, when a research team headed by Yuri Stroganov arrived in Yeisk and surveyed the 49yds (45m) wide oval, whose stems were laid down counter-clockwise. In the middle the corn stood upright, forming an oval of 41ft x 6ft (1.5m x 2m). While radiation measurements didn't yield any results, the researchers found changes in the colours of the corn within certain areas of the circle. Furthermore, visitors reported headaches after entering the pictogram – a phenomenon which we also know from England. Moreover, Stroganov managed to interview an eye-witness, who had observed a blue and white shining object on the night of 19th June around 3.00am, which resembled the arc of an arc-welder.

Also in the Caucasus, in the area around the Georgian capital of Tbilisi, mysterious 'UFO-nests' turned up amongst bushes, often after sightings of mysterious luminous objects. These 'bush circles' I personally managed to see when, in December 1990, as the only western participant, I took part in the first International UFO Conference of Georgia, which was organised by Professor Thales Shonya of the Georgian Academy of Sciences.

The two examples which Professor Shonya showed me lay next to each other and had a diameter of 10yds and 13yds (9m and 12m). All the bush branches seemed to have been pushed down counter-clockwise in spiral-shape and appeared like a large whirl. Furthermore, the bushes within the circle were covered by a kind of white powder which, as Professor Shonya explained to me, consisted of diverse minerals with a high proportion of magnesium. The circle exhibited heightened radioactivity, and participants in the visiting group complained of sickness, circulatory trouble and headaches. Professor Shonya was certain that there was a connection between the bush whorls and the UFO-sighting wave which, since July 1989, had caused a stir in Tbilisi. Besides thousands of sightings, Shonya had investigated 200 cases of direct contacts and UFO 'abductions' – their real numbers he estimated to be ten times higher – partially linked with surprising healings for contactees (see Hesemann, 1990).

At the Tbilisi conference, I met Dr Nikolai Nowgorodow from the Polytechnic Institute of the University of Tomsk, who handed me a 20pp report about his thorough investigation of three pictograms near the town Jigulja aside the Volga, a pretty little country town at the foothills of the Urals. Dr Nowgorodow had discovered a whole group of circles, ovals and pictograms when he investigated the numerous UFO news reports in the local press in Toljetti, the main town in the district – sightings of mysterious flying objects, which almost always disappeared in the direction of Jigulja.

On 14th June 1990, he set off to Jigulja together with a some friends. Shortly behind the Morschkaya

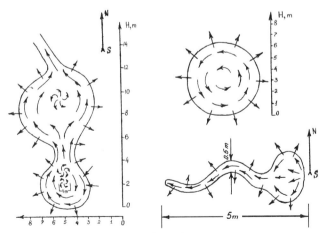

The corn patterns at Jigulja on the Volga.

Circle centre at Jigulja. (Photo: N Nowgorodow).

dam lay the wheat fields of Jigulja, and Dr Nowgorodow couldn't believe his eyes when he saw what had happened here: circles, English-style circles! In an area less than a mile in length lay no less than a dozen peculiar formations: perfect circles and strange ovals, elongated and deformed shapes, everything was present, with diameters between 13yds (12m) and 44yds (40m). The wheat lay either in a clockwise or counter-clockwise manner, and within the elongated shapes it was mostly brushed in a northerly direction. But also within them Dr Nowgorodow discovered spirals of 13yds (12m) in diameter, just as cleanly formed as in the British circles.

In many circles, the young corn had stood up again, which gave the formations quite a 'tousled' impression. Single stems were peculiarly twisted or woven into each other, and others stood there bent in a curved manner, seeming to have grown upwards again after having been laid down flat.

One member of the group got headaches in one of the circles, and one woman perceived a tingling and pressure feeling when she took stems from the circles into her hand, a feeling which she didn't have when she touched a control sample from outside the pictogram. I was surprised about another detail in Dr Nowgorodow's report: he mentioned that even in October 1989, a group of ten 'analogous circles' had been discovered in the high grass of a meadow near the village Woronino in the area around Tomsk in central Siberia. Thus the crop circles had turned up here as well, in the middle of Siberia way away from anywhere.

The formation was investigated by a group of researchers of the Polytechnic Institute of the University of Tomsk, headed by Dr Vladimir Luneva. One of the circles was 4.1yds (3.75m) wide and 4.65yds (4.25m) long, containing an equilateral triangle in its midst, while on the rim of the circle three equal-sized semi-circles were arranged, giving a triangular bias to the circle. The researchers emphasised the pattern's beauty and symmetry in their report. The grass within the formation was bright green and shorter than the surrounding meadow, while the triangle consisted of normal grass like that outside of the formation. All of the ten circles had the same size and were equally round, as if drawn with a pair of compasses, according to Dr Nowgorodow's report to me.

Dr Vladimir V Rubtsov reported quite a special kind of circle. At Merefa, about 20 miles (30km) south-west of the city of Kharkov, Ukraine, an angler named A E Vorontsov was a witness on 7th January 1990 to an approximately 25yds wide, top-shaped disc hovering above the frozen river Mzha, before it shot vertically into the air. On the ice, Vorontsov discovered a ring of 22.6yds (20.7m) diameter – the first 'ice ring'!

CROP CIRCLES OUTSIDE EUROPE

Australia

On the evening of 19th January 1966, around 9.00pm, in the middle of the Australian summer, banana farmer George Pedley was driving back home on his tractor. Work was done, and he was looking forward to a few quiet hours. However, a loud hissing sound, which even drowned out the tractor's noise, jerked him from his eventide mood. He looked up, wondering where the buzzing could have come from, when a bluish-grey disc rose up out of the nearby marsh and shot into the sky. Pedley described the eerie object as 26ft (8m) wide, and about 10ft (3m) tall. Had it landed in the marsh? The farmer took a look. In the midst of the marsh grass he located a spiral-shaped circle of 33ft (10m) in diameter.

"The reed was bent without exception below the water surface, and lay whirled around in a clockwise manner as if it had been exposed to an unbelievable rotational force", he explained later. *"The air smelled sulphurous and seemed somehow electrically charged"*. Pedley got his neighbour and a friend to have a look, and they in turn informed the press. Little later, two similar circles were found about 27yds (25m) away from the first one, both about 11ft (3.50m) wide. Further findings followed in the same region, near Tully in Queensland – there were six of them there, between 10ft (3m) and 16ft (5m) wide.

An investigation by the Royal Australian Air Force reached the conclusion that an unknown energy must have pulled the plants out of the marsh ground and whirled them into these spiral patterns. A hoax could be excluded. Slight traces of burns on some of the stems indicated the action of a mysterious energy. The official report ended with the conclusion that a 'heavy weather turbulence', a local whirlwind, must have been responsi-

ble. This explanation was rejected by meteorologists: on the day in question, the weather was dry, still and sunny. At least 40 circles followed after 1971, most of them in 1977. Beforehand, luminous spheres, red lights or metallic discs were observed in most cases.

In recent years, reports came increasingly from the states of Victoria and South Australia. Twelve circles in two groups were discovered in 1989 at Speed, Victoria and investigated by a research group from Melbourne. John Pinkney from the newspaper *Weekend Truth* quoted a farmer in the edition of 16th December: *"Evidently, something has gone down there which radiated unbelievable energies. Outside the circles one could penetrate the ground with one's fingers. But within, the soil was unbelievably hardened, like cement. The wheat seems to be interwoven, almost like a basket. Quite incredibly, the plants are totally undamaged and are fully ripe"*. At another location, even a quintuplet formation was discovered.

New Zealand

On 6th October 1972, the *Wellington Times* reported that Henry Thomas and his family had heard a 'strange sound' during the night of 30th September. On the next day, they found a 30ft (9m) wide circle with flatly laid down grass stems on their meadow.

But New Zealand's real crop circle summer was the summer of 1992–93. The inhabitants of Ranfurly, South Island, reported dozens of circles, up to 16yds (15m) in diameter, which appeared in January and February (summer in the southern hemisphere) in their region. While sceptics regarded them as rutting patterns of the almost extinct Moa bird, the more popular theory claims that they are UFO landing sites.

Japan

The first known Japanese crop circle appeared on 30th June 1979 on a rice paddy near Toyosato, north of the

'Science City' Tsukuba in the district of Ibaraki, northeast of Tokyo. Its diameter measured 13ft (4m). The rice plants seemed at first glance to be damaged – a closer investigation revealed that they had been pressed deeply into the mud in which the rice grows. Japan's crop circle expert Professor Yoshi-Hiko Ohtsuki of the Tokyo Waseda University counted thirteen circles in the period between 1979 and 1989.

But no press sensations arose until two circles appeared which the rice farmer Shunzo Abe discovered on the morning of 17th September 1991 in his rice paddy at Sasaguri near Fukuoka on Kyushu: a large circle of 20yds (18m) in width, and next to it a smaller one 7yds (6m) in diameter, surrounded by a ring. The stems lay counter-clockwise. No footprints were discovered indicating the work of a 'joker', although visible footprints would have been left within a marshy rice paddy.

Two weeks later, further circles turned up in the vicinity of the historic site of Yoshinogari on Kyushu: a circle of 11yds (10m) in diameter, which soon after was surrounded by a ring, and later still four smaller satellite circles of 3–4yds (3–4m) in width joined them. Altogether there were eventually seventy-six circles which turned up before June 1991 in Japan's rice paddies, as Professor Ohtsuki told me.

Afghanistan

I was informed by Colin Andrews that a team of geologists from the University of Cambridge discovered about thirty circles 'with the detail of crop circles' in deep snow, on an expedition in the highlands of Afghanistan in 1990.

Turkey

Further 'snow circles' turned up in 1975 in the highlands of Anatolia: seven extreme whirls, one next to the other, at the foot of a mountain slope.

Egypt

One of the most fascinating reports of pictogram formations I have ever received came from Charlotte Wüsthoff from Düsseldorf, Germany. Ms Wüsthoff had flown from Cairo to the Red Sea on 28th November 1992 with Egypt Air. Around Port Safaga, she discovered a mysterious pattern in the desert sand: a circle, which had an 'F' key attached to it, whose shaft was surrounded by a ring. Interestingly, the 'F' is the Egyptian Hieroglyph 'neteru', literary 'The Watchers', the Egyptian word for the gods of the Nile. Have they returned?

Brazil

On 17th June 1969 around 2.00am, a married couple observed an oval, bright-shining object, *"like a mercury-vapour machine with elongated rays"*. It hovered forty-five minutes above the same place, while it projected a light ray into the trees. Then it disappeared. At daylight, the two discovered a 9yd (8m) circle, in which the plants lay in a counter-clockwise direction on the ground.

Nine days later, likewise at night, a local judge heard a *"noise like the buzzing of a bee swarm"* and sighted an object which swung to and fro in the sky and finally sank down into the bushes, to climb up again shortly thereafter. At the 'landing place' in question, he found a second, flatly-pressed circle and broken branches.

Puerto Rico

As my friend and colleague Jorge Martin, chief editor of the magazine *Enigma*, told me, several circles and concentric rings in stone turned up in the middle of August 1991 on a rocky plateau near Ajuntas in the south-west of this mountainous Caribbean island. Martin, who investigated the traces on the spot, described them to me *"...as if something had burned or marked them in the stone, something which landed here and left its traces"*. He is convinced that the circles are linked to a wave of UFO-sightings and landings which were reported in this area at the same time. Unfortunately, the circles survived only few weeks. Then, one night, a convoy of olive-green cars were seen in the region, and on the next morning they were literally smashed out of the stone – by governmental agents, as Martin suspects. Puerto Rico is an American protectorate and 'playground' for the US military and secret services.

Mexico

On July 11, 1991, the date of an eclipse of the sun over central America, millions of citizens of Mexico City directed their cameras at the sky to film the historic event. But, to their surprise, they also captured something else on film – a shining, metallic disc hovering beneath the clouds for about an hour. Even the TV cameras of

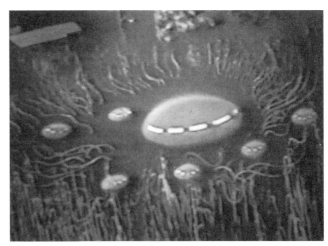

Eyewitness drawing of a UFO, hovering over a sugar-cane field in Metepec, sending out small balls of light, creating the pictogram.

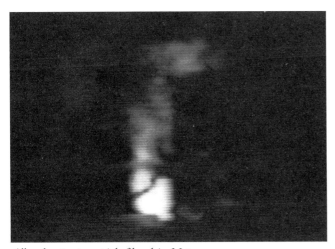

Alleged extra-terrestrial, filmed in Metepec.

Mexico's biggest private station, TELEVISA, recorded this strange phenomenon which, of course, resulted in nationwide headlines. Indeed, it marked the beginning of the biggest wave of UFO sightings in history which is still continuing today.

"Since then, we regularly record flying objects demonstrating strange flight patterns, on radar, sometimes as often as twice a week," a civilian air traffic controller informed me when I went to Mexico City to investigate the sightings.

On 16th September, 1994, starting at 8.00pm and continuing for five hours, he recorded a strange object hovering in the direction of Metepec, west of Mexico City. And it was on this night that the strangest event in the history of crop circles took place.

At about 11pm, Sara Cuevas, accompanied by her daughter Erika, used her camcorder to film a luminous, disc-shaped object hovering over the city of Metepec. Shortly afterwards, she noticed a strange, luminous being standing, only about 90ft away, in the middle of a nearby sugar-cane field. Grabbing her camera again, she filmed until the 4ft tall humanoid slowly moved away. Next morning, Sara Cuevas and her neighbors discovered a strange formation of flattened sugar-canes in the field in question. Even the footprints of the entity were found. After the 'Metepec Case' had been featured in a TELE-VISA documentary, another woman, a neighbor of Sara Cuevas, contacted local UFO investigator, Daniel Munoz Tovar and revealed that she had taken a second film that night, from a different position, a bit further away. Other witnesses reported that, later that night, they, too, had observed the landing of a luminous, dome-shaped object in the middle of this field. Small balls of light had shot from it and whirled through the field, creating the crop formation in seconds, before returning to the mothership which then took off and flew away. Subsequent investigation showed not only that many sugar-cane leaves had been burnt, but also that the ground temperature in the centre of the circle was higher than that recorded in the rest of the field. A higher radio-activity reading – $3\frac{1}{2}$ times above normal – was also recorded.

In fact, the Metepec formation was not the first but the second event of its kind to have occurred in Mexico. During the previous night (September 15th) a pictogram, 400ft long and 210ft wide, appeared in a sugar-cane field near the village of Jocotitlan/Toluca. Again, the canes were found lying flat on the ground, bent but not broken and, again, witnesses reported having seen a luminous object that night. Some of the first villagers to enter the formation suffered from nausea and skin burns, possibly caused by radiation from the formation.

In fact, many Mexicans believe that these UFO sightings and events were indications of the 'return of the gods', as prophesied in the calendars of the ancient Mayas and Aztecs. According to the Dresden Codex, a pre-Columbian astronomical manuscript, the eclipse of July 11th, 1991 – which had been accurately predicted more than a thousand years earlier by ancient Mexican astronomers – would herald "the end of the fifth sun and the beginning of the sixth sun, the sun of Quetzalcoatl, the plumed serpent." According to the prophecy, this would indicate "earth changes".

TELIVISA journalist, Jaime Maussan, who interviewed leading experts on Mexico's pre-Colombian history for a UFO Special edition of his Sixty Minutes programme (which normally covers political, social and ecological issues) gave me this intepretation of the prophecy:

"The new lord is coming, the old lords will die or leave. A new order will be born. The eclipse indicates a return to roots, the knowledge of the Ancients, of the indigenous people, to the reign of the gods. In the sixth sun, we will meet the Lords of the Stars."

Canada

According to a report which was sent to me by Christian Page from the Organisation for Collection of Information on Extraordinary Phenomena (OCIPE), in Manitoba alone there were ten crop circles in 1990, and twenty-five throughout Canada. Most of them were investigated by the North American Institute for Crop Circle Research with headquarters at Winnipeg, Manitoba, who coined the specialist term UGM – 'Unusual Ground Markings'. The history of the phenomenon in Canada can be traced back to the seventies.

The first circle appeared in September 1974 on an oilseed rape field at Langenburg, Saskatchewan. During the rape harvest, farmer Edwin Fuhr noticed a strange metal object in the midst of his field which, as he saw, began to turn. When looking around, he recognised four further steel hemispheres to his left, which also hovered about 1ft (30cm) above the ground. As if immobilised, he observed the peculiar spectacle for fifteen minutes, until smoke formed underneath the objects, a strong wind sprang up and the objects shot straight up into the sky. There where they had hovered, Fuhr discovered five circles of 3.5cm (1.4in) in diameter. The plants were pressed flatly on the outside and were twisted clockwise into a ring. The farmer called the police.

A few days later, Fuhr's neighbours' dog started barking around midnight and acted crazy till about 3.00am. No-one could see anything – until the next morning when Fuhr drove to his field and discovered a sixth ring next to the five other circles.

In the following years, there were repeating reports about the mysterious circles' appearance, sometimes in tobacco fields, at other times in sweetcorn fields, and then again in the wheat fields of Ontario, Newfoundland and British Columbia – about twenty in number. But it was not until 1990 that the phenomenon literally exploded. All the formations were situated in wheat fields, and about half of the cases had the corn laid down clockwise. An especially nice example from Tweedsmuir, Saskatchewan consisted of concentric rings which alternately rotated left and right. Only in one case did it come to a UFO sighting during the night of a circle appearance: a student observed strange lights.

There was, as in England, an evolution of the phenomenon. The first reports spoke only of simple circles. But by the end of the 1990 season there were some cases of 'double rings' and even a perfect cross with a pair of compasses at the middle, surrounded by two concentric rings. This evolution continued in 1991. Pure circles were now the exception – in almost all cases they were agriglyphs, complex pictograms. At the centre of circle phenomena this time was the state of Alberta.

The first cases in this sensational series weren't exactly timid – they appeared on 21st August 1991 only 55yds (50m) in front of the main entrance of the local TV station CFCN-TV at Lethbridge, Alberta: one large

circle, next to it a threefold dumb-bell of three circles linked by corridors. The TV station invited experts from the Canadian Farmers Association, the Astronomical Association, the police and a local UFO organisation for a local investigation. The UFO researchers knew of five reports of mysterious lights in the region during the week preceding the discovery of the formation. Six days later, a farmer at Okotoks, Alberta, south of Calgary and 80 miles (130km) from Lethbridge, reported an almost identical crop pattern. On 1st September, news about fresh circle findings arrived from the whole area around Lethbridge.

But probably the most beautiful formation was the 'Warner Brothers', as people named the four-fold pattern which was discovered on that day at Warner, Alberta. Majestically, the circles lay on the ridge of a flat hill in the midst of a field of golden-yellow wheat. The farmer Roy Teztlaf noticed them during harvest. Two of the four spirals lay clockwise, two in the opposite direction, and quite evidently in several layers, of which each was arranged at an angle to the previous one. Individual stems still stood upright, others were bent at half height at right angles. The pictogram was located in the midst of a several hectare field without tram-lines. There were no footprints or indications of intruders, and it would have been impossible for humans to penetrate one hundred yards of ripe wheat unnoticed (two tracks recognisable on aerial photographs were made by Tetzlaf himself). The crop was so dry and brittle that the slightest disturbance would have been visible.

While Canadian cereologists were still bowled over by the fascinating beauty of the 'Warner Brothers', they soon were confronted by their next puzzle: a pictogram at Codhurst, west of Lethbridge, which had turned up on 31st August on the land of farmer Fred Watmough. It could most accurately be described as a chain of circles, 2–8yds (2–7m) wide, which, spirally arranged, ended in a gigantic, 27yds (25m) long 'F'. Watmough reported how his dogs had barked for hours the night before. Many visitors to the crop circles reported feelings of dizziness, sickness or headaches. Wild geese were observed to avoid the crop circles by flying large detours around them – not once did a wild goose fly over one of the circle groups. Sometimes, a flock of geese divided, a few birds flying around the pictograms on the left side, others on the

right, and yet in one case they returned together when flying in the other direction. Everything indicates that they consciously avoided the agriglyphs.

In 1992, there were more crop circles in Canada. According to a study by the North American Institute for Crop Circle Research, 47 formations were found that year, most of them in the states of Manitoba (20), Alberta (18) and Saskatchewan (8). It wasn't only quantitatively that the phenomenon grew. As well as simple circles, dumb-bell formations turned up more and more frequently, and in 10% of cases there were UFO sightings beforehand. At Ipswich, Manitoba during the night of 14th August, a UFO was observed hovering over a wheat field. On the next morning, the farmer found a pictogram in the shape of the astronomical sign for the planet Mars, 9.3yds (8.5m) in diameter. Two further 'Mars' symbols were discovered on the same morning at Strathclair, Manitoba.

But the most mysterious incidence happened on 22nd August 1992 in the vicinity of the community of Milestone in Saskatchewan. There a farmer Joe Rennick discovered an irregular pattern of flattened corn about 7yds wide and 21yds long in his wheat field. At first Rennick thought of wind damage, but then he noticed that the stems were laid down in a concentric, anti-clock-wise direction – and in the midst of the pattern lay a flattened, dead porcupine. When Rennick examined the carcass, he realised the animal was neither ill nor hurt – it evidently had been crushed by something very heavy, or by a strong unknown force. A porcupine weighed around 25lbs (11kgs) and was as big as 16in (40cm) in diameter, but it was just 1in (2.5cm) thick, its legs were stretched, and somehow it looked like a cartoon figure. Broken-off porcupine spines and a drag-mark at the edge of crop formation hinted that the porcupine had been hurled from there into the middle. Moreover, the long spines from its body lay in the same orientation as the wheat stems surrounding them. Rennick realised an immense force must have acted here, in which the porcupine accidentally mixed up.

Until now researchers had always asked themselves: if the crop circles really were produced by a strong energy, why did an animal never become victim of the process? Perhaps because the forming of a circle is preceded by some danger indication – maybe a high frequency sound – which warns animals away. The porcupine however, originating from the hedgehog family, reacts to danger by rolling itself up and pointing its spines towards the threat, instead of escaping.

The farmer noticed yet another special feature: while the rest of the field was still muddy from frequent rainfall, the soil within the formation was hard and bone-dry.

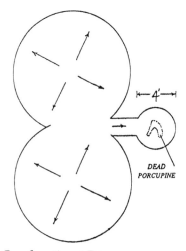

Crop formation at Estevan, Saskatchewan, showing position of dead porcupine, found in August 1989.

The laid stems had left behind imprints – as if they had been laid down before (or while) the ground dried. And while the corn on the field as a whole was green and soft, the stems within the pattern proved to be dry and brittle. A few days later, a farmer named Don Hagel discovered two 39yds (36m) wide circles inside his wheat field, which touched each other to form an 'eight', at Estevan, Saskatchewan, 100 miles southeast from Milestone. A short corridor led from the place of their touching to a smaller circle, about 1.3yds (1.20m) wide. And in this small circle were located the remains of another porcupine. It must have been there for some two weeks. Flesh and skin were completely decomposed – only bones and black, rotting remains were left. (Report by Chad Deetken)

USA

It had to be at Gulf Breeze, Florida, of all places, in the midst of a local UFO-sighting wave, that America's first crop circle turned up. Gulf Breeze is the UFO-Mecca of the United States, since local businessman Ed Walters took a photograph of a mysterious flying object and thereafter was hit by a blue ray which lifted him into the air, in November 1987. A married couple by the name of Somerby also saw the blue ray, and since Mr Somerby was editor at the local newspaper, he wrote about his experience the next day. Further witnesses then reported their experiences, and Ed Walters made his photos available. In the following months Walter had a number of experiences with the mysterious luminous objects, including an 'abduction' (being involuntarily taken inside an ET craft), which he recalled under hypnosis when researchers of the US UFO organisation MUFON investigated the case.

It all developed into hundreds of UFO sightings by local residents, and they still happen to this day. One of the most peculiar incidences in the region of

Gulf Breeze.

Gulf Breeze was the appearance of a 6yd (5m) wide circle in the grass of Shoreline Park in Gulf Breeze in November 1989. A second circle followed in January 1990. The two whorls signalled the beginning of the first circle year in the United States – sixty further circles followed during the twelve months thereafter, twenty of them in connection with UFO sightings, according to statistics from the North American Institute for Crop Circle Research.

It is significant that the majority of circles turned up in grass, followed by sweetcorn, wheat, barley, beans, sugar cane, alfalfa, cotton and marsh-grass. All of them were simple whorls, not pictograms or formations. The statistics of NAICCR for 1991 show only fourteen cases by 5th September 1991 – which however doesn't mean much since the circles are often only discovered during harvest, for American fields are often large.

America's circle country is the rural Mid-West, particularly the states of Missouri and Kansas. In the middle of September 1990 the farmers Roger and Lynda Lowe noticed two circles on their sugar cane field, each one about 11yds (10m) wide. Sugar cane grows up to 2yds high and breaks very easily. *"The circle was perfect when we found it"*, the Lowes explained to the local press. *"The plants weren't broken. They lay nicely next to each other on the ground".*

Shortly thereafter Michael Newcomer discovered two 22yd (20m) circles in the hip-high grass on his pasture at Oskaloosa. A perfect circle of 17yds (15m) in diameter in a sweetcorn field near Milan, Illinois was investigated by UFO researcher Jeff Fischer from MUFON in October 1990. The plants lay in a clockwise manner and were bent at the ground or at a height of 16in (40cm). Two weeks before the circle's discovery – and nobody knows when it was made – several witnesses had seen UFOs in the surrounding area, *"geometrical shapes, surrounded by lights of all colours".*

Soil samples from the circles in the year 1991 – in the states of Tennessee, Iowa, North Carolina and Oklahoma – were tested for heightened radioactivity by American physicist Marshall Dudley. He detected that their alpha-radiation was in some cases up to 27% below, but in other cases up to 198% above the rate for control samples.

According to a report by the North American Institute for Crop Circle Research, the number of crop circles again increased to forty-six in 1992 – the centres of gravity this time lay in Pennsylvania (12 cases), Tennessee (9) and Illinois (8). This time they mainly chose wheat (21 cases) and grass (15) as their medium. Usually they are simple circles, but also dumb-bells (as was in Minnesota), T-shaped patterns (in Pennsylvania) and rings (in Illinois).

The appearance of a circle in flat-laid grass at Raeford, North Carolina, was preceded by a UFO sighting. Startled by a loud noise *"like a freight train"*, a farmer and his wife ran to the door and went outside, where an object *"the size of a swimming pool, surrounded by orange-coloured lights"* hovered over the pasture 100yds away from the

farmhouse. The couple ran back into the house and called their children. When they went outside again the UFO was gone.

Then, in February 1993, the first 'ice circles' appeared overnight on a thin layer of ice covered with light snow on the Charles River in Boston, Massachusetts. The next morning, hundreds of employees of the

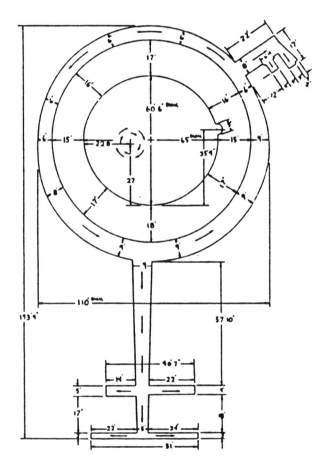

Pictogram at Kennewick, WA, 29th May 1993.

(Drawing by Jerry Phelps)

renowned Massachusetts Institute of Technology (MIT), which lies on the banks of the Charles River, were witnesses of the phenomenon: dozens of circles and concentric rings, linked with each other by passages, not unlike the 'stone circles' which had appeared in Puerto Rico.

A good omen for the crop circle year of 1993 arose on 29th May when the first American pictogram of the year appeared at Kennewick in the state of Washington: a ringed circle with two extensions, an 'F' and an 'antenna'. Its stems were interwoven and bent such that Professor Levengood definitely excluded a hoax. It was the first of about forty crop formations in the summer of 1993. One of them appeared on 26th July at Route 28 at Columbia, Herkimer County in the state of New York, about ten miles south of Mohawk, discovered by passing motorists. It consisted of four circles linked with each other, the greatest 9yds (8m) in width, in an oat field. On the night of its forming, a truck driver from North Carolina observed a 'cylindrical object' in the night sky above the field in question.

6. The UFO Connection

On the evening of 13th July 1988, Mary Freeman, a young woman from Marlborough, was invited for dinner by friends in Avebury. The evening ended around 11.00pm, and she said goodbye and got into her small Renault. She drove along the A361, which crosses the stone circle, and took a smaller road which follows the so-called 'Avenue', two rows of standing stones which are part of the 'sacred landscape' of Avebury.

The road was quiet, it was a dark, cloudy new moon night, and on the horizon Miss Freeman recognised the outline of Silbury Hill. But what was *that*? An intense golden-white glow came through the clouds and descended slowly, silently and majestically, brighter than a full moon. A quick look at the road in front of her, then back to the mysterious luminous object. At this moment, a thin beam of white light seemed to come out of it, falling at an angle of 65° on to the area in front of Silbury Hill. *'I couldn't believe my eyes, but I wasn't frightened"*, Mary reported later. *"The whole thing somehow had something ethereal about it"*. Seconds later, her car was caught by a kind of 'energy current'. Objects on the dashboard, a book and a pack of cigarettes, suddenly flew in a wide loop into her lap. She drove on slowly, following the UFO and the beam, and finally turned on to the A4 towards Silbury Hill to observe the object at closer range. For a few seconds trees blocked her view. When at last Mary saw the impressive Silbury Hill in front of her, the shining object had disappeared.

Irritated and deeply moved by all this, Mary turned around and drove back home to Marlborough. Thirty-six hours later, on 15th July 1988, farmer Roger Hues discovered the first of five 'Celtic Crosses' which were to appear that summer in the region of Silbury Hill. The five-fold circle pattern, 96yds (88m) in diameter, was located at exactly the place where Mary Freeman had seen the 'narrow beam of white light' going down two nights before. Chance? Or had 'somebody' made the formation? Had the UFO perhaps programmed the wheat stems to lay down twenty-four hours later in a pre-arranged pattern?

Mary Freeman's experience is only one of a number of cases which suggest a connection between the crop formations and the UFO phenomenon. 'UFO' doesn't necessarily have to mean 'space-craft from outer space', for much indicates that it quite possibly could also be vehicles of inter-dimensional travellers who don't have to be physical in nature.

In September 1976, the German parachutist Willy Gehlen slept inside his car which he had parked on a field-path near Upton Scudamore at Warminster, when he was awakened by a buzzing sound. He opened his eyes and saw a tall figure in front of him, whom he thought was the farmer who owned the field. When Gehlen apologised for his 'unauthorised parking', the figure didn't answer. Instead, minutes later, Gehlen saw a red pulsing light which ascended out of the field and finally flew away. A little later the first known crop circles turned up on exactly that field. Is there a connection?

Mrs Joyce Bowles from Winchester claims to have met extra-terrestrials four times in 1976 and 1977, and she contends that once she was even taken aboard a space craft. At one point the UFO landed on her field at Chilcomb near Winchester. *"This is our field"*, explained the UFO traveller to her, and one of his colleagues showed her a kind of map with *'...all kinds of lines. In the middle there was a circle, surrounded by rings"*. From 1977 onwards, crop formations turned up on this field. An encounter with the circle-makers?

As we have seen so far, in many cases – and throughout the world – there have been UFO sightings in the context of circle phenomena. The UFOs mostly turn up when or before the circles appear, or when the phenomenon experiences a quantum jump. In the case of the first five real German pictograms (Damp, Marburg, Heinzenhausen, Grasdorf, Netze) UFOs were reported, but then reports ceased. Similarly, this happened in other countries, such as Canada. In relation to the circles at Langenburg near Regina, Saskatchewan, in 1974, George Wingfield thoughtfully commented: *"This account... is certainly reminiscent of many crop circle events today, and yet now there is an entirely different perception as to their cause. If it's UFOs today, they really have to be invisible. Why then did Edwin Fuhr give such a graphic account of shiny, metallic nuts-and-bolts flying saucers? Perhaps it is humanity that has changed, or at least its perception of the external world ....or is it the UFO phenomenon itself?"*

I believe it's neither of the two. More likely, it seems to have something to do with the strategy of the beings who seem to visit us in UFOs – a strategy of 'gentle approach', of slow familiarisation, of gradually habituating us to the fact that we are not alone. Occasional individual sightings of UFOs can be sufficient to suggest a connection with crop formations and 'circle-makers', without it being necessary to make regular and constant showings. What is certain is that *most* of the crop formations appear 'just so' and out of nowhere, without previous UFO manoeuvres. At most, 20% of all circles are preceded by a UFO sighting. 'UFO' in this context stands for all forms of unusual though intelligently-behaving light phenomena in a wider sense.

This was the case on the night when the enormous tetrahedron at Barbury Castle appeared – the 'mother of all pictograms'. On this night, Brian Grist, Gary Hardwick and his girlfriend Alison from Bristol had been circle-watching in the region of Beckhampton. Shortly before midnight, they noticed three strange lights which silently crossed the sky. During the next hour they saw many white lights, objects which pulsed with green, red and white lights, and which disappeared sometimes towards the north, and other times towards the south. Finally, an enormous, dark object passed noiselessly over their heads. One of the lights stopped and didn't move for minutes, and several times the pulsing UFOs seemed to fly towards the three people. The trio categorically exclude confusion of these lights with planes, satellites or shooting stars, for the sightings were too close, too breath-taking and clear. Brian described the experience with the words: *"It reminds me most of scenes in the film 'Close Encounters of the Third Kind'. I simply couldn't believe what was happening there."*

Other circle researchers in the vicinity saw the lights that night, mostly in the direction of Barbury Castle, an ancient hill fort. The warden at Barbury Castle, who lives in a bungalow on the hill, heard a *"colossal thunderous din"*, and thereafter a *"pulsing buzzing sound"* that morning around 3.00am, *"...as if a hundred planes were passing overhead"*. It stopped suddenly, after only a few minutes. Without getting up, he turned over and went back to sleep. It should be added here that Barbury Castle lies nearby the RAF Lyneham air base and that the warden was accustomed to low-flying planes. But this noise was louder, more intense, different.

Two weeks later, when a circle surrounded by a ring with ten (!) satellites turned up near Hopton, Norfolk, UFOs were sighted. A large red light surrounded by a Saturn-like ring and as large as a full moon apparently descended at the site of the formation in the corn field. When it touched the ground, it suddenly went dark, according to several witnesses in their report to the police.

Anthony Dodd, a retired police sergeant, now involved in researching crop formations in the North of England, is convinced: *"I don't have the slightest doubt that these formations are produced by UFOs. There has always been an increase in UFO sightings when crop circles appear. One goes hand in hand with the other, and it has been like that for some years. Much links the UFOs with the crop formations. One example, which members of our organisation investigated, was in Bristol, where a pictogram turned up after a whole number of witnesses observed UFOs above the area".*

That was on 29th June 1991 between 11.30pm and midnight. A witness described how a red ball of light, which flashed sparks, flew at low altitude overhead. At some distance, the object seemed to go down in the area of some nearby corn fields. The witness ran towards the fields to see what would happen, but lost sight of the UFO. A little later, a helicopter turned up, illuminating the fields with a searchlight. Enquiries revealed that Bristol police received dozens of calls by people who also claimed to have seen the mysterious red object.

Around 11.50pm on the same night witnesses observed a circular object with a red ring, with about ten smaller, red lights on the underside, crossing the sky at low altitude. The space-craft was buzzing audibly, stopped for a short time above one of the nearby fields, then disappeared in a westerly direction. The witnesses explained that while the luminous object flew away, a helicopter had appeared suddenly and began to chase the UFO. Only

when the craft shot away at high speed did the helicopter pilot give up, turning round and slowly crossing the field, with search-light bearing on the field. Then he turned around and disappeared in the direction he came from. On the next morning local residents discovered a large, dumb-bell shaped pictogram on the field above which the UFO had been sighted.

In my investigations I regularly meet people who have observed odd phenomena in circle country. One woman reported that during the night on which one of the smaller 'Delphinograms' appeared on the grounds of Firs Farm at Beckhampton, she couldn't sleep and went for a walk in the vicinity of her house. *"Then I saw a light coming from this hill and flying towards me. At first I thought it was a car's headlights, but then it stopped in front of me. It was an object of light. Finally it flew away."*

A couple by the name of Hallet, who were on their way back home to Bishops Cannings in a taxi on 8th July 1991, saw a lenticular-shaped flying object hovering over a prehistoric burial mound. In July, a Japanese TV crew filmed a light in the night sky which suddenly 'blinked out' – and a new crop formation was discovered there the next morning. On 22nd June, 'crop-watchers' of the Centre for Crop Circle Studies (CCCS) observed an orange-glowing sphere, and one of them was quick enough to record it for a few seconds on video, with the moon in one corner. One of the witnesses, John Holman, remarked that the ball of fire hovered above Milk Hill, three miles away from where they stood. On the basis of this distance he calculated the size of the object to be 80–110ft (25–35m) in diameter. A closer inspection of the film showed that the UFO had disappeared in a flash, in a time-span of between $1/17$ and $1/25$ of a second. Ironically, one of the hills in this area is called 'Golden Ball Hill'.

At the Japanese-British observational station in 1991 at Adam's Grave there were spectacular sightings. At the beginning of August, the 'permanent staff' noticed a flash

The first 'UFO nest' was found at Tully, Queensland, on 19th January, 1966.

After a night of unusual electrical disturbances in 1986, a reed circle was found in wetlands near Nishikawacho in Northern Japan.

In mid August 1991, several concentric circles and rings appeared on a rocky plateau near Ajuntas, Puerto Rico.

(Photo: Jorge Martin)

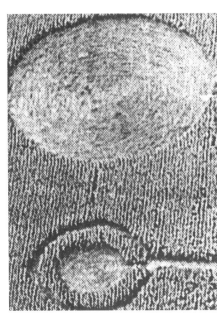

These circles in a rice paddy in Japan, which appeared on 17th September 1990 near Fukuoka, attracted world-wide attention.

The way the crop is laid in these photographs gives an impression of the energy involved in creating the patterns.

Detail of the swirling 'floor pattern' in a crop circle.

The clean and precise edges are visible here.

A different part of the same pictogram, viewed at ground level, with Silbury Hill in the background.

Characteristics of authentic crop circles: a precise and clean centre.

How the stalks are laid: here they flow around a stone.

A clean edge: here a ring, only a few centimetres wide, flows anti-clockwise round a clockwise circle.

One can clearly see that the stalks are bent, not broken, on the edge of a tractor path.

In most authentic crop circles, the floor pattern displays several layers.

The stalk is bent, not broken.

The joints on the stalks are thicker on those from within the crop circle than from without.

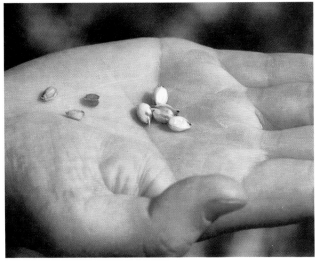

The seeds from the crop circle are misshapen; those from plants outside are unspoilt.

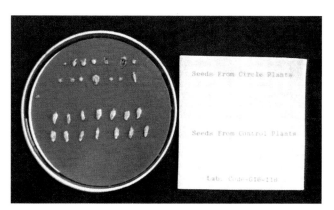

The biochemist Dr Levengood discovered that these seeds (from the pictogram near Bath in 1992) were deformed. Compare these with different samples (below) from the same field.

(Photo: Dr W. C. Levengood)

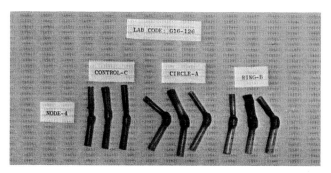

He also found that the joints of affected plants were abnormally large. These are samples of the 'triple stalks' from Lockeridge.

(Photo: Dr W. C. Levengood)

 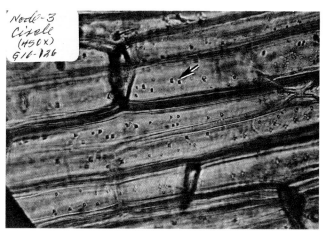

Microscopic studies of enlarged plant cells (x450); on the left from a control sample; on right from a crop circle. The dark lines are 'extending scars' as a result of expansion of the cell walls. The spots (indicated by arrow) are the pores by which the plants take in nutrients. Dr Levengood achieved a similar effect when he placed the stalks in a microwave oven for several hours.

(Photo: Dr W. C. Levengood)

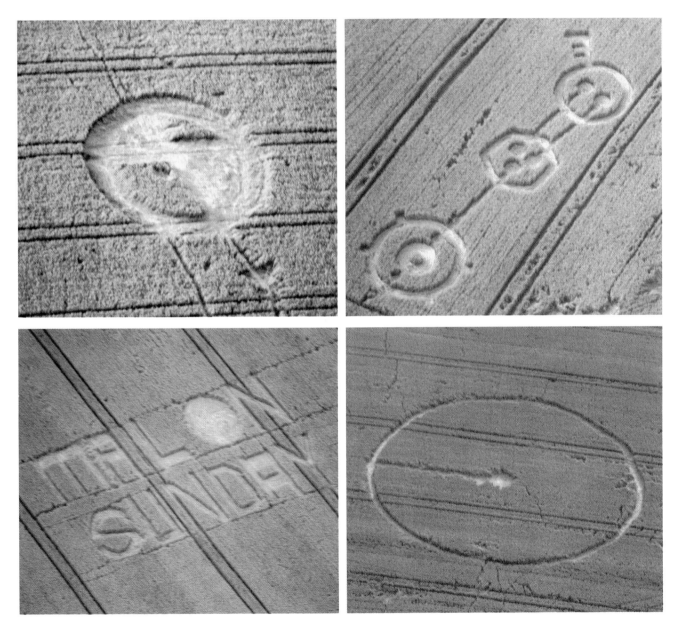

Can you spot the tell-tale signs in these faked circles?

Two of the mysterious white horses that keep on turning up on the green hills of the Wiltshire downs. Were they signs for the gods – and did the gods respond? In fact, crop circles often appear below the white horses, especially these two. Above is the Westbury, near Warminster; below the Allington White Horse, near Alton Barnes.

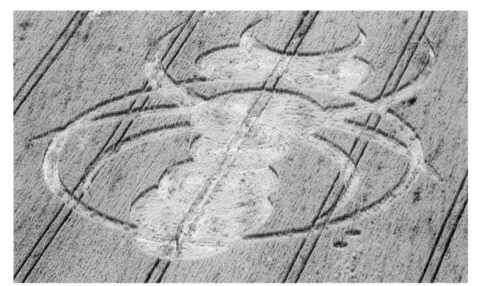

'The Bee': Barbury Castle, Wilts.
7th July 1994.

'The Eye of Horus': Alton
Barnes, Wilts. (240ft. diameter),
21st July 1994.

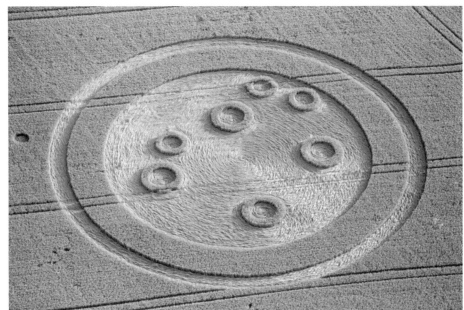

*Froxfield, nr. Hungerford, Wilts.,
24th August 1994.*

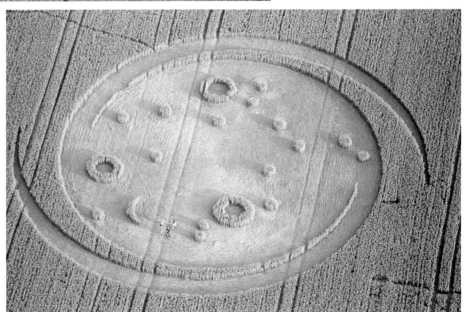

*'Galaxy': West Stowell, nr. Pewsey,
Wilts. (160ft. diameter), 23rd July
1994.*

'Triple Crescents': Oliver's Castle, Devizes, Wilts. (320ft. diameter), 27th July 1994.

'The Flower': Froxfield, nr. Hungerford, Wilts. (350ft. diameter), 4th August 1994.

'Infinity': West Overton, Hants., 28th July 1994.

Uffington White Horse, Berks., 15th July 1994. (the White Horse is in the top left hand corner)

Ashbury, Oxford, 26th July 1994.

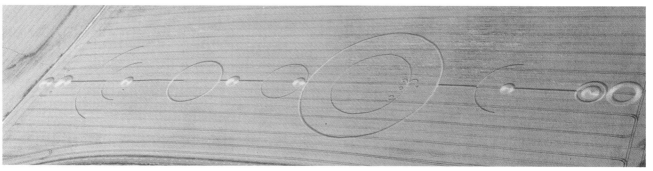

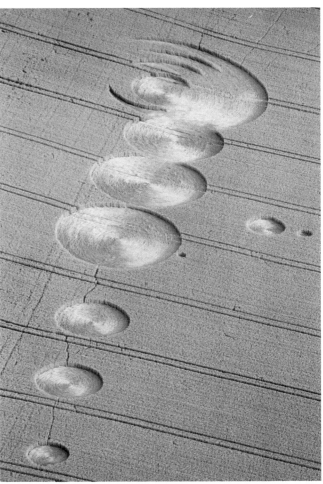

'The Claw': Hackpen Hill, nr. Marlborough, Wilts., July 1994.

Left: 'The Scorpion': Devizes, Wilts. (550ft. long), 15th July 1994. (the huge scale is shown by the lone figure in the lower circle)

Thought Bubbles': Wilsford, nr. Amesbury, Wilts., July 1994. **Inset:** *'The Bicycle': Andover, Hants., 28th July 1994.*

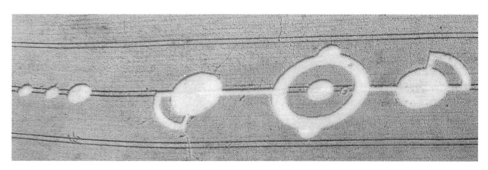

The Devil's Punchbowl, nr. Hazelmere, Surrey, July 1994.

Bourton Stacey, nr. Andover, Hants., July 1994.　　　　*'The Labyrinth': The Avenue, Avebury, Wilts., July 1994.*

of light in the sky, then "a luminous disc" turned up, *"which hovered over our camp and seemed to be observing it"*. Observing it? *"Yes, so I believe, and it seems to me as if the extra-terrestrials are also behind the crop circles, and are watching us now, to see what our next step is going to be, before they plan theirs"*. So thought one of the crop-watchers.

Some of the most interesting phenomena associated with crop formations are the enigmatic small white spheres which have been observed and filmed several times, in the vicinity of the formations. George Wingfield has seen them repeatedly, once with two witnesses during the 'Wansdyke Watch' in June 1990. He describes them as *"mysterious lights… very small and matt, which slowly and thoughtfully glided closely over the wheat, perhaps 200–300yds away from us"*. For one hour, Wingfield observed how the small objects came together and shot apart, and when he tried to approach them, they simply glided away.

A similar observation was made by the Vogt couple the night before the pictogram at Marburg in Germany appeared on 20th July 1992: *"About football-sized, not quite round light-spheres flew at high speed through the air, at 3–15ft height, along the road"*.

A single object of this kind, a small white-shining disc, was photographed by Busty Taylor by chance on 8th August 1987 when he, together with Pat Delgado and Colin Andrews, inspected a newly-made circle at Westbury. And then, in July 1990, such a mini-UFO was filmed for the first time.

Steve Alexander from Andover had driven with his wife to Alton Barnes on 26th July 1990 to marvel at the gigantic 'classic' pictogram – as did thousands of others. He had his video camera with him, and since he wanted take some pictures from a bird's-eye view, the couple climbed Milk Hill, above Alton Barnes, and Steve did his filming. It was around 4.30 in the afternoon, and the Alexanders were just going to leave when Steve saw something flashing in the field down below. Looking closer, he noticed a small, shining object which flew towards him, then turned around, dived into and then out of the corn field. In a flash he put down his camera-bag, took out the camera and began to film. *"The object flew very low amidst the corn, and it glittered all the time, sparking"*, Steve Alexander told me when I interviewed him in August 1991. *"Finally it stopped in the corn for almost three minutes, then it started again, flew closely over the field, glittered and flashed, crossed the field boundary and a few nearby gardens and houses and continued its course over a neighbouring field. There it passed a tractor driver, until it finally disappeared in the distance."*

The first person Alexander told about this remarkable piece of film was Colin Andrews. When Andrews saw the video, he noticed the tractor driver, whom the object passed. Here was a witness who must have seen the mysterious UFO at close quarters. He found out whom the field belonged to, drove to Stanton St Bernard, and asked whether anyone on the farm had observed anything unusual on 26th July. An 18-year old farm worker called Leon Besant had come back to the farm that evening, having been applying fertiliser on the field, and had excitedly told everyone he had seen a UFO. He was laughed at, and in the days that followed people pulled his leg about it. This continued for about a week, and they calmed down only when Leon stopped mentioning it. But he knew what he had seen.

"I reckoned that if I continued to insist I'd seen it, I would be declared insane", Leon reported. The situation changed instantaneously when Colin Andrews appeared at the farm with the film, and showed to the assembled staff. Suddenly Leon was the hero of the day. Everybody insisted they had always believed him. After all, who could have doubted his word! *"On 26th July 1990 I was fertilising the field with the tractor when this silver-gleaming object flew past me, just over the corn, and finally disappeared in the sky. I watched it. It was some distance from me, but I remember it was the size of a beach*

ball, and it glittered in the sun, as if it was made of silver paper – a constant glittering."

Colin Andrews gave the Alexander film to the Japanese for analysis. The result: the object had a diameter of only 8–16in (20–40cm) and reflected the sun's light on its surface, which seemingly consisted of a kind of special steel. The object moved directly over the crops, touching the wheat ears and pushing them aside.

The mystery grew when, in August 1991, two German students, Constantin and Dominik von Dürckheim (great-nephews of the German Zen philosopher Karlfried Graf Dürckheim), filmed a similar object in a newly-formed formation near Manton, Wiltshire. Six times the bright object crossed the pictogram – only 8in (20cm) wide, again at the crop ear's height, again in straight flight paths. Once it dived into the corn and little later it came back up, before it finally disappeared in the field. The mini-UFO gave an ethereal rather than a densely physical impression and seemed to become *smaller* as it came closer to the camera.

A third, far more striking film I received from Dr Fred Bell, a NASA scientist who has been working for some years in UFO research. Dr Bell used this piece of film for his video, which is provocatively called *The UFO Conspiracy and an Introduction to Extra-terrestrial Science*[1]. The piece of film, an amateur video of excellent quality, was recorded with a high-quality Sony camera, by music producer David Tickle. *"It was 7th May 1990"*, he explained. *"I drove from Gilford to Stonehenge to film a few scenes with my video. I filmed the stones of Stonehenge and the pastures which surround them, and my attention was drawn to the man-made tumuli around the site. Scientists describe them as burial mounds, but excavations extracted neither skeletons nor burial objects, and so nobody knows what they really were. They rather remind me of UFOs, and my impression is that the native inhabitants in this area possibly built them after the model of something which had landed there a long, long time ago.*

"When I had filmed my scenes, it was around 3.00 in the afternoon, and I noticed a bright light which hung above one of the tumuli. I have visited Stonehenge many times at night and often enough I saw amber-coloured lights which danced up there in the sky, but never before had I seen something in daylight. So I focused my camera on to the light, until it began to move after some time. It definitely wasn't a helicopter, or a plane, or a balloon, for it was brighter and hovered for minutes at one place."

But that wasn't all. When Tickle later examined the film on a monitor, he saw that two small, shining spheres manoeuvred in the field in front of the tumulus, finally ascending parallel to each other and flying past the stationary light. A careful analysis, picture by picture, revealed that the two lights seemed to flicker with the same rhythm as the 'mother ship'. Throughout the film it flashed again and again in the field, as if it were making electric discharges, and it shot small lights at unbelievable speed through the corn stems below. Dr Bell calculated that the speed of these spheres of light was more than 125mph (200kph). On the individual 'frames' of the video, they were visible only as a bright stripe. All these manoeuvres clearly exclude the possibility that the luminous objects are ball lightning, geomagnetic discharges or

An official photo by the British Airways: a luminous sphere circled Concorde in June 1973 over southern England.

plasma bubbles. *"It is one of the most impressive UFO films of all those shot so far"*, explained Dr Bell, *"and it clearly proves that these objects are under intelligent control and that it is they who are responsible for the crop circles"*.

These very fast, seemingly remote-controlled spheres or disc-shaped mini-UFOs have been known to us for years in the UFO literature. On a film taken in 1959 in Mexico by the American UFO contactee George Adamski, who passed away in 1965, one can see such a small luminous sphere and the way it flies to and fro next to a landed, dome-shaped space craft, hidden behind a bush. Paul Villa, who took a series of outstanding pictures in 1965, had photographed a whole group of football-sized, highly reflective spheres, whose surface appeared to be made of a special steel. In 1969 the crew of Apollo 12 filmed a luminous object which shot over the lunar surface at great speed. And in June 1973, a bright, football-sized sphere flew around Concorde during one of its test flights, hovering for a few seconds next to Concorde's circular portholes, then to shoot up into the sky at great speed. Luckily, a second British Airways plane was flying next to Concorde, documenting the flight on film. The most impressive part of the film was examined by international experts, who couldn't find a 'conventional' explanation.

That these spheres aren't just remote-controlled space probes, but have a number of other abilities available, is demonstrated in a fascinating photo which was taken in summer 1989 in the vicinity of Moscow. It shows how a luminous sphere projected a human face. Presumably, they are thus capable of making holographic projections, which explains reports of these balls of light 'converting' into human-like beings. One of the most interesting cases of such a 'conversion' or projection happened in 1917 at Fatima, Spain, and went down in the annals as a classical Mother Mary manifestation. Dozens of UFO contact cases of similar holographic projections have received less attention, one of which I describe in my book *UFOs: Die Kontakte*[2] (in German), and which I shall recount here.

A young man from South Africa, James Forbes, experienced the following. *"Outside, a strong wind was howling. Suddenly James noticed how a blue fog formed in the middle of his room. In the middle of the fog hovered a sphere of blue light, which finally exploded noiselessly, illuminating the whole room. Out of the light a human figure formed, about 7½ft (2.3m) tall, reaching almost to the ceiling…"*.

The most detailed picture of a 'telemetric disc' was made on 29th January 1963 on the grounds of the Nordic

Photos by Christian Lynggard.

Cable Company at Aalborg, Denmark. Guard Christian Lynggard photographed a light-sphere from only one yard's distance, while it moved around the company's property. On the photos it appears etheric, almost transparent, similar to the spheres filmed by Steven Alexander, and Constantin and Dominik von Dürckheim.

It is therefore highly probable that a connection exists between the UFO phenomenon and the crop circles. But what do we make of the 80% of all crop circles which turn up without a definitive connection with a UFO sighting? If we suppose for the time being that the crop circles and pictograms are produced by the intelligences in UFOs or spacecraft, then the question which immediately follows is *how?* For one thing the circles certainly are not: imprints of landed UFOs – even though the first circles gave the impression of being 'UFO nests'. The shapes of pictograms are too varied, and too often they turn up without a UFO being seen.

There remain two alternatives: either they were produced by 'invisible' UFOs – this could be due to multi-dimensionality as well as to a possible clever visibility-shield – or through an energy, such as an energy-beam from a very high altitude. One factor seems certain: there is an 'aerial component' in the phenomenon – too frequently the pictograms lie aligned to tram-lines in the fields, which are seemingly used like the lines on a writing page. Often the pictograms are so perfectly placed in the landscape – in relation to a prehistoric site, natural features, a parallel road or a field boundary – that it appears as if ingenious landscape artists had been at work.

From reports by UFO contactees we have found that at least some UFOs contain very powerful 'floor-lenses', with the help of which they can presumably recognise the smallest details on earth, even from great heights. There are a number of indications that crop formations could be made in exactly this way. Why? Perhaps it is the next step in a widening and deepening of humankind's consciousness, influenced from outside.

John Michell came to a similar conclusion when I asked him about his impression of the connection between crop circles and the UFO phenomenon. *"Every researcher admits"*, he said, *"that the mysterious lights in the sky, the peculiar noises, and the strange effects and things which people experience in connection with the crop circles point at the UFO phenomenon. There isn't just a **connection** with the UFO phenomenon: both are expressions of the same phenomenon. After the great UFO waves in the '60s and '70s, a process of rationalisation started, and people tried to explain away everything. Some said everything had just been imagination anyway, or some natural effect. Finally the phenomenon became physical, thus leaving physical traces behind, and these attracted the attention of scientists, who now can no longer ignore them."*

REFERENCES

1. *The UFO Conspiracy and an Introduction to Extra-terrestrial Science*, video.
2. *UFOs: Die Kontakte*, Michael Hesemann, 1990. Verlag Michael Hesemann, D-4000 Düsseldorf 1, Worringer Str. 1, Germany.

7. A Solution to the Mystery?

Friday 16th August 1991 was a fruitful day for me in my attempts to get to the root of the mystery of the crop formations. On the previous evening, at the weekly meeting of local crop circle researchers at the Waggon & Horses pub at Beckhampton, we had met Thomas Roy Dutton, a leading research engineer at British Aerospace, involved in aircraft and space exploration projects. Dutton, who has spent years investigating the UFO riddle in his spare time, had computer-analysed dozens of aerial photographs of crop formations, which had been handed to him by Busty Taylor. He found out that all of them were designed on the basis of the same mathematical model. This fundamental pattern didn't correspond to the behaviour of a plasma-vortex and couldn't possibly have been produced by hoaxers on the ground. His conclusions sounded convincing: a beam from very a great height had etched the circles and pictograms into the corn.

We arranged a meeting for 11.00am the next morning at one of the latest pictograms, a gigantic three-fold dumb-bell which had turned up on 13th August on the organically-farmed land of Martin Pitt at Marlborough. After Peter, my cameraman and co-producer, had installed his camera and tested the sound, I interviewed Roy Dutton about his highly interesting theory.

"Mr Dutton, you are of the opinion that the crop circles and pictograms were produced in a mechanical way

Roy Dutton.

by an unknown intelligence. How do you support your thesis?"

"The corn inside the circles is undamaged and laid down very gently in very interesting and often overlapping lengths. I have tried to analyse the spirals which we find in the circles. I started with the simple circles, because it was easier, and every single one of them could be simulated in a mathematical model. The circles are made according to proper mathematical laws, and I managed to produce similar designs on my computer screen following the same laws. These mathematical laws do not correspond to the behaviour of an ordinary vortex. I think the circles were made in rows of spirally-shaped strokes, bit by bit in sequence, one after the other, filling in the gaps between the initial outlines of the circles. When you look at the circle on which we are now standing, you see that the spiral goes in a large bow from the centre in a clockwise direction to the outside with an angle of perhaps 270°. It is the same mathematical law used in this spiral which we find in a crop circle of only 57° rotation."

"Could you demonstrate this with an example?"

"Of course. Busty Taylor gave me an aerial photograph of a simple crop circle, which I analysed. I tried to find the rules by which the spiral was produced. I managed to determine it quite accurately, and the same rules which were valid in that example are also used in larger spirals such as this one here, which is much larger than the one I analysed. But if I could look at it from above, I could tell with certainty whether it is real, for it would have to follow the same rules. What we have here, I think, has to do with a kind of scanner ray which lays the corn in rows in the right place, and this is only possible when a beam, similar to a laser, is directed from above onto the fields, a beam which programs the corn to follow these mathematical laws. The reason why it couldn't have been an ordinary vortex – for vortices also follow mathematical laws – is that here in the spirals we have a constantly-flowing radial component which can stop abruptly at the borders to produce the cleanly cut edges which we see here. No vortex follows such a pattern."

"Which energy was used?"

"This is the big question. None of the energies known to us is capable of doing this. A very strong laser would cause considerable damage, and would most probably even burn the corn. Young, green corn would especially be in a bad state afterwards. For that reason I don't think that electro-magnetic or laser energies have been used here. If we look at further possibilities – and this is the point where I have to go beyond my own sense of reality and beyond the present level in science – we have here, I believe, a new form of energy, which hasn't even been discovered yet and which can affect the corn without causing damage. I could imagine that it is a kind of gravitational radiation. We are still very much at the beginning of discovering gravitational radiation, and nobody has ever measured it with certainty. But judging by a recent publication by the Italian physicist G D Palazzi of the University of Rome, there is hope, for he says it could soon be possible to gain microwave-gravitational radiation from a Synchrotron. A synchrotron is a particle cluster generator which accelerates particles to almost the speed of light."

"What can be concluded from this about the makers of the crop circle phenomenon?"

"It looks as if we are dealing here with a technology which is far ahead of ours. For that reason we have to suppose that it is of extraterrestrial origin."

I asked Roy Dutton for a detailed explanation of his theory, which you can find in the next chapter. On the same day I became aware that he had a solution to the riddle of the origin of the crop circles.

After we had filmed the Dutton interview, we drove back to Winchester where we met Steve Alexander, whose film – which I later saw for the first time – confirmed my conviction that the UFOs are behind the crop circle phenomenon. When we said goodbye to Steve in the late afternoon, his father-in-law, himself an ambitious circle-enthusiast, suggested we drive up to the Punchbowl at Cheesefoot Head. We gladly accepted, although we had filmed the Punchbowl only a few days before from a helicopter.

Dusk was already falling and the ripe corn was set in a golden light when we parked our car at the side of the Punchbowl. After I had taken a look at the impressive scene of this natural amphitheatre – in which was a pictogram in the form of an old Saxon world-tree or *Irminsul* – I noticed a group of people on the slope of Telegraph Hill, which rose above the Punchbowl. One of them had a camera attached to a tall pole, and others seemed to be doing measuring: they had to be crop circle researchers. Apparently a new pictogram had turned up the previous night.

When we approached the group, I recognised Pat Delgado and Colin Andrews, who were leading the investigation. Yes, Colin Andrews confirmed, this formation had been discovered this morning. It was in the shape of a six-petalled star, surrounded by a double ring. Everything indicated that it was a real pictogram. I had to smile to myself. Two weeks before, George Wingfield had told me how often the crop circles seemed to react to desires and thoughts by researchers. *"Try it yourself and wish a pattern. Maybe it will appear."* I 'wished' a Star of David surrounded by a ring, closed my eyes and focused my attention on the symbol. And now it lay here, in front of my feet. It wasn't a Star of David, but a six-petalled flower, which resembled the Babylonian symbol for the planet Venus. Nevertheless, thank you, Circle-makers!

I asked Peter to set up the camera and attach the microphone, wanting to interview Pat Delgado after completion of his investigation of the new formation. *"I am very happy with the circle here – it shows all characteristics of a real formation"*, he explained. *"We have here some interesting features: where the corn is laid down inside the central circle and the petals – I call them 'petals', for there are six of them, and from the air they look like a flower surrounded by two rings. It is a very pretty circle, and it shows details which very convincingly agree with those of another pattern which appeared about one week ago behind the hill in that direction, and was real. Also this one here, which formed last night, is real."*

Later I was to hear about the strange circumstances under which this six-petalled star had formed. In the night in question, Richard Andrews and Leonie Starr had been at watch on Cheesefoot Head and had neither heard nor seen anything. Only when it was getting light did they discover the formation. Shortly thereafter, a motorcyclist approached and stopped, to 'see whether a crop circle had formed again'. He told Andrews that he had driven past on the way back home to Petersfield around 2.00am and had seen, exactly above the place where the pictogram now lay, a 'dome of light' which hovered over the field. Immediately he had the idea that the 'UFO' could form a crop circle, and for that reason he had come back here immediately after dawn.

Andrews and Starr had heard a passing vehicle around 2.00am. And another thing was remarkable about this pattern: it lay exactly at the place where six crop circle researchers, among them Colin Andrews and George Wingfield, had had the strange encounter with the 'trilling sound', in 1989.

Still thinking about the Roy Dutton interview in the morning, I asked Pat Delgado whether there were any hints of the way this formation had been created. His answer confirmed my suspicion: *"The likely method corresponds quite accurately to what I described in my last book: that every possible shape can be made by a kind of brushing of the corn with a kind of energy which tells every stem where it must lie. This formation looks as if it has been brushed with an 8in (20cm) wide brush, and as if it had first started to draw the outlines of three pedals, and then had said, 'No, we don't want to fill them in'. Let's take a single petal: first they brush its outlines, then they fill them in, just as one would do it on paper. So I think all these formations were created through pencil-lines of energy, which programmed every stem to go down in a predetermined direction, possibly very much later – perhaps weeks later, at night when nobody sees it. That's the way I think they are made, and here we have a perfect and beautiful example of that."*

What is behind this energy? Who creates the circles? *"My theory is that it is an intelligence, a highly developed intelligence, which uses an energy we still don't understand. It's that simple."*

Now, Delgado's 'pencil-lines of energy' are another word for Dutton's 'scanner'. This would explain a detail which was already observed in the pictograms of 1990. There the separately lying 'boxes' were always connected with each other via a fine track, only a few inches wide, as if the artist couldn't manage to lift his pencil.

A further pointer towards the riddle's solution arose during a meeting I had with Stanley Morcom, a circle-surveyor for CCCS, whom I later met in a delphinogram at Firs Farm at Beckhampton. Morcom has been especially keen in investigating the various crop 'floor patterns' which make up the pictograms. Could conclusions be drawn from them about their creation? In front of a running camera, Morcom lifted the layers individually – which somehow reminded me of fibre-mats – and showed what was laid down first: a thin, 6–8in (15–20cm) wide line which ran the full length of the formation, from one end to the other. Taking this line – which was too narrow to have been drawn by humans – as the starting point, the whole pictogram was built up layer by layer.

"This is typical for all the formations I have managed to investigate this year", Morcom explained to me. *"In this case the first line runs through the whole formation, and further lines extend from it on both sides till they reach the edge. The middle line finally forms a ring at both ends and continues on the other side. Starting from that narrow line, quite evidently all of the corn was laid down in one go, for there is no place where the laid-down corn meets upright-standing stems – as should be the case if the*

corn were laid down in a sequence. I think it is all laid down simultaneously, in the shortest possible time."

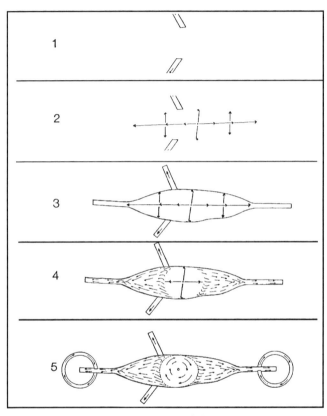

Diagram of the lay of the Lockeridge delphinogram.

During a second 'layer analysis' which Morcom did with the American physicist Michael Chorost on the enormous delphinogram at Lockeridge, he found similarly interesting results. In this case, the dolphin's 'fins' were formed before everything else. Then the central axis was followed by three roughly perpendicular 'rips', which defined the formation's shape and structure, then the outlines were drawn. Finally, the corn was laid down flat, starting at the centre. In the centre itself a vortex formed, and around the delphinogram's two sharp 'ends' there appeared two rings. This didn't correspond at all to the method demonstrated by Doug & Dave, and it is not likely that hoaxers begin with the pattern's extremities and are able to draw such fine axial lines. Yet it fits all too well into the model which Roy Dutton suggests.

There is still further evidence which seems to confirm Dutton. Everything indicates that the affected corn really has been influenced by an unknown radiation, as he proposes. Serendipitously, as the six-petalled flower was bathed in golden evening sunlight on that same significant day, I met Kenneth and Rosemary Spelman. The Spelmans were the people who had done the first chemical analyses of corn from a circle, at their 'Signalysis' laboratory at Rodborough, Stroud, described in Andrews' and Delgado's second book *Crop Circles – The Latest Evidence*.

Their results were fascinating. *"The energy pattern of the crystals produced by a distillation process from the plants inside the circles was dramatically different to that from control samples taken from plants in the same field"*, as Andrews and Delgado wrote. Spelman reported to me in greater detail about the results of his crystallisation analyses, developed in Germany, given the name 'Spagyric' and normally used in the diagnosis of illnesses.

"We took samples from different parts of a circle, and we clearly found a dramatic change took place in the corn from inside the circle as compared to corn from other parts of the field which, we believe, wasn't influenced. The inner structure of the stems was totally different. The structure of the corn from inside the circle looked similar to the structure we find in the blood of our patients. It was a clear, regular pattern which showed that an intensive energy had acted on the circle. We compared it with the corn from outside the circle, which contained a very much more irregular pattern and didn't show the same strict structuring. This was a remarkable difference. We repeated the experiment in other circles and found the same changes."

This was a very promising initial result, although for science it had no great relevance, for it was based on a subtle diagnostic method and couldn't be reproduced in an ordinary laboratory. But it pointed in the right direction, and it fell into the right hands.

On 2nd January 1991, Pat Delgado received a letter from Professor W C Levengood, a biophysicist from Michigan, USA, who specialised in the analysis of bio-electrochemical energies in plants and seeds. Dr Levengood is a scientist with a worldwide reputation. For ten years he had a professorship at Michigan State University, before he set up on his own. He obtained a patent for his 'automatic seed analyser', and the analyser is used worldwide. Apart from five further patents, Dr Levengood has written forty-nine papers for specialist international journals, among them *Nature* and *Science, Biochemistry and Biogenetics, Electroanalytical Chemistry* and the *Journal of Bioelectrochemistry and Bioenergetics*. He had become aware of the crop circle phenomenon through Andrews' and Delgado's book, had read about Spelman's analyses and wished to use the scientific methods available to him to get more solid results. So he had asked Delgado to send him plants from crop circles and control samples from the corresponding fields.

The first package, with samples from the 1990 season, arrived with Dr Levengood at the beginning of February 1991, and further samples followed at the end of April and through the summer of 1991. The first samples, originating from a pictogram which appeared in July 1990, gave indications that a genetic change had indeed taken place.

"Outwardly," wrote Dr Levengood, *"the glumes* [husks] *appeared to be filled out to the same degree as the control plants. This did not prove to be the case; all of the glumes from within the circles were empty of seeds. However, this is not the end of the story.*

"On further examination a condition known as 'polyembryony' was observed in over 90% of the glumes. Polyembryony is an uncommon genetic aberration and is manifested as the

formation of multiple embryos within a single glume. The endosperm does not form, therefore they are not seeds.

"*So that I might obtain some prospect of finding seedless heads in a normal field of wheat, I contacted experts in the growing and breeding of wheat at Pro Seed Inc, Michigan, for whom I am a consultant. I have two associates there, one an agronomist, the other a plant breeder. Without giving them any details, I posed the question, 'What is the probability of randomly removing a single, normal-appearing wheathead in a field and finding it completely empty?' In essence the answer was, 'About as likely as winning a lottery three times in a row.'*"

Dr Levengood gained similar results with the second sample. Encouraged by these promising results, Delgado sent Dr Levengood further samples from the first pictograms of the year 1991. "*In the parenchyma cells of the stem nodes*", Dr Levengood found, "*the cell wall pits were much more prominent and sharply outlined in the nodes from the circle than in the control node tissue.*

"*Externally, the heads and glumes as in other previous samples were of normal appearance. The seeds from both samples were not completely mature. They were white and the endosperm had not completely filled out. About a hundred seeds were obtained from each sample. It was very apparent there was a large number of malformed seeds in the circle sample: about 40%, compared to 0% in the controls. These malformations consisted of brown coloured, completely flattened seeds, compared to those with the embryo exposed and extending out of one end of the seeds.*

"*Most of these deformations can be explained by a premature dehydration of the seeds. For this to have occurred the development must have been arrested in the circle samples at the time of the pictogram formation. The control plants apparently continued development during the eleven day shipment period. This is the second sample group in which embryo or seed development had been altered or suppressed.*"

Analyses of further samples from pictograms of the summer of 1991 also gave similar results. In ears from del-

phinograms at Lockeridge, 32% of the seeds were abnormal, and in the case of the ears from the 'dumb-bell' at Alton Barnes at least 20% were abnormal. Obviously, the changes were smaller, the riper the corn already was. Dr Levengood concluded that an ionising radiation triggered these genetic changes, a radiation which could be caused by gamma rays, electron and proton rays, from which one would also expect other damage, such as burns.

Most revealing about the nature of this radiation was Dr Levengood's microscopic examinations of the cells in the enlarged spots on the wheat stems' knots. 'Spots' or cell-wall pits are tiny holes in the cells which enable the transport of ions and electrolytes into and out of the organism. On his microscopy pictures is clearly recognisable that these spots grew from originally flat, undefined areas to sharply outlined trapezoid-like shapes. This would happen, according to Levengood, when water within the cells is heated so quickly that the cell walls swell and force the spots to expand. Some photos very clearly show 'expansion scars' leading off the spots, which would indicate an expansion of the cell walls.

By the way, you can observe this for yourself. For this you only need a microscope with 450x magnification and a few stems from a crop circle. The enlarged knots are a conspicuous detail, especially with young corn in June crop circles. In June 1991, we already had drawn the attention of our German 'crop circle tourists' to this, and Johannes von Butlar showed it to an accompanying *Quick* magazine reporter, who unfortunately omitted to follow this theme in his report.

To test whether these cell wall expansions really could have been caused by short-term heating, Dr Levengood placed a few stems from the control sample into a microwave oven for thirty seconds. The cells swelled so much that the cell wall pits expanded, and under the microscope they resembled samples from the pictograms. Was this therefore the clue: does a kind of microwave energy heat the plants quickly while it forms the crop formations?

In one of the control samples heated in the microwave oven the cell membrane broke. Similarly, the cell walls of stems in a grass formation in Cornwall were broken, while the stems themselves were covered by a black, non-reflecting substance which looked like soot. Dr Levengood found that the substance was a trace of charring. Grass leaves are covered with a thin layer of paraffin. When the grass is heated from above, fast, but not enough to catch fire, the paraffin actually burns to a char. Grass stems are finer and therefore more vulnerable than wheat, and one can suppose that its 'limit of tolerance' is lower than with normal wheat, which probably explains why we don't normally find such radical outcomes in the case of wheat.

A microscopic examination of the stems found that the grass-blade cells underneath the paraffin coating were totally destroyed. The cell walls showed large holes and cracks. A parallel investigation of the Cornwall circle by Kay Larsen, a retired biologist and member of CCCS, led to the same result, and Larsen concluded that *"an enormous force running in one direction had acted on the affected stems and made the cells on one side of the knots burst and swell"*.

Only one sample from a wheat field – it originated from a formation at Alton Priors – showed similar symptoms. Here a pitch-black substance *"was spread on to the surface of ears and leaves"*, as Pat Delgado put it, which also proved to be heavy burns when examined under a microscope. The heating must have been very short and intense, for deeper layers of tissue weren't affected.

Can this heating also be identified in the ground? To find out, Pat Delgado sent soil samples to the biochemist D DiPinto of the Delawarr Radionic Laboratories at Oxford, from a circle which formed near Cullompton, Devon. She found out that the contents of important nutrients such as nitrate, phosphate and sulphur were reduced by 50% compared with a control sample, while the sample contained an excess of cobalt, carbon, molybdenum, titanium, plutonium and zinc. Her conclusion: *"I have carried out radionic analyses of the samples. I can only refer here to elements and trace elements, but my impression is that violent, intense and quick heat rather than environmental poisons has denatured the soil and destroyed the natural elements"*.

A further aspect was investigated by the nuclear physicist Marshall Dudley from Oak Ridge, Tennessee, in co-operation with the physicist Michael Chorost, who in summer 1991 blossomed into being America's leading crop circle expert, and who surprised the British scene again and again with refreshingly new approaches. Chorost supplied Dudley with soil samples from five formations and two control samples from each field, taken 10yds and 100yds away from each formation, and asked him to examine these in terms of a possible increased radioactivity.

The first samples originated from a 'dumb-bell' which had appeared on 17th June at Jaywick, Essex. It showed only slight deviations. The second sample was quite different. It was taken from the 'Mother of all Pictograms', the gigantic tetrahedron at Barbury Castle. While it didn't show any special deviations from the control values in the first experiment, a second examination about two weeks later resulted in clearly increased radiation. Dudley attributed this to the fact that the samples had dried out by then, and that the alpha and beta particles were no longer hindered from coming out by the water present in each sample. One sample from within the formation showed a 31% lower alpha value compared to control samples, while samples from other formations showed a value which was heightened by 17%. The anomalies thus are in themselves abnormal.

Similarly unusual were the results of a soil sample from the Alton Priors 'Key', which first lay 26% below, then 17% above that of the control sample. Dudley concluded that something had changed the soil chemically, and that the changed soil absorbed or stored more water, which would cause it to bind alpha particles. Accordingly, the initial low values would be explicable in that they simply dried out more slowly than the control samples. Dr Levengood, on the other hand, proposed that the addition of negative ions could have neutralised the alpha-particles. As a matter of fact, plasma is a possible source of negative ions, however it may come to be used.

But what was confusing was that samples 4 and 5 showed highly increased alpha and beta values, namely 198% and 103% respectively for alpha and 48% and 57% for beta radiation, above the values for control samples for sample 4, and 45% and 27% above the alpha control value and 35% and 22% above the beta value for sample 5. Both samples originated from the Delphinograms on Firs Farm at Beckhampton. Dudley thinks that the soil there was either enriched with radioactively contaminated material, or that something had radiated its cell nuclei with neutrons or protons. Analyses of spectrographic data indicated a neutron activation, but only further investigations can provide conclusive information.

Does this mean a health risk for crop circle researchers? Probably not, thinks Dudley, as long as circles aren't entered within the first hour after their being laid down. A Geiger counter could be a valuable instrument in circle research. But how can the contrast between the abnormally high and the abnormally low values be explained? One possibility is that differing weather or soil conditions may be the cause, and another is that only certain areas of the formation were contaminated, by whatever does the contaminating. The only safe fact is: it is unlikely that a macroscopic technique such as physical stamping or rolling down of a circle can cause changes on the microscopic or even atomic level, of the kind that Levengood and Dudley have found. Much more, these results indicate that an unknown energy was involved.[1]

This conclusion is confirmed by a paper by Dudley and Chorost in the *MUFON UFO Journal* of February 1992. According to this, Dudley discovered thirteen short half-life radioactive isotopes which do not exist in nature, in two soil samples from one of the Fish formations at Beckhampton, of which eleven isotopes were not to be found in comparison control samples from the immediate surroundings of the pictogram. None of the isotopes could be traced back to Chernobyl or any other known cause. Furthermore, they had a common denominator: they formed when the soil is radiated with deuterium nuclei.

The British UFO researcher Dr Armen Victorian presented the results of Dr Levengood's and Dudley's investigations to a microwave expert at the Kirtland air force base in New Mexico, USA, who called all the changes 'typical' for microwave action. In exactly the same way, Victorian quotes the report of his research colleague Omar Fowler, who documented traces of burns in formations in the Midlands of England, such as at Mansfield, Sutton-on-Trent, Southwell and Husbands Bosworth. Fowler came to the following conclusion:

"During a seven year period of investigating crop circles and pictograms, one common denominator emerged. This was the discovery of single standing stems, with top sections bent over at a height of 55cm (22in), in an otherwise flattened circle of wheat or barley. It has also been discovered that the single stems, apart from being bent 55cm, show a number of other common features. These are small 'crease' and burns marks at similar points on the crop stems. It is believed that the 55cm stem measurement is indicative of high frequency (H/F) wavelength in the lower GHz (gigahertz) range.

"The 'crease' marks and small burnt areas on the stems could be consistent with microwave action during the formation of a crop circle. It is common knowledge that microwaves in the low GHz frequency can be beamed thousands of miles to within an accuracy of just a few millimetres. They can also be programmed to transmit a 'footprint' of almost any desired pattern to its

destination. By this means, a microwave beam programmed with either a pictogram or circular pattern could be directed to the target area."

George Wingfield is convinced that an 'invisible pen', a 'force field of unknown consistency' wanders around in the corn and bends down the stems. *"The energy seems to be capable of focusing narrowly, as well as being able to widen itself, while it draws the pattern. Often its path is recognisable, following the tram-lines for a short time, before it makes a course correction to execute the pattern. Where the 'more clever' signs have their 'inscription' broken – as with the rectangular 'boxes' of some pictograms – the 'pen' sometimes has to move through standing corn to get to a new starting point to draw the separated segment. Where there are no tram-lines available, one finds a few centimetres-wide, extremely thin line of bent corn, along which the pen wanders to reach the necessary new starting place."*

He also interprets the results of Dr Levengood and Marshall Dudley to mean that a kind of microwave, and possible gravitational waves (in the sense of Dutton's gravitational waves) are responsible for the phenomenon. *"They could supply an explanation for many effects which have been observed in crop circles, for one must suppose that they are able to penetrate nuclei of atoms and split these. This again could explain the change in alpha radiation and the presence of radioactive isotopes with a short half-life time."*

Some kind of high-frequency electromagnetic waves could *"cause an excitement of electrons in the atoms of the soil or the plants, which afterwards drop back into their original energy level by sending out this low-level radiation found in them. Such radiation also could weaken plants at a certain height and cause the observed bends. As a matter of fact, stems can also be bent after they have been heated for one or two seconds in a microwave oven – the stems soften and are sleek enough to be bent. Should this be the mechanism, then the weight of the ears or the inflorescence of the plants would be enough to let them sink to the ground. And the quick heating of the plants, which are radiated by such microwaves at a certain height, would evaporate the moisture within the stems and cause the swellings and cracks which are sometimes observed."*

There remains the question, who can use microwave gravitational radiation in such a clever way? And what do they want to achieve with it?

REFERENCES

1. See Jürgen Krönig's *Spuren im Korn*, Verlag Zweitausendeins, Frankfurt, 1992.

8. The Mathematical Simulation of Crop Circles

by Roy Dutton

What's it all about?

The recurring creation, usually overnight, of flattened crop 'circles', particularly on ancient sites – and close to military test areas – in the English counties of Wiltshire and Hampshire, has aroused considerable public interest, but only limited scientific response. Despite the claims of the hoaxers Bower and Chorley, serious researchers of the crop circles are aware that a significant new phenomenon is manifesting itself annually; and that the phenomenon is not restricted to the crop fields of southern England.

Publications on the subject have brought these strange localised events to the attention of a wider audience. Dr Terence Meaden has attempted to explain the phenomenon in meteorological terms, by suggesting that a hitherto unknown electrical-airflow (plasma) vortex is involved. However, my research led me very quickly to dismiss the vortex hypothesis, on the grounds that the circular evidence in the fields could not been produced by such means. Having realised that such extraordinary evidence demanded unbiased thinking, I set aside the problem of trying to define the physical nature of the stimulus and instead, sought a behavioural model which could account for the features observed in the circles.

Analysis of the features of several well-defined circles, based on measurements and photographs provided by Colin Andrews and Busty Taylor, together with my own observa-tions within the circles, revealed that an extraordinary degree of mathematical conformity underlay wide variations in the appearance of the specimens. It is important to record that pictogram evidence was not used in these studies, because pictograms were considered to be undoubtedly contrived.

Mathematical Modelling of Spiralled Circles

Detailed examination of the varied and complex spiral patterns in the flattened crops led me to the idea that a simple mathematical model might adequately simulate them all. This model was then programmed into a PC and produced very acceptable reproductions of a selection of complex patterns kindly provided by Colin Andrews as test cases.

Basically, the motion of a point P, which is constrained to move in a controlled manner relative to a fixed point O is modelled in the following manner (fig 1):

Imagine a point S moving along a line O to P in accordance with a given law of motion.

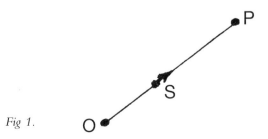

Fig 1.

Imagine, next, that the line OSP is rotating about point O at a given angular rate at any instance. If we assume that S is progressing from O to P then the locus of S will be a spiral; and its shape will be determined by the relative lines of linear and rotational motion at each location of S on OP, as shown below in fig 2:

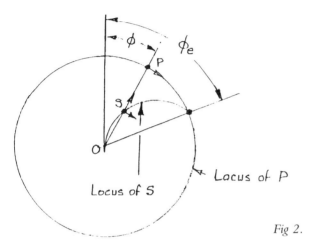

Fig 2.

The simplest form of this motion is one in which the radial velocity of point S and the angular speed of rotation of OSP have constant values; surprisingly, it was found that this form could create the spirals found in the genuine crop circles. It can be said therefore that the tangential (swirl) and radial components of flow to be found in crop circles are defined mathematically as follows:

Tangential component = w x r

(where w is a constant and r is the local radius), and

Radial component = a constant greater than zero.

Although the tangential component typifies that of a classic forced vortex, the radial component does not. Indeed, this combination of flow vectors eliminates, I would say

unequivocally, an aerodynamic vortex of any kind as the crop-flattening stimulus. Both components of flow suddenly cease to exist at the peripheral radius R, though sometimes this cut-off is masked by a circumscribing peripheral ring of flattened crop.

However, the process just described determines only the shape of a single spiral. The visual evidence suggested that most of the specimens had been flattened in a series of spiralled strips. Additionally, over-layering indicated that sequencing of the strips had also been a feature of the flattening process. With the aid of computer graphics, I was able to reproduce the spirals and the observed sequencing, very satisfactorily, for each circle analysed. This was achieved by assuming that the flattening stimulus (represented by S in fig 2) ceases to function on reaching P at the periphery of the circle and returns, instantly, to the centre O, via the radial line joining P to O. The next spiral is then commenced. The number of spiralled strips in any circle is given by the simple relationship:

number of strips = revolutions x strips/revolutions

Both the number of strips as well as the number of complete revolutions must be integers. The number of strips per revolution is given by 360 divided by the sweep angle (φe) in degrees.

The concept has been so successful in explaining not only the shape of the crop patterns, but also the ridged appearance of many of them, that it is not difficult to imagine that there is some form of discrete physical stimulus which behaves in a programmed way, like point S. Given also that the crop stalks, even ripe and brittle ones, are persuaded to lie flat on the ground, without structural failure at the base of the stalks being evident, I submit that it is wellnigh impossible to find any known stimulus which could produce such effects. It therefore becomes even more reasonable sensible to speculate that some form of unknown technological device might be responsible.

The Challenge of Winterbourne Stoke

The idea that an artificial solution to the problem is more likely than a natural one is reinforced by my observation that some of the complex patterns can be reproduced only by assuming that there are several point-stimuli operating in different modes, whilst in principle rotating around the same central point. An example of the latter is the Winterbourne Stoke crop circle of 1989. Mr Colin Andrews supplied me with drawings made by two different witnesses and a xeroxed composite oblique photograph. The drawings are reproduced here (fig 3) and appear to differ significantly on the segmentation of the largest ring by over-layering. The available photographic evidence did not resolve this difficulty.

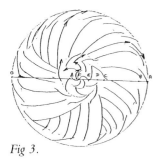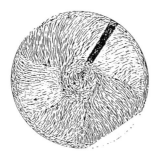

Fig 3.

My first attempt to reproduce this complicated pattern caused me to have to introduce operation-mode options into my program, which resulted in the creation of the first approximation shown in fig. 4:

The over-layering, however, continued to baffle me until I recognised that this pattern involved progressive movement of the virtual centre of rotation of the line OP (see fig 2) during the formation of the largest annulus, which had been combined with very much more sophis-

Fig 4.

ticated sequencing than that written into the PC programme. The result, eventually produced by superimposition, is shown in fig 5.

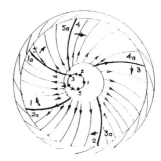

Fig 5.

The overall sequence seems to have been as follows:
 (i) The flattening operation commenced with the laying down the peripheral annulus;
 (ii) This was then followed by an outward sequence of flattening, in three distinct modes, from around the true geometrical centre of the formation;
(iii) Finally, flattening in the largest annulus began at sweep (1) in the diagram in a clockwise direction, and proceeded in the manner programmed for the PC, until a 72° segment had been swept by sweep (1a). At this point, the stimulus executed a 144° backwards (anticlockwise) leap before recommencing the clockwise flattening procedure.

From the start of this sequence it seems that the virtual centre of rotation of the stimulus began to precess anti-clockwise, following a circular path of 2.4m (7.87ft) in diameter, with its centre situated 1.2m (3.9ft) to the left of the geometric centre, as shown before. The 72/144° flattening sequence continued around an ever-changing centre, until the entire annulus had been swept. As corn laid down in any segment was unaffected by a stimulus which swept across it in a different direction during flattening of the subsequent segment, this produced the observed discontinuities in the floor pattern.

It is interesting that the simulation diagram (fig 4) also sheds light on the disagreement between the two on-site drawings of the pattern. There are, in fact, five divisions of the large annulus: but the division at sweep (3) is not very distinct and that at (4) is not detectable.

What Kind of Causative Stimulus is Involved?

Major problems arise in identifying the nature of the corn-flattening stimulus involved because, to my knowledge no such stimulus exists. However, we can conceive the kind of device which might be involved, given that such technology is currently available to someone, somewhere.

Acknowledging that most of the crop 'circles' are in fact elliptic and that their major axes tend to lie along the lines of maximum field-surface gradient (also that the crops are undamaged, other than being 'steamed' through 90° angle at soil level), the discrete crop-flattening stimulus required seems to be some form of radiant energy, beamed laser-like from above.

It is easy to imagine, as being one possibility, some kind of phased, active linear antenna system, which is rotating in the horizontal plane about one end, while the radiation source is being traversed radially, in the programmed manner just described, until a complete disc of crop is flattened. Saturn-like rings of flattening surrounding the central pan, which are sometimes present, could be produced by rotating a similar stimulus without radial movement; while straight-line spurs projecting from the circular area into the surrounding crop could be produced by a non-rotating stimulus being traversed into, or away from the location of the circle, prior to or following formation of the circle.

If such a piece of technology exists, we can be sure that its primary purpose will not be to irritate the long-suffering farmers in southern England or to baffle the rest of us with mind-bending enigmas. Beamed radiant energy which can flatten crops, yet not visibly affect the ground from which they grow, could be finely tuned for the real task being performed. My suggestion is that, sensibly, that task might be seismic (geological) investigation, executed remotely (possibly from extremely high altitudes): but by whom? And what kind of radiation could possibly produce such effects?

Could it be, as I personally guess, microwave gravitational radiation, such as that which Palazzi suggested can be produced with the help of a synchrotron? (see: G D Palazzi, "On the production and detection of gravitational waves from artificial sources", University of Rome, 26th April, 1988).

Has anyone any other, less exotic ideas which fit all the known facts? As far as I know, Dr Meaden did not attempt to explain the intricacies of the Winterbourne Stoke patterns in terms of his vortex hypothesis.

Things yet to be Revealed

The implications of the mathematical modelling work, as described above, are supported by the findings from another aspect of my research. I have discovered that those circles which have been observed during the process of creation have occurred at very interesting times of the day; the same times at which UFO Close Encounters could be expected to occur. Both Close Encounters and crop circles seem to be linked by the same sidereal (star) time connections; which means that the times of their appearances, on any day and in any year, are now predictable, given this behaviour pattern continues. But that is another story, which has yet to be fully told.

9. The Ground Component

I sat with Busty Taylor in the Waggon & Horses pub in Beckhampton, near Avebury, and we discussed the previous week's experiences during our film shooting in England. Busty has probably seen and photographed more crop circles from the air than anybody else. I liked the calm, thoughtful, appraising manner with which he approached the phenomenon. He was not only *the* crop circle pilot, but also he was a first rate crop circle expert, a man with a lot to say. One of the things he said concerned his personal theory about the circles' origin.

"What causes them?" I asked Busty. *"Well, my opinion hasn't changed since 1985. It has an aerial component together with a ground component. At the moment, we can't prove either of them. There are Earth energies, involved with what we call 'ley-lines', and there is an aerial component, luminous objects, which people have observed where later a crop circle appeared. Both go together. We have the tram-lines to which many formations seem to orientate, such that there must be an aerial component. And then we can identify the 'ley-lines' to which they are aligned. The big question is how to bring the two components together to be able to say exactly where all the factors come together, where the missing link lies."*

Busty's words still resounded in my ears while I worked on this book. Didn't everything indicate that we had solved the mystery of the crop circles with the 'aerial component' and its connection with the UFO phenomenon? Not quite: we would have forgotten an important aspect without our friend Busty Taylor's insistent warning.

What are 'ley lines'? One of the early researchers into the site of Stonehenge, Rev Edward Duke, speculated in his in 1846 publication *The Druid Temples of Wiltshire* that there once existed a direct link between Stonehenge and the stone circle at Avebury. According to Duke, this line represented an 'axis of power', and each prehistoric site on it represented one of the seven astrological planets. Some years later, William Henry Black, a member of the respected British Archaeological Society, extended Duke's theory with the suggestion that all ancient sites in the British Isles, and possibly in the whole world, could be linked with each other by 'Great Circle Lines'. Although the Establishment ignored Black's ideas, a small circle of enthusiastic followers soon collected around the researcher, meeting regularly in the Green Dragon hotel in Hereford.

Years later, a certain Alfred Watkins joined the circle, and he soon became the white knight of the ley-hunters. Watkins' term 'ley line' was later to become a household word, and soon was used to encompass any straight alignments. Watkins came to this realisation about such a network of lines on a hot summer day, 20th June 1921, when he roamed on horseback through Herefordshire. He halted on a hilltop to orientate himself. He looked around over the landscape spread in front of him. Suddenly it became blurred, as if in a haze, and in front of his eye there slowly formed a new image, at first indistinct, then getting clearer and clearer – an image from an epoch long gone.

Spread over the whole country he saw a network of lines by which ancient sacred sites were connected: mounds, standing stones, crosses, churches erected over pre-Christian sites, old trees shrouded in legend, moats and sacred springs. They were all arranged along exact alignments which proceeded over valleys, mountains and hills. Watkins had experienced the magical world of pre-historic England in a moment of transcendental vision – a world which long ago had sunk into the darkness of the past. *"It was a moment of flash-like illumination"*, wrote Watkins later. *"The whole plan of the Old Straight Tracks had unexpectedly revealed itself to me."*

When Watkins looked for alignments involving churches and prehistoric sites on a topographic map, he found his vision confirmed. Not unusually, five to ten sites aligned with each other in a relatively short distance. Many of them showed common characteristics, for example place-name endings with the affix '-ley', place-names involving 'White' or 'Red' or other terms – or churches dedicated to the 'dragon killers' St Michael and St George were common. Furthermore Watkins found that the courses of alignments were often identical with old Roman or ancient British roads.

The straight lines are not solely an English phenomenon. In China they have been known since ancient times

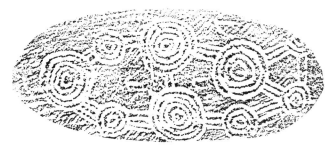

Churinga stone of the Australian Aboriginals.

as 'dragon paths' and are an essential part of Chinese geomancy, *Feng Shui*. The Australian Aborigines identify paths or 'song-lines' along which the energies of creation crossed the country. They erected their sanctuaries on the 'Churingas', at which they still celebrate their ancient sacred ceremonies. On Churinga-stones which act as 'maps' for journeys into the Dreamtime or astral world, they are shown as an arrangement of interlinked rings and circles.

The best known of the 'sacred lines' of England is the St Michael line, which runs from Cornwall to Hopton in Norfolk. Not only does it link Glastonbury Tor (the long axis of which roughly aligns with it) with Avebury, but also it runs in the direction of sunrise on 1st May each year, and over fifty churches, chapels, ancient sites and stone crosses lie along it. Most of the churches are dedicated to St Michael and St George, and many of them are located on the top of hills. Two British geomancers, Hamish Miller and Paul Broadhurst, wrote a whole book, *The Sun and the Serpent* about this 'sacred line'.

Their comprehensive studies and field research with dowsing instruments showed that the St Michael line is coiled into two energy-streams (like the serpent's rod of Aesclepius), which Miller and Broadhurst called the 'Michael' and 'Mary' lines – not only because of the churches located on them, but also because one of the streams carries 'male' and the other 'female' energies. This corresponds to the principles of Chinese *Feng Shui*, in which *"in the Earth's crust there are two different, I would say magnetic, streams, one male, the other female, one positive, the other negative"*, as *Feng Shui* expert E J Eitel wrote in 1873. Where both streams meet each other many of the great sanctuaries of prehistoric times are located – sites like Avebury and Glastonbury. There is a parallel here in the human microcosm, through which, according to Indian yoga teachings, two subtle energy channels, *Ida* and *Pingala*, the one male, the other female, coil around a central axis

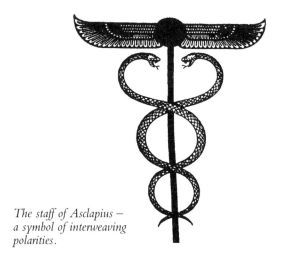

*The staff of Asclapius –
a symbol of interweaving
polarities.*

tested the circles for this connection. Their findings were that most circles seem to lie on top of energy lines.

This involves not only the great 'sacred lines' like the Michael line, but also the Earth's countless lesser local energy channels – comparable to the *nadis*, man's subtle nerve fibres, which supply the body with *prana*, cosmic life-energy. These Earth channels are not measurable by physical means, but can be measured with man's psyche or subconscious, which articulates itself through instruments like pendulums and divining rods. However, it is conspicuous that only rarely do two dowsers get the same result. This disturbs them little, since they are convinced of the multi-dimensionality of earth energies and they believe that every dowser perceives them in specific ways, which differs from individual to individual.

"The subtle energies of the Earth (called ch'i by Chinese geomancers, the Holy Spirit by early Christians, and symbolised by medieval mystics by the number 1080) are conditioned in their flow by the characteristics of the local landscape, its mountains, forests, rivers and valleys", wrote John Michell. *"They can also be directed by human activity, and the ancient science of the priests thoroughly studied the possibilities of discovering and manipulating the Earth's sacred energies. The traditional eastern method of locating a new temple involved localising a 'Dragon's Head' (the dragon being a universal symbol of the Earth's spirit) and driving it a stake into it, to fix and concentrate its energies for the inner sanctum at the appropriate place. Plutarch, a priest in Delphi in the first century, refers in 'Decline of the Oracles' to the streams of earth energies, which activated oracles and places of invocation. They are influenced, so he writes, by the Sun and the celestial bodies."*

named *Sushumna*, running up the spine. They meet each other in the chakras, the seven energy centres of man.

When Miller and Broadhurst examined the area around Avebury, looking for the Michael and Mary lines – it was the summer 1988 – the crop circles turned up again, fifty-one in the area just six miles around Silbury Hill. The two dowsers weren't greatly surprised when they found that all of them lay *"exactly on the course of the 'female' energy flow"*. This was the first hint of a connection between crop circles and earth energies. From then on, legions of diviners

In 1935, two French archaeologists, Merle and Diot, found, after a thorough investigation with divining rods, that *"without exception, every megalithic monument is in a certain relationship with subterranean currents which pass, cross or surround them"*. Guy Underwood came to a similar conclusion in 1969 in his book *Patterns of the Past*, in which

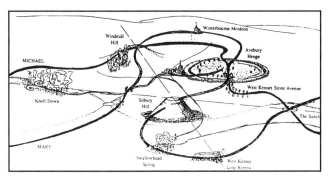

The energy lines around Avebury, according to Miller and Broadhurst.

he concluded from his investigations in Wessex that *"every ancient monument or building was erected in relation to the flow of earth energies"*.

Now we know already that the crop circles mainly turn up in the environs of prehistoric sacred sites, stone circles, moot places or burial mounds. For the dowser it is certain that these monuments were built on top of energy lines, and often enough they served to harmonise these lines, in the sense of an 'earth acupuncture'. This, so dowsers believe, led to smaller lines radiating from them. And on these radiating lines, the circles often appear.

Dowser David Tilt thinks that they formed through 'energy discharges', which would happen from time to time under certain conditions. His first encounter with the phenomenon goes back to 1984 when he examined a stone circle at Seaford, Sussex. On 28th July 1984, according to Tilt, *"...the energy level at this site had risen to an unbearable degree, which made the continuation of my work extremely uncomfortable. Under these conditions one experiences disorientation, feelings of dizziness and difficulties in concentration, and hence it is better to leave such a place until the energy falls to an acceptable level. When on 3rd August I came to Seaford again, I felt that something unusual must have happened, for the energy level was extraordinary low. A crop circle had turned up in the meantime."* The energy had presumably been discharged.

This moves in the direction of one of the most interesting and beautiful theories about the crop circles' origin. According to this theory Mother Earth is speaking to us and warning us of the consequences of the environmental destruction. Its best-known advocate is Colin Andrews, who met with Hopi Indians, who interpreted some cereological symbols for him. The symbols, they said, were no script or language, but spoke directly to man's consciousness. It is necessary only to look at them to receive their message. The Indians reacted very emotionally to photos of pictograms and interpreted them as follows: *"Mother* (the Indian term for our Earth) *is in serious difficulties. Mother is crying. Our Brother* (mankind) *is responsible. Mother doesn't let snow fall on the mountaintops anymore. It can't melt anymore and flow into the rivers. Her blood* (oil) *is taken from her. Her lungs* (trees) *wilt in every town in the world."*

An intelligent Earth which speaks to us with crop symbols? This would correspond to the Gaia hypothesis proposed by British biologist James E Lovelock, naming it after the Greek Earth goddess. He says that our blue planet is none other than a living, self-preserving, self-regulating super-organism, which constantly adjusts its chemical, physical and biological processes to maintain optimal conditions for life. Human civilisation has had a similar effect on the Earth body as a cancer tumour has on the human organism.

According to the theory of the Cambridge biochemist Rupert Sheldrake, the systems of this organism Earth are not only regulated by physical laws, but also by 'morphogenetic fields', the invisible, organising, 'form-producing' consciousness in nature. Does the organism Earth thus 'appropriate' the symbols in the corn from the 'collective unconscious' of humankind? Is our home-planet an intelligent being, which can articulate itself in such a beautiful, clear and artistic way? Are these whirls and patterns of the pictograms formed from *within* planet Earth?

As much as we might sympathise ideologically with every mythical-ecological explanation, the indices rather speak against this hypothesis. Too often they orientate along field boundaries and tram-lines, indicating that a force coming from above acted here. Still, the 'ground component' is an important part of the phenomenon, a jigsaw-piece contributing to a solution of the riddle, which needs to be taken into account.

Dowser Richard Andrews, who has researched crop circles since 1985, noticed that in the stone circles of Stonehenge and Avebury as well as in the crop circles, the energy flows spirally towards the centre. He found out that all genuine crop circles show organised energy-fields in the ground – a fact confirmed by other dowsers – and that these patterns can still be located the following year, when all exterior traces of a formation have long disappeared. Furthermore, Andrews noticed energy patterns in some pictograms which weren't manifested in the laid corn – then some days later the pictogram 'developed' into just that pattern, adding rings or further extensions.

Andrews' conclusion, which I personally think is logical and possible, is that the circles form in two steps. *"First an intelligent force acts from above on earth energies and thus creates an invisible pattern which predetermines the direction in which each individual corn stem will fall. At a later time, a subterranean force starts the process which creates the visible form in the corn field."* Could this mean that the crop circles, similar to the stone circles of prehistoric times, are a method of 'earth acupuncture', that they are supposed to activate southern England's energy lines? Are they thus preparing a frequency-rise of the Earth, as in the 'New Jerusalem' prophecies of old?

10. THE WATCHERS

I have become sceptical of psychics and 'channels'; their statements are often too contradictory, too unspecific and sometimes incorrect. If however a psychic, several times in a row, correctly predicts the location of new crop circles, then at least they deserve our attention. Isabelle Kingston is such a medium. She repeatedly demonstrated this ability in 1990. In March, George Wingfield asked her where the most important circles of that year might appear. After a short meditation, she referred to the fields below Adam's Grave, at Alton Barnes. For one week, Wingfield and his colleagues from the CCCS watched from Adam's Grave, a hilltop, and nothing happened – disappointed they withdrew. This was in the middle of June 1990.

Four weeks later, on 12th July, the most impressive and largest of all of the pictograms of 1990 appeared exactly at the predicted place – this was the 151yds (138m) long Alton Barnes formation, which caused a stir worldwide. Understandably, George Wingfield and others have since then listened out for anything Isabelle Kingston says!

Isabelle Kingston, a soft, portly woman, probably lives up to most stereotypes of a British medium. But her story goes beyond this, for it was she who supplied us with another key to the crop circle riddle.

In March 1987, she gathered her circle in her Victorian house in Ogbourne St Andrew, to find out more about the mysterious Silbury Hill, the prehistoric mound south of Avebury, erected 4,600 years ago, whose purpose is still

The psychic Isabelle Kingston in front of Silbury Hill.

unclear. After a longish meditation, Isabelle received the first message. It originated, according to her, from *"an intelligence outside this planet"* who called themselves 'the Watchers'. Since ancient times they had guided humankind's fate, though they had acted out of the public eye until now.

The Watchers told her that it had been they who, millennia ago, instigated the construction of Silbury Hill. The syllable 'Sil' had had the meaning 'shining beings'. Temples like Silbury had the purpose of helping humankind at some time in the future. Avebury itself, said the Watchers, was energetically linked with places of power worldwide. At present it is the Watchers' task to prepare Earth for the

'New Jerusalem', a new age. England was located at the centre of a great 'pyramid of light' which they had set up. For this purpose they were 'charging' the 'ley lines', the energy channels of the Earth, at various points. This was visible in the form of large, swirled circles on the fields, circles in the corn.

"This old country holds the balance. It is the key to the world. Many of these places are purified such that they can become channels of the new energy", explained the Watchers. *"The pyramid of power which surrounds this country is the key – in your words, a button which must be pressed for activation. You are your planet's immune system, the healing system which will create the changes, but there are other keys which must be activated. This country is a test area – it has to be right before the whole can be lined up the other dimensions. Things are changing at Stonehenge – an energy field is above the stones. Some crop circles are the exact dimension of Stonehenge. Circles have appeared as a blueprint for humankind to mark that place as a place of power. It is as if these places are being unlocked. Centres are being awakened – it is part of the plan."*

In June 1988, Isabelle received new messages from the Watchers. *"There will be a sign at Silbury Hill"*, she predicted. *"It will clarify our presence for you"*. Two weeks later the mysterious 'quintuplets' turned up there. *"The number of circles will grow enormously in 1989"*, she said at the beginning of 1989. There were around 120 in 1988, and over 300 in the year 1989. *"The circles will be different in 1990. There will be different formations and various physical manifestations"*, she said at the beginning of 1990. This was the year of the great quantum jump, the year of the first pictograms.

On 10th July 1991, Isabelle received the request: *"Go to the hills and call for the Brethren. Link yourselves with the cosmos and draw the energies in to help. Become lightning conductors. Channel the light into the very soil. Transfer it into pure love and wait for the explosion."* On 11th July, Isabelle's group met for a meditation, following the Watchers' plan. On the same night a pictogram appeared on a field at Ogbourne Maizey,

near Isabelle's home, and within one week seven large and impressive agriglyphs formed, among them the exceptional tetrahedral formation at Barbury Castle.

I had to get to know Isabelle. We arranged to meet on a cloudy August afternoon at Silbury Hill, that *axis mundi* of Kingston's cosmology. After we had found a suitable filming place, I began to interview her before the running camera. *"It started when a new energy spoke through me, and this energy announced that a sign near the old temples of Avebury would appear, a sign which showed that they are raising the consciousness of the Earth"*, she explained.

Who or what was this energy? *"They called themselves 'the Watchers', but this is only an expression for a cosmic universal consciousness, for beings which are very concerned about this planet and what is happening on Earth at present"*. What do you think the crop circles are, what do they mean? *"The crop circles have a multi-layered meaning, many components, many types of energy coming together, energies of the Earth and the Universe. The nature realms and spiritual spheres are creating formations which have a profound effect on people who see and experience them."*

How do the circles form? *"They are created by an energy-form, a form of consciousness, possibly out of our own self, possibly from other spheres or dimensions."* Now, an evolution of the phenomenon took place from normal circles towards complicated patterns and pictograms. How do you explain this? *"Certainly there is a development. We began with the simple circles, and as the energies built up and the consciousness developed, the formations also became more complex and we were given more and more pieces of the puzzle."*

What meaning did the quintuplet formation have, the first one at Silbury Hill in 1986? *"This was, as I have been told in a channelled message, an input of energy into the Earth, into the ley lines and energy lines, to balance the energy and to harmonise all of us."* Silbury Hill is certainly one of the main energy centres in southern England. For what purpose was it built by our ancestors, and what is the connection with the crop circles? *"Silbury Hill was really built before the stone circle at*

Avebury. They erected it as an energy centre which would connect cosmic energy and earth energy with each other, to then direct these into the stone circle where they used the energies for their own purposes. Its name means 'the hill of the shining ones', who evidently – although they possibly had no physical form – supervised the erection of this site."

Now, Silbury Hill, itself like a pyramid, was erected at the same time as Egypt's pyramids. Who were the constructors? *"I believe that at that time there was a raising of consciousness and that the Old Ones, as we might call them, were linked not only with the Earth, but also with the Cosmos. I am certain the people who lived here were influenced from outside to erect this site. I think these places were thought of as a kind of insurance policy for a time in which humanity would open up and gain its energy from the opening of these centres."*

Who were the 'Shining Ones'? *"The Watchers use this expression because they are the ones who help us in our evolution. Various cultures gave them different names. We can say that they come from the Cosmos, the Universe or the universal understanding. We can also call them the guardians of this planet."*

Silbury Hill is, as it were, the 'Archimedean point' of the crop circle phenomenon. George Wingfield even believes that the crop circles have steered from Warminster and Winchester towards this target, and only went through their 'quantum jump' when they eventually reached it. Says George: *"I think that in this region, Silbury Hill is the centre of activity... It is a big energy centre. We always knew that, for we knew about the Earth energy lines which cross Silbury Hill, similar to Stonehenge. If you mark previous years' crop circles on a map, you see that they lie on a certain energy line which starts at Silbury Hill. When the circles reached Silbury Hill in 1988, this became the point from which they really exploded in number and variety."*

Perhaps the mysterious 'Hill of the Shining Ones' really supplies us with a key to the identification of the circle makers. Terence Meaden identified it as a symbol of the *axis mundi*, or world-centre, which, at the beginning of Creation, stuck out of the primeval ocean when the gods descended to it. *"It could have its spiritual counterpart in the Ziggurats of the Sumerians in the 4th millennium BC, four-sided mountains made of clay bricks with a sanctuary on the top, where heavenly and earthly forces came together in harmony."*

Silbury Hill was built around 2,700BC as a six-stepped limestone round pyramid – today it is 144ft (44m) high. Likewise, around 2,700BC, Imhotep, the 'divine architect', erected the similarly six-stepped quadratic limestone pyramid of Zoser at Sakkara near Memphis in Lower Egypt, about 198ft (60m) high. Who was this Imhotep? According to ancient records he was an Egyptian Leonardo da Vinci. He was high priest at Heliopolis, chancellor of the empire, the second man after the pharaoh. He is credited with the first large stone building in history – the pyramid at Sakkara – and the invention of hieroglyphics, astronomy and medicine.

The author in front of the step pyramid of Zoser at Sakkara, built in the same century as Silbury Hill and, as with the latter, six-stepped.

The Greeks called him Asclepios and made him their god of medicine. He was a pupil of Thoth, the god of wisdom, whom the Greeks identified with their messenger of the gods, Hermes. As Hermes Trismegistos ('thrice-greatest Hermes'), Thoth is considered to be the initiator of esoteric knowledge, and the hermetic scriptures deal with the great questions of humankind in the form of a dialogue between Hermes=Thoth and his pupil Asclepios=Imhotep. Thoth was one of the original gods of Egypt, the *neteru*. Literally translated, *neteru* means – 'the Watchers'.

The Egyptians claimed that their gods originated from a distant mountain country and that they came in the dim and distant past on ships and 'heavenly boats' from the south. Their homeland was *'ta neter'*, the 'land of the Watchers'. Southwards, Egypt is reachable only by ship

The emblem of 'the Watchers', the sun disc crossed by serpents, above the frieze of an Egyptian temple.

along the Red Sea. If one follows the Red Sea and rounds the Arabic peninsula, one reaches a country which in old times was called 'Shumer' – literally, 'the country of the Watchers'. It is the 'land Sinear' of the Bible, the homeland of Abraham, Noah and his ancestors. It is seat of the oldest advanced culture, the culture of Sumer.

The British archeologist Henry Austin Layard found the first traces of Sumerian culture when in 1840 he excavated the biblical Nineveh, capital of the Assyrian empire, near Mosul in Iraq. It owed its splendour to king Sennacherib (died 681BC), who, according to the Bible, was forced by an angel of the Lord to return to his homeland during a siege of Jerusalem. The British Museum at London exhibits impressive treasures of Assyrian art, which came to light during this excavation – among them monumental reliefs which show the Assyrian king hunting, campaigning or receiving foreign ambassadors.

But, for the specialists, a far more important find came in the form of hundreds of plain clay tablets, often not larger than a hand, full of information about this culture between the Euphrates and Tigris. Most of them originated from the library of Assurbanipal, a successor of Sennacherib. Assurbanipal, a highly educated ruler of the 7th Century BC, ordered his scribes to collect all old texts from his empire, to copy and to translate them. Many tablets of this library carry the remark "translated from...". On some of them it says, "...from the language of Sumer". An inscription from Assurbanipal himself reads:

> *"The god of the scribes has bestowed me with the ability to know all about my arts.*
> *I was initiated into the secrets of writing.*
> *I even manage to read the difficult tablets in Sumerian.*
> *I understand the mysterious words carved into stone from the days before the Flood."*

For the Assyrians, Sumer was a country of prehistory, the cradle of their civilisation, even of humankind. Many texts translated from Sumerian proved, to the surprise of archaeologists, to be very ancient precursor scripts of the Old Testament – the Creation, the Flood, the Tower of Babel – which was rooted in the scripts of the Sumerians.

When, during excavations in the 1920s, the first Sumerian cities were discovered, archaeologists came upon a civilisation of riddles and superlatives. When in 1956 the sumerologist Noah S Kramer endeavoured to do a stock-take of their literary inheritance, he dedicated each of the twenty-five chapters of his book *From the Tablets of Sumer* to an innovation we owe to the Sumerians. Among them are the first schools and universities, the first two-chamber parliament, the first historian, the first pharmacist, the first hospital, the first medicine and surgery, the first cosmology, the first love story, the first literary debates, the first laws and social reforms and the first search for world peace, harmony and immortality.

The oldest star map of the world is part of an Akkadic cylinder-seal which today lies in the Berlin Pergamon Museum. It shows a demigod who leads a mortal with two goat-sacrifices to the god Enlil (sitting). The gods carry the characteristic 'horned crown'. The detail drawing shows the nine planets around the Sun, in the right proportions and in the correct order – and a tenth planet, the planet of the gods (top left, between Mars and Jupiter, its closest point to the Sun).

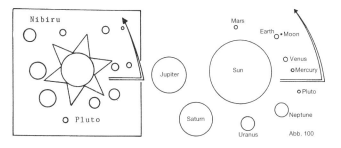

The Sumerians had at their disposal a seaworthy fleet for trading and a network of artificial canals between the Euphrates and Tigris as waterways and for irrigation. They invented the kiln and erected enormous walls of fired clay bricks, such as in the first high-rise building, the seven-storey high Ziggurat, visible for miles around. It was a temple and observatory for the priest-astronomers. At its top was located, like a penthouse, the 'House of the Gods', always ready for deities to move into at any time.

One of the most astonishing discoveries by researchers of Sumerian culture was that their astronomers quite obviously had surprising knowledge about our solar system. A drawing on an Akkadian cylinder-seal from around 2,400BC shows our solar system astronomically correctly: the sun at the centre, the planets circling it true to scale in the correct order – small Mercury, equal-sized Venus and Earth, the Moon, Mars, the giants Jupiter and Saturn, the 'twin planets' Uranus and Neptune, and the small Pluto. The cylinder-seal, stored under catalogue number VA/243 in the Middle Eastern department of the Pergamon Museum at Berlin, shows a demigod guiding a man who pays tribute to heaven's god Enlil and sacrifices two goats when receiving the plough from the god. Obviously it illustrates an important step in human evolution when man, formerly hunter and shepherd, became a farmer under instruction from the gods. Now, cylinder-seals were the predecessors of the printing press and were used among other things at the schools and priestly universities of Sumer for duplicating scientific models and symbolic expressions. Presumably, the star map in Berlin – man's oldest – was such a 'teaching book' for both history and astronomy.

People of classical antiquity, of the Middle Ages and even of the Renaissance knew of only six planets. Uranus was discovered in 1781 by Herschel, Neptune 1846 by Galle, and Pluto only in 1939 by Tombaugh. These three planets, however, are correctly depicted on the Sumerian cylinder-seal, plus a mysterious tenth planet. Sumerian sky catalogues describe ten planets in detail. Uranus is called *Kakkab Schanamma*, the 'twin planet' to Neptune, and Neptune is named *HUM.BA*, 'March land vegetation'. Another Sumerian name for Uranus is *EN.TI.MASCH.SIG*, 'planet of the bright, green life''. This sounded mysterious until we explored closer to the two planets.

In August 1977, the US space probe Voyager 2 started its odyssey into space. It transmitted pictures from Jupiter and Saturn back to Earth. Then the NASA engineers managed to swing it past Saturn's gravitation such that took another course towards Uranus and the unknown. On 25th January 1986, Voyager passed the planet, transmitting pictures of its green-bluish surface to Earth. Analyses showed that the planet has a solid centre surrounded by a marsh of super-dense hydrogen and ammonia. Then, on 24th August 1989 the flight passed Neptune. Again a green-bluish world which resembles Uranus like a twin, probably similarly-structured underneath the dense cover of methane. The Sumerians had known it. Where from?

"When the heavenly kingdom came to Earth before the Flood…", began the oldest known chronicle, the Sumerian list of kings from the 3rd millennium BC To earth? From where? Nobody knows where the Sumerians originate. Suddenly, as if from nowhere, they had appeared around 3,800BC, and with them their culture. No preparatory stage, no evolution – culture already developed.

The texts in cuneiform script also have an explanation for this. According to them, the gods once descended 'down from Heaven' to the Earth and created man at Sumer, paradise. Their first colony was the city E.RI.DU, literally 'house built far away', erected on an artificially-piled hill at the mouth of the Euphrates, in the midst of the land *edinu* ('plain') or *E.DIN* ('Home of the Righteous Ones') – the Garden of Eden in the Bible. Eridu was to give our planet its name in some languages – *Ereds* in Aramaic, *Erd* or *Ertz* in Kurdish (and *Erde* in German), *Eretz* in Hebrew. Then other gods followed, founding further cities. Like a general

staff, they settled the earth, dividing up their areas of responsibility. To the 'under-gods', the *Anunnaki*, they entrusted the building of the Garden of Eden: *"Coming from (the god) Anu to execute his instructions, he appointed three hundred of them as heavenly Watchers, to fathom the Earth's paths from Heaven; and on Earth he ordered six hundred to live on it. After he had given all his instructions to the Anunnaki of Heaven and Earth, Enlil divided up the offices."*

Who were the Anunnaki? Their Akkadic name *An-nun-na-ki* literary means 'those who came from Heaven to Earth'. The Anunnaki's 'heaven' was, according to Sumerian texts, *NI.BI.RU*, the 'crossing planet', 'heaven's mediator', a planet of our solar system. Were the Anunnaki extra-terrestrial visitors?

That is what the New York orientalist Zecharia Sitchin believes, after studying Sumerian writings for decades, which he – as one of but few experts – could read in the original. In the five books of his *Earth Chronicles* series, Sitchin claims that Nibiru is an undiscovered tenth planet of our solar system with an orbital period of 3,600 years and an irregular trajectory, whose perihelion (closest point to the Sun) lies between Mars and Jupiter, its aphelion (furthest point) somewhere out in space, far beyond Pluto. It is apparently a planet which produces its own warmth and atmosphere (or has it artificially produced).

The 'gods' of Nibiru apparently came to Earth because of gold. They needed gold and platinum for their planet's life-support system. Gold in all cultures was the 'metal of the gods'. They mined it in Africa, in today's Zimbabwe, which, according to Sitchin, they called *AB.ZU* (deep deposit). Even today, gold, in all Semitic languages, is called *ZA-AB*. Their heavenly port was Mesopotamia, linked with the mines via the *MA.GUR UR.NU AB.ZU*, the 'ships for minerals from Abzu', controlled by Anunnaki under the command of *EN.LIL* ('Lord of the Earth').

Sitchin suggests that the names of early Sumerian cities indicate a function of the country as trans-shipment centre

Zecharia Sitchin, who expects the 'Anunnaki's' return.

and base for the Earth operations of the 'gods' and 'under-gods'. *BAD.TIBIRA* was the 'bright place at which the ore was processed', *LA.RA.AK* ('to see the gleaming shine') a kind of runway light to aid the orientation of space craft. *SIPPAR* ('bird city') was the space port, *SHU.RUP.PAK* ('place of highest well-being') the medical centre. Enlil himself apparently erected *NIBRU.KI* ('Nibiru's place on earth'), whose Ziggurat carried a *DIR.GA* ('dark, glowing chamber') on its top, in which star maps were stored, and in which *DUR.AN.KI* ('connection between Heaven and Earth') was maintained.

Man emerged as a slave of the gods, according to the Sumerians. When there was *"trouble too great, toil too heavy, and much hardship"* for the Anunnaki, it led to the first revolution of history, the under-gods mutiny:

> *"Every one of us has declared war.*
> *The exhausting work kills us.*
> *Their lamentations were audible in heaven."*

The Bible later names the leader of the 'fallen angels': *Lucifer*. Enlil wanted him to be executed, but Anu and his son Enki had a better idea: a *'lulu amelu'*, a primitive worker, must be created: *"Let him carry the yoke, let him perform the laborious work of the gods"*. In other words: let's create humans.

The solution was soon found. *"The creature whose name you mentioned exists. We need only to link it with the image of the gods."* It hadn't escaped the Anunnakis' notice that hominids existed. By fertilisation of an egg of a female hominid with the 'godly' semen of the Anunnaki they formed the *'lulu'*, literally 'the mixed', which they called *Adama* ('from Earth'). *"In the image of the gods and from their blood they made humans, and imposed service on them to relieve the gods. It was an incomprehensible task."*

The Sumerian texts, in Sitchin's interpretation, describe in detail how several genetic interventions were needed to complete this act of creation. *"When man was created, they didn't know bread for food and knew no robes. They ate plants with their mouths like sheep, drank water from a ditch."* Only through long-term observation of this evolution, with occasional genetic interventions and the extinction of degenerated species (for example through the Flood), the gods made man, whom they allowed to settle around their bases in clay huts. They appointed kings as their rulers, and priests as intermediaries, making these their pupils, while they commuted in their 'heavenly boats' between Heaven and Earth.

Actually, the Sumerian chronicles even state man's creation in terms of time and place. According to them, the 'rule of the gods' over Mesopotamia began with the foundation of Eridu around 428,000 years ago. For 144,000 years or 40 'Shars' or solar orbits by Nibiru, the Anunnaki had tolerated the labour before they revolted. This means that the *'lulu'* were created about 280,000 years ago, 'above *Abzu*' – north of Zimbabwe. This was exactly the time which palaeoanthropologists and biochemists recently set for the evolving of *Homo Sapiens* in East Africa.

If all this is true, where are the Anunnaki today? Sitchin supposes that visits by the 'gods' have taken place every

3,600 years, when Nibiru approached the Earth. And there are a number of indications that the time of the 'return of the gods' might not be all that far away.

In 1981, five years after publication of Sitchin's first book *The Twelfth Planet*, the US Marine Observatory in Washington DC speculated whether observed deviations of Pluto's orbit could indicate the existence of a hitherto unknown tenth planet. According to calculations by the astronomer Thomas Van Flandern, who bases his thesis on complex comparisons of attractive forces, this 'planet C' should be at least double the size of Earth, and should be about 2.4 billion km (1.5 billion miles) away from Pluto. Its orbital time was calculated to be at least one thousand years. Van Flandern's well-founded assumptions brought NASA into the search, promising to set their Pioneer probes to search for the mysterious tenth planet.

Finally, in 1982 the space telescope IRAS (infra-red astronomical station) was launched, to search outer space for infra-red radiation – for objects which emit heat but are too far away to reflect sunlight. And IRAS made a find. On 30th December 1983, the press reported that the space telescope *"discovered a celestial body in the direction of the constellation Orion, which possibly is as big as the gigantic Jupiter and perhaps so close to the Earth that it could belong to our solar system... When IRAS researchers saw the mysterious celestial body and calculated that it was possibly but eighty billion kilometres away from Earth, they speculated that it is moving towards Earth."* Later, a report by the US magazine *Newsweek* on 13th July 1987 stated: *"Last week NASA announced something unusual at a press conference: it seems possible that an eccentric tenth planet orbits the Sun".*

For Sitchin, the possible discovery of Nibiru in 1983 symbolised a trigger for the numerous rapid political changes in the eighties. *"The Sumerians learned from the Anunnaki about Nibiru, just as they could only have gotten such accurate data about Neptune and Uranus from them"*, Zecharia Sitchin explained in an interview for *MAGAZIN 2000*.

"This means, if Nibiru exists, then the Anunnaki are also probably a reality. This would mean that there are other humans in space, who have visited our Earth for 450,000 years, and have created us; this is something completely different, something with enormous consequences for governments and religions of this world. This explains the chain of events which we have observed since 1983, since these IRAS pictures. Our whole picture of the world has changed since then. Ronald Reagan, who previously spoke of the Soviet Union as 'the Evil Empire', became friends with Mikhail Gorbachev, they disarmed together, and suddenly started working together on outer space programs. It became ever clearer that their first common aim should be Mars."

Why Mars? Sitchin believes this is because it was described in the Sumerian sky catalogues as a 'midway station'. The Mars pyramids and the now famous 'face on Mars' indicate that an extra-terrestrial base must have existed there. Sitchin is convinced that clues which the two Soviet Mars probes Phobos I and II transmitted back to Earth indicate that these bases are possibly being reactivated by the Anunnaki.

Statements by Ronald Reagan at summit talks gave cause for speculation: *"How easy his task and mine might be in these meetings that we held if suddenly there were a threat from some other species from another planet outside in the Universe. We'd would forget all the little local differences that we have between our countries, and we would find out one and for all that we really are human beings here on this Earth together."* Reagan used this formulation at a summit in Geneva in 1985, in his speech before the United Nations in 1987, at the summit at Washington in 1987, in 1988 at the National Strategic Forum and in 1988 at the summit in Moscow.

When would Nibiru again reach its perihelion? Taking Sitchin's dating of the Flood at 11,600BC, and further passages around 8,000BC, 4,400BC and 800BC as his starting point, one would next come to the year 2,800AD This would mean that the planet of the gods, after it had reached its aphelion in 1000AD, would now have already covered more than half of its return journey towards Earth. And perhaps the Anunnaki's harbingers are already here...

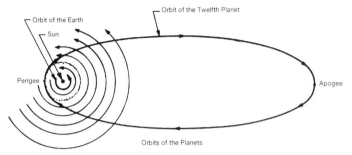

The orbit of Nibiru according to Zecharia Sitchin.

The consequence for our society of the gods' return was indicated by Sitchin in our interview: *"Although the different religions, especially Judaism and Christianity, speak of a 'time of the Messiah', the 'dawning of the Heavenly Kingdom on Earth', the 'New Jerusalem' etc, whether in the books of Daniel or Ezekiel or in the Revelations of John, I don't think that the heads of these religions will really be looking forward to this event with great joy. For ultimately, many old beliefs would have to be given up, and this could lead to great unrest. Then there are the governments, the authorities, the industrial-military complex, the intelligence services, the space programs, which would be affected, and which would have to give up their position of supremacy, if we were confronted with this higher knowledge... In one of my books I quoted a number of clear indications that the first preparations for this event are being made. Those in responsible positions already know that they are coming – not in a thousand years, not in a hundred years, but possibly very much sooner."*

One of the indications: in 1985, shortly after the Reagan-Gorbachev summit at Geneva, the Department for Advanced Technology of the US State Department brought together a study group of scientists and diplomats, NASA experts and representatives from the (then) Soviet Union, which was to investigate extra-terrestrials – or more

accurately, what we should do if we discovered them. The first report was published in 1989. It was a two-page document with the title "Principles concerning activities following the detection of Extra-terrestrial Intelligences".

It contained nine clauses and an appendix. Its main part dealt with the offices which should be entrusted with control after this discovery became known. In the first instance, so it said, it would be essential to prevent the general panic which would be expected if the public found out that we humans are not alone in the Universe. For this reason it is to be forbidden that any discoverer make observations publicly known. Instead the study group should be informed, to coordinate all further investigations.

In paragraph 8, it literally said: *"No response to a signal or evidence of extra-terrestrial intelligences should be sent until appropriate international consultations have taken place. The procedures for such consultations will be subject to separate agreement."* Should a signal first have to be decoded, it is essential in the meantime to prevent rumours from forming and to stop the situation becoming uncontrollable. The government should react with 'calming explanations' in response to pressure from the press and the public. In this light, the 'calming explanation' involving Doug and Dave and *Today* newspaper become increasingly comprehensible. They were just pawns in a larger game.

I asked Sitchin: do you believe that the UFO phenomenon is related to the return of the Anunnaki? *"Yes, but I should mention that the 'UFO phenomenon' has been known since ancient times. Also in the Bible there is talk of what we would describe as UFOs. I would remind you of the descriptions by the prophet Ezekiel or Jacob's 'dream' of 'heaven's ladder', the 'chariots of fire' of Elias and others. They therefore have evidently visited Earth not only since 1947, but since very ancient times. In fact, it has intensified in the last 45 years. If this, as I suppose, is only a repetition of what we experienced in biblical times, the solution of the UFO riddle also lies in the past, with the gods. It isn't the return of the gods themselves yet – the Anunnaki or Nefilim –*

*but it is the return of their messengers. The Bible calls them angels, Watchers or, in Hebrew, **Malachim**, 'ambassadors'.*

"The Malachim aren't gods themselves. In my books I show pictures of them which are millennia old and which astonishingly resemble some of the drawings made today by people who claim to have had encounters with extra-terrestrials. Both have the same smooth skin, the same almond-shaped eyes, very much larger than those of humans, both are asexual, and I personally consider them to be robots or androids. Perhaps the Anunnaki have stationed them on a nearby base, maybe even Mars, so that they monitor our evolution and possibly regularly transmit back to them data about us."

One of the best documented cases of ongoing 'surveillance' by extra-terrestrials is the case of the American Betty Andreasson, which Raymond E Fowler, a renowned American UFO expert, investigated in detail. It is documented in Fowler's book, which interestingly bears the title *The Watchers*!

Betty Andreasson's story began with a power cut on the evening of 25th January 1967, when she sat with her family in their house in South Ashburnham in Massachusetts. While her husband tried to fix the fuses, Betty noticed a bright light in their garden. The blackout lasted only for

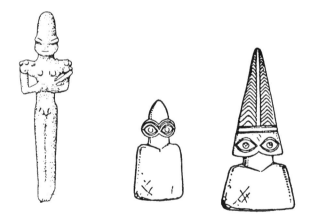

'The Watchers' in the form of old Sumerian statuettes.

minutes, and when it was bright again, it seemed to Betty as if she suddenly had found herself in something of a nightmare. Her family stood motionless in the room, as if frozen, and through the closed door stepped four small beings, around 4ft (1.20m) tall. Their heads were large and pear-shaped, in place of a nose they had two small holes, with a narrow slit of a mouth and enormous, almond-shaped eyes which reached beyond their temples. They wore dark-blue, skin-tight uniforms, with a symbol of a bird with stretched wings on them.

Then Betty heard a voice inside her head. The beings seemed to want to communicate with her telepathically. Their leader, who introduced himself as *'Quazgaa'*, had Betty brought into his oval space craft, which hovered over the garden. On board, she was physically examined in a frightening and painful way. Thereafter she was sat on a chair, and a kind of air filter was placed over her mouth and nose, and around her seat a kind of glass dome was put, which slowly filled with a fluid. For Betty, the pulsing feeling of this warm fluid was pleasant and relaxing. It prepared her for the next phase of this contact – a visit to another world.

She saw a place with a red atmosphere, with lemur-like beings crawling and climbing up concrete-like buildings. Another place was green. Betty saw a gigantic bird, which transformed before her eyes into a bright source of light, and then a voice spoke to her, which filled her with deep joy. She learned that she was chosen for a task, of which she would become aware only years later. *"They have come to help the human race"*, Betty remembered. *"They say they love the human race. If we don't accept, we will not be saved. We will not survive... But because of their great love, they can't allow man to continue the path which he has trodden... They will come to Earth. Man will be afraid of this."*

When Betty was brought back home, her family was still in a paralysed state. Betty was brought to her bed, and fell asleep. Next morning, life again took its usual course, and

Betty couldn't remember anything that had happened during the previous night. But the contacts continued. In 1973, she woke up at night because a mysterious light shone through her bedroom window, while her husband was sleeping soundly. Again four beings entered her room, led her outside, where she was 'sucked' by a beam on board a UFO hovering above her house.

This time, the aliens showed her how two foetuses were taken out of a woman. Betty was horrified when she saw how the beings pushed long needles into the foetus' heads and ears, before they put the contents into a container with fluid, which was attached to a strange apparatus. *"We have to do this, because humankind will in time be sterile because of pollution of land and water and air, and bacteria and other horrible things on Earth"*, explained one of them.

During the next encounter in 1975, one of the aliens said to Betty that the time had now come to remember. Indeed, this time she recalled the initial images of these strange encounters, and Betty contacted the American UFO organisation MUFON, who passed her on to Raymond Fowler. So, the basis for what was to be a 15-year cooperative effort between Fowler and Betty Andreasson was set up. Through a neutral hypnotherapist Fowler arranged for Betty to be taken back to the time of her UFO contacts, enabling her to re-experience what had happened to her in detail – which the aliens made her forget until the time was ripe. In this way, they found that Betty has had forgotten encounters with these humanoids since childhood, and members of her family, under hypnosis, remembered Betty's 'abductions' and even their own close encounters on board a UFO. Moreover, the contacts were to continue to this very day.

During the encounter in 1973, when one of the beings explained to Betty why they had shown her the treatment of two foetuses, she asked, bewildered, *"Who are you?"*. The answer (given by Betty in the third person) was: *"He says that they are the overseers of nature (of the Earth) and of natural forms – the Watchers. They love mankind. They love planet*

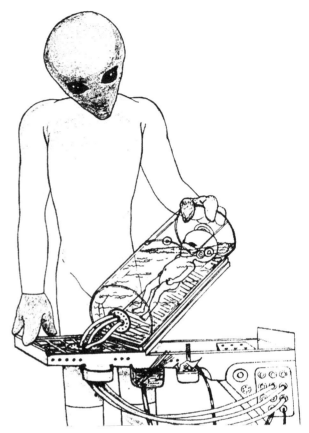

A 'Watcher', from a drawing by Betty Andreasson.

Earth, and they have cared about humankind since the dawn of humanity. They observe the spirit of all things... they are the administrators, and they are responsible. This is why they take away human forms... for many centuries... They have collected the semen and eggs of men and women."

This harkens back to genetic operations by the Anunnaki. According to Sumerian texts, they once before tried to raise humankind's consciousness through genetic manipulation, to prevent a catastrophe: the Flood. An indication for this we find in the *Book of Genesis* (ch 6, v1–4):

"When men began to multiply on the face of the Earth, and daughters were born to them, the sons of the gods ('bene elohim') saw that the daughters of men were beautiful, and they took to wife such of them as they chose… At that time, the Nefilim were on the Earth, and also afterward, when the sons of the gods came in to the daughters of men, and they bore children to them. These were the mighty men that were of old, the men of renown."

The 'Nefilim' or 'Anakim' of the Bible are the Anunnaki. Their name comes from the Hebrew NFL, 'be thrown down' from Heaven to Earth, while 'Anakim' is a corruption of 'Anunnaki'. *"The expression for the 'sons of the gods' however, who were involved in events before the Flood, is 'the Watchers' in old biblical and apocryphal scripts"*, states Sitchin. *"For in those days, the angels of the Lord descended to Earth – those who were called the Watchers – and they taught man's children to let justice and uprightness on Earth to prevail"*, as it says in a Jewish Apocrypha, the *Book of the Years of Jubilation*.

Another Apocrypha, the *Book of Enoch*, describes how the 'Watchers' made a human, the patriarch Enoch, their messenger. He woke up one night to find two 'shining ones' standing at the end of his bed. They brought him to a 'house of crystal stones, engulfed in tongues of fire', in which he ascended to Heaven, where a voice spoke to him, requesting him to warn mankind of the approaching Flood and to prepare for the return of the Nefilim.

The parallels to Betty Andreasson are obvious. Both were in contact with a group of non-terrestrial intelligences who called themselves 'the Watchers', and who felt responsible for humanity's evolution. As in the case of Betty, so also in the Book of Enoch there is talk of 'Watchers of Heaven and Earth', and it adds that *"everything which he undertook during his life, took place with the Watchers and the Holy Ones"*.

Does continuing environmental destruction threaten us just as much as the Flood once did? Is our development influenced by an unknown power, and are the mysterious symbols in the corn one of their methods to influence our thinking? Are they – like the UFO phenomenon – part of

a 'policy of gentle approach', with the aim of preparing growing numbers of the public for the 'return of the gods', without causing panic?

One of the best experts in the UFO phenomenon is Anthony Dodd, a retired police officer, who has worked intensively in this field since a strange encounter while on duty 15 years ago. Dodd is research director of the British UFO organisation Quest International and a publishers of Britain's best UFO magazine. That alone was enough for me to drive to Yorkshire to interview Dodd about his views on the crop circle mystery. *"I am convinced they are messages, they want to tell us something"*, he explained. *"I believe the authorities already know what this message is. In my opinion, the messages tell us that we're running into a dead-end, a point of no return, concerning the destruction and pollution of our planet – a point at which we can no longer change anything."*

Why do they choose such mysterious symbols for this, which nobody really understands? *"Perhaps these symbols were chosen so that only high-ranking scientists could read them, or maybe they don't want everybody to understand them, for possibly they understand that this could lead to panic. But according to my information, the cryptologists of our governments have already decoded some of the pictograms, and now NASA and some leading universities are also interested."*

Where does this lead? How do you see the future of the phenomenon? *"The phenomenon is developing fast, it is growing in number and complexity, everything is increasing rapidly. The number of UFO sightings increases equally. I am quite certain that everything is running towards a climax and that very soon something 'Big' will happen."*

Why is the 'return of the gods' being announced mainly in southern England? Is it because the network of ancient temples and sacred landscapes here, making contact with the larger cosmos, is the most intact one? Or do the numerous Wessex White Horses play a role – since they are really best seen from the air? The white horse was regarded by the Celts as a symbol of the Beyond, the Otherworld, of the

Sun and the heavenly chariots of the gods. The oldest of them is located at Uffington, its creation estimated to be around 800BC; the most recent dates to the 1930s, when the white horse still had a symbolic significance.

There are figures with other motifs, like the club-brandishing Cerne Abbas giant or the Long Man of Wilmington, who holds a staff in each hand – a motif we also find on Sumerian cylinder-seals. Nobody knows any more why these gigantic structures ever were made. Were they marker signs, tribal totems? Or signs for the gods, like those on the Nazca table-land in Peru? Strikingly, the crop circles often appear at the feet of the White Horses. Have the gods answered...?

Perhaps there is still another explanation. A 'far out' one. The region around Avebury is an artificially-formed sacred landscape, whose model lies on the planet Mars – the US author Richard Hoagland believes this.

Before the Viking 1 NASA space probe landed on Mars in July 1976, it transmitted around 300,000 photos of the Mars surface to Earth. One of them shows a structure in the Mars region Cydonia which is reminiscent of a human face.

In 1980 the photo came into the hands of computer specialists Vincent DiPietro and Gregory Molenaar, who were so fascinated by the 1,500yds long figure that they analysed it with aid of digital techniques and modern image-analysis methods such as edge-enhancement, amplification of grey shades through altered colour separation and the 'staircase effect' or graduation of image elements (pixels).

When they found a second photo, on which the Mars face is seen from another perspective and with another sun position, they managed to prove that it really does seem to be a symmetric, artificially-made monumental structure, *"...the awe-inspiring image of a human countenance against the background of the Martian landscape"*, as DiPietro stated it. But that wasn't all. Only ten miles from the structure the two NASA scientists discovered six gigantic pyramids with sym-

metrical outer edges and corners. Just as with the Egyptian pyramids, they were obviously astronomically-orientated.

At that time, the science journalist Richard C Hoagland became aware of the investigations by DiPietro and Molenaar. Hoagland had studied natural sciences, had been director of planetariums in West Hartford and New York

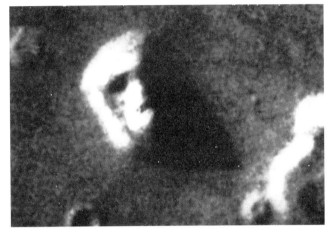

The Face on Mars (NASA Viking photo 35A72).

The 'Mars City' (NASA).

City, was editor-in-chief of *Star & Sky Magazine* and an adviser at the NASA Goddard Space Flight Center. In the middle of the '70s he was scientific adviser on space flight programs at the US TV stations CBS and CNN, and made live commentaries on NASA's Voyager mission. Additionally, it was he who, with Eric Burgess, developed the Earth's first interstellar message: the engraved disc installed on the Pioneer 10 probe into the further regions of our solar system.

For Hoagland the Mars structures were an architectonic 'Pioneer disc', an extra-terrestrial message for the people on Earth. He felt called to decode it. In his book *The Monuments on Mars* he proved that 'Pyramid City' and the Mars face were but part of an enormous area, orientated in the direction of sunrise at the Mars summer solstice some 500,000 years ago. Furthermore he discovered that the 'Mars City' was arranged according to similar laws of harmonic geometry to ancient temple complexes on Earth.

This is remarkable, insofar as the 'arrival of the gods' on Earth and the foundation of the first colony, Eridu (in Mesopotamia), was dated by the Sumerians at 428,000BC. One can thus suggest that the 'Mars City' was the first base of the 'Anunnaki', before they came to Earth – and millennia later, taught humankind their 'sacred geometry'. For Hoagland, this geometry wasn't accidental. Rather it had to be a code, a mathematical message for posterity, in the same way as the Pioneer disc had been intended. Soon he found out that it was not the Mars face which is the most important structure in the Cydonia region – rather it served the purpose of attracting our attention towards the 'time capsule' of other Mars structures – such as a five-corner pyramid whose top points at the face, which Hoagland called the 'D&M Pyramid' in honour of DiPietro and Molenaar.

Its geometry was decoded by Erol Torun of the cartographic department of the US Department of Defence (who, ironically, had his office in the five-cornered Pentagon). He not only found that the 1.5 x 2.2km (0.9 x 1.4 miles) large, almost thousand yard-high structure was arranged according

to the 'golden mean', as depicted in Leonardo da Vinci's famous figure of the man inside a circle. He also discovered that the angles and distances and mathematical constants which he distinguished in the D&M pyramid could be found throughout the whole region.

These constants are formed by dividing two other constants by each other. One of the constants is e, the base of the natural logarithm, the other one is pi (π), the ratio of the circumference and diameter of a circle. e divided by pi gives a ratio of 0.865, a trigonometric function and, amongst other things, the tangent of the angle 40.87 (tan 40.87°). Now the apex of the D&M pyramid lies exactly on the Mars latitude 40.87°. This means that the pyramid's position is coded in its internal geometry.

But what was important about e divided by pi? The answer to this question was supplied by Stan Tenen, who had occupied himself for 20 years with geometric symbols in antique texts. What he found again and again were 'tetrahedral metaphors', the same code as in the Cydonia geometry and the sacred geometry of ancient temple complexes from Teotihuacan in Mexico to Gizeh in Egypt, from Stonehenge in England to Zimbabwe in Africa. This led to the figure of the tetrahedron inside the circle. If one places a tetrahedron, a three-sided pyramid, with the top at the 'north pole' of a sphere, its corners touch the sphere at a latitude of 19.5°S. Many old temple complexes on Earth lie at a latitude of 19.5° – and also the most powerful geological structure on our blue planet, the volcanoes on Hawaii.

Most interestingly, the red spot of Jupiter, the Schild volcanoes on Venus, the gigantic Mars volcano Olympus Mons, the dark spot on Neptune and the main region of sun spot eruption on the Sun are located at a latitude of 19.5° of northern or southern latitude. A coincidence? Or a still-undiscovered law of astrophysics?

In this phase of his work, Hoagland came across a further piece in this cosmic puzzle. He met Bruce DePalma, a physicist at the respected Massachusetts Institute of Tech-

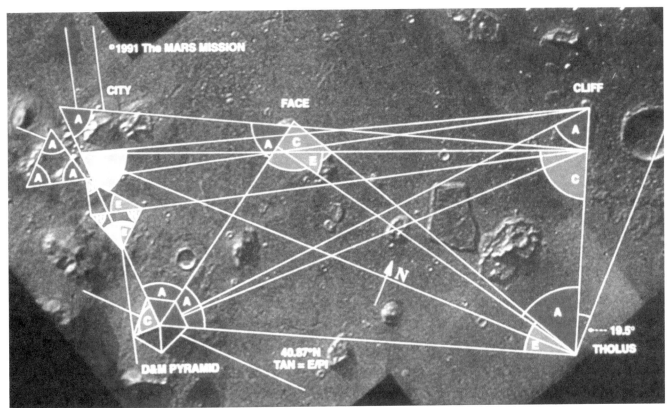

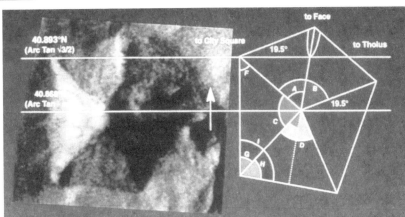

Above: *Richard Hoagland's reconstruction of the Cydonia geometry.*

Right: *The 'D&M' Pyramid: central point of the 'sacred geometry' on Mars.*

nology (MIT), who busied himself with the physics of rotating bodies. DePalma believes (together with a number of Japanese scientists, the Indian Paramahansa Tewari and the American Adam Trombly), that rotation opens a 'gate' and that energy flows in from the 'void', a higher sphere, another dimension or from hyperspace, in a coherent, electrical form – and that it comes to such an energy-exchange between the dimensions at a latitude of 19.5°.

A first proof for this hypothesis is the planet Neptune: when the American Voyager II space probe passed this planet in autumn 1989 and transmitted its data to Earth, surprised astrophysicists had to acknowledge that all their predictions were wrong. Neptune wasn't an ice world at the edge of the solar system which they thought it was – instead it was a marsh of methane gases with bizarre weather conditions and winds of up to 2,000kph (1,250mph). Neptune radiates three times as much energy as it receives from the Sun. Only Trombly's hypothesis answers the question of where it gets this energy from. (Also: Zecharia Sitchin's thesis of the 'planet of the gods' Nibiru, with an eccentric orbit around the Sun of 3,600 years becomes plausible, through this model of a Sun-independent energy-production).

The Cydonia structures thus appear to contain knowledge about 'that which holds the world together in its

Ring and 'Tholus' on Mars: models for Avebury and Silbury Hill?

innermost' to quote Goethe, a world formula, a secret of unlimited, free energy, which perhaps could change our lives in the near future, as a clean, gentle and natural alternative to nuclear energy and fossil fuels. Interestingly enough we find the same 'magical shapes' of 'tetrahedronic geometry' in some crop circle patterns. And so many of the circles have been concentrated around an area which seems to be the terrestrial counterpart to the Cydonia region: Avebury and the mysterious Silbury Hill.

East of the mysterious 'Mars face' is a ring and a hill, the 'Tholus'. A spiral path apparently leads to the top of the Tholus, as once there was such a path on Silbury Hill. North of Silbury Hill lies the stone circle of Avebury, whose two inner circles deviate from north towards the west at an angle of 19.5°. North of the 'Tholus' on Mars is a crater ring with two elevations, two hills near it – exactly at those positions where the Avebury ring also has elevations. The proportions of Tholus to Ring and of Silbury Hill to the Avebury stone circle correspond. *"Have the ancient British, the builders of Avebury, tried to reproduce the Mars monuments?"*, asked Hoagland – perhaps directed by the 'Watchers', the Anunnaki?

Although much has been destroyed over the centuries in the Avebury region, still other parallels can be drawn to the Cydonia region. For example, if one superimposes topographic maps, scaled proportionally to each other, then where in Cydonia we find the five-corner D&M

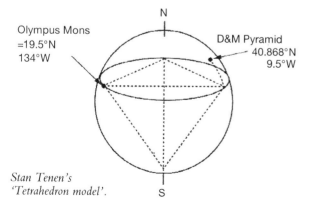

Olympus Mons
=19.5°N
134°W

D&M Pyramid
40.868°N
9.5°W

N

S

Stan Tenen's
'Tetrahedron model'.

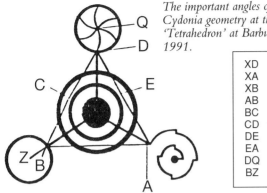

The important angles of the Cydonia geometry at the 'Tetrahedron' at Barbury Castle, 1991.

XD	0°
XA	120°
XB	234°
AB	268°
BC	24°
CD	30°
DE	148°
EA	150°
DQ	0°
BZ	234°

pyramid, we find a five-corner of enclosure on the grounds of Firs Farm, Beckhampton. Where the 'Mars City' is located, we find old fortifications and tumuli in Avebury. The Mars face itself would be located north of the A4 main road, west of Beckhampton, in the region of a prehistoric long-barrow.

The measurement unit of the megalith culture was the so-called 'megalithic yard' of exactly 2.72ft. But 2.72 is equally the constant **e**, which is of significance in the Mars monument's construction. Chance? Also the north-east orientation of Stonehenge, at an angle of 49.6° corresponds to the Cydonia geometry: in this case the angle of the D&M pyramid, equivalent to the **e**/*pi* formula of 0.865, the central mathematical value present at Cydonia.

An investigation of the crop circle patterns was done by Hoagland's colleague Colette Dowell, which suggested that almost all genuine formations contain values associated with the Cydonia geometry. Moreover, the long pictogram at West Kennett of 16th July 1990 was arranged such that its axis pointed exactly at the east side of Silbury Hill, while an angle of 19.5° takes in the west side[5]. The long pictogram at Old Sarum from 1992 contained angles of 45° and 52°, which, divided by each other, results in 0.865, or **e** divided by *pi*. But the most complex collection of Cydonia data were found during a thorough analysis of the 'tetrahedron' at Bar-

bury Castle, which proved to be a perfect tetrahedron (and a symbol for the energy-exchange with the fourth dimension).

A projection of the concentric rings located within the pictogram on to the latitudes of a planet yielded the following values:

19.5°: the point of energy-exchange between the dimensions in a rotating body;

22.5°: the angle of inclination of the Mars face;

49.6°: one of the angles of the triangles making up the D&M pyramid and the axis-angle of the Stonehenge Avenue (**e**/*pi* in degrees);

52°: the (rounded-up) latitude of Barbury Castle (exact: 51.30°N), a similarly 'self-referred' coding as in the Cydonia region, where the geometry of the structures contains their position;

45°: exactly half the angle between equator and pole;

45°/52°: 45 divided by 52 gives 0.865, the 'Mars formula' **e**/*pi*;

60°: the angle in which the three sides of a tetrahedron stand to each other;

69.4°: **e**/√5 in degrees, a relation which we find as much as three times in the Cydonia region;

60°/69.4°: again 0.865, or **e**/*pi*.

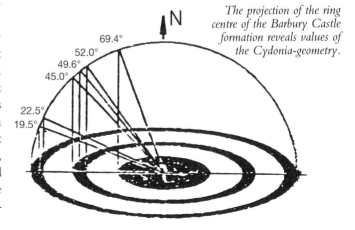

The projection of the ring centre of the Barbury Castle formation reveals values of the Cydonia-geometry.

So the pictogram from Barbury Castle is none other than a terrestrial counterpart of the D&M pyramid: it carries in it all important numbers of the Cydonia geometry. Or, in Hoagland's words: *"The whole damn thing is through and through tetrahedric and 'Cydonian'!"*. And this down to the smallest detail. Do you remember the pattern's single 'crooked beam', the only untidiness of the otherwise-perfect formation – and for hoaxer-theorists the *corpus delicti* for the 'true culprit'? Hoagland, with others, suspected that this 'kink' was important. Which angle would he have found if the kinked line had intersected the inner ring – which it avoids? The answer: 49.6°. *"Bingo!"*, exclaimed Hoagland, *"Damn, these guys are elegant!"*.

For 49.6° is not only the key angle of the D&M pyramid and the 'Avenue-angle' on which Stonehenge was orientated, but it also is **e**/*pi* in degrees (degrees = radians x 180/*pi*), the Mars formula. Hoagland:

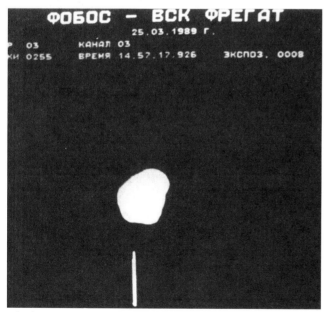

The last photo by the Mars space probe Phobos 2.7.

"Our discovery and verification of Cydonia geometry in the midst of the corn confirms an unusual suspicion: 'somebody'... obviously uses the same geometry as those who placed their remarkable geometric stamp in the Cydonia region half a million years ago... has at last returned to Earth..." – in the 'terrestrial Cydonia', the region around Avebury.

Isabelle Kingston, the psychic, was once again proven right. When I interviewed her in July 1991, she had explained to me, on camera: *"In the Barbury Castle formation, indications of different dimensions and the gates to these dimensions are given to us, which are contained in the power of the pyramid... I feel that we can learn more about a new form of energy through studying this pictogram, which possibly can be used in humankind's future, an energy which won't have any side-effects like many of the forms of energy which we use today."*

But there is yet another indication that the originators of the Mars structures have returned. With remarkable international participation, the Russians sent two space probes to Mars in 1988, Phobos 1 and Phobos 2. Their task was first to photograph the Mars surface and collect data – and then to turn to the Mars moon Phobos, which gave the mission its name. But the project didn't succeed. Phobos I never made it to Mars, disappearing "suddenly and inexplicably" during the approach to the Red Planet.

Phobos 2 reached Mars, entered into orbit around the planet and began to transmit photos from its surface. On one of the pictures which the probe's infra-red camera took – which photographs not light and shadow, but heat emissions – there appeared a grid-like pattern, as if a whole city lay below the planet's surface. On another photo an elliptical shadow appeared on the planet's surface – the shadow from "something which shouldn't be there", as the Russians explained at that time. Two days later, when the probe left Mars orbit and was redirected to approach the Mars moon, it came to a "sudden interruption of the radio connection". Phobos 2 went into a spin, as if it was "hit by something" – such were the Russians' words. The screens turned black and the space probe went silent – for ever.

For a long time rumours circulated about what could have hit the probe. But finally, in June 1990, the famous Russian test pilot and cosmonaut, Dr Marina Popovich, visited our 'Dialogue with the Universe' conference at Munich – and had the last two Phobos 2 photos with her. The two infra-red pictures showed the Mars moon in the background – and, an elongated object which left behind a luminous trace and moved towards the space probe.

In his book *Genesis Revisited*, Sitchin draws parallels between the Phobos incident and the story of the building of the Tower of Babel, when man had tried once before to reach the home of the gods. Are 'they' again active on Mars? Are they preparing their return to Earth? Are the crop circles part of a 'cosmic Menetekel' (warning sign)? Whether or not this is the case, Sitchin's interpretation received a boost when, five years later, a terrestrial Mars probe again disappeared. On 25th September 1992 the American 'Mars Observer' was launched, and eleven months later it was supposed to enter orbit around the Red Planet.

Since its camera had a fifty times finer resolution than the Viking probes, Hoagland and his followers expected new proofs of the artificial origin of the Cydonia structures. But on 21st August 1993, the Mars Observer also went silent. Something had gone wrong, and even speculations that the space probe had 'exploded' filtered through to the public from NASA-circles. Was the time still not ripe for terrestrial technology to lift the veil of mystery about our possible origins? Do 'they' alone want to determine the time of a possible return, for the next open rendezvous? Do we have to be prepared slowly, step by step, through 'signs in heaven and on Earth', before seeing our creators again?

Malachim.

11. THE RETURN OF THE GODS

Robert Emenegger is a well-known American documentary film-maker, a member of the Republican Party and experienced in working with American governmental offices. He had already shot documentary and propaganda films for the US Department of Defence and the air force, before he and his co-producer Allan Sandler were presented a new project from a government office in 1972: a documentary about UFOs. Although Emenegger had never before been involved with UFOs, he was interested. He was invited to the Norton air force base in California.

In the presence of an officer of AFOSI (Air Force Office of Special Intelligence), he discussed the project with Paul Shortle, leader of the audio-visual department at Norton AFB. What Shortle offered him left Emenegger speechless. For the film he could have 200yds of 16mm film material which the US air force had shot when three UFOs had landed at Holloman AFB in New Mexico. The UFO crews had met and communicated with the base-commander Lieutenant-colonel Emmanuel F Bonvincin and two intelligence service officers.

Emenegger was willing to accept all conditions to get this material. In the following months, Emenegger travelled to Washington DC many times to present his script to the Pentagon, and air force Colonel Coleman confirmed the existence of the film to him. He would have to take a secrecy oath, and then he would get the material in

few months. General Haldeman, chief of staff during the Nixon era, explained to Emenegger that he had heard about the film. Meanwhile, Sandler shot film at Holloman, one showing buildings 383 and 1382 at the end of 'Mars Avenue', where the 'encounter of the third kind' was supposed to have taken place.

But at the last minute, the handing over of the film was cancelled by the Pentagon. The reason, colonel George Weinbrenner from Wright Patterson AFB at Dayton, Ohio, explained to Emenegger, was the MiG 25 affair and... Watergate. The nation was worried enough. He encouraged Emenegger to finish the film, as planned, as a television special. Instead of the original pictures, he should get the scenario of the Holloman landing graphically composed and present it as "something which *could* happen in the future – or *perhaps* has happened already". Emenegger followed the advice. The film *UFOs: Past, Present and Future* went out on nationwide TV, and *UFOs: It has begun* was later brought out on the video market.

In his book, *UFOs: Past, Present and Future*, Emenegger describes the scenario:

"Two military interceptors are dispatched to escort the unidentified craft out of the area. By chance, cameramen, a technical sergeant and a staff sergeant of the base photographic team, are aboard a base helicopter on a routine photographic mission at the time, and they run off several feet of film of three objects in the sky over Holloman. One of the objects breaks away and begins a

descent. *A second high-speed camera crew, set up to photograph a test launch, turn their camera toward the object and run off approximately six hundred of feet of 16mm film.*

"The camera continued to roll as the extraordinary vehicle comes into view. It hovers, almost silently, about ten feet off the ground for nearly a minute, and yaws like a ship at anchor. Then it sets down on three extension arms.

"The commander and two officers, along with two base Air Force scientists, arrive and wait apprehensively. A panel slides open on the side of the craft.

"Stepping forward, there are one, then a second and a third — what appear to be men dressed in tight-fitting jump suits. Perhaps short by our standards, with an odd blue-gray complexion, eyes set far apart. A large pronounced nose. They wear headpieces that resemble rows of a rope-like design.

"The commander and the two scientists step forward to greet the visitors. Arrangements are made by some inaudible sort of communication, and the group quickly retires to an inner office in the King I area. They are met and guided to the end of Mars Street to the west area building number 930. Left behind stand a stunned group of military personnel."

Although this may sound like science fiction, the existence of the Holloman film was officially confirmed. On 14th October 1988, the nationwide TV station CBS broadcast *UFO-Cover up: live.* In the programme Paul Shortle, chief of the audio–visual department of Norton AFB, explained that he had seen the film himself and was certain that it was no experimental film, but an authentic document. In a government briefing of 1977, leaked in 1985 to the US UFO researcher William L Moore, it says that the Holloman meeting took place on 25th April 1964 – as result of an experiment by the US government to come in contact with the UFO pilots. To quote:

"Project SIGMA (was) originally established as part of Project Gleem in 1954. It became a separate project in 1976. Its mission was making to establish communication with Aliens. The project met with positive success when, in 1959, the United States established primitive communications with Aliens. On 25th April 1964, a USAF intelligence officer met two Aliens at a prearranged location in the desert of New Mexico. The contact lasted approximately three hours. Based on the Alien's language given to us by EBE, the air force officer managed to exchange basic information with the two Aliens. This project is continuing at an air force base in New Mexico."

A similar document which likewise confirms the Holloman incident (and also puts it on 25th April 1964), was presented in 1983 to the US journalist Linda Moulton Howe during a visit to the Air Force Office of Special Intelligence unit at the Kirtland AFB. As Howe found out, the extra-terrestrials are supposed to have claimed that they had created man and had controlled his evolution repeatedly through genetic manipulation. Now it was their interest to carry out genetic experiments on earth-humans. In his book, Robert Emenegger published a drawing of one of the two extra-terrestrials who landed in 1964 at Holloman.

When I saw them for the first time, I had something like a *déjà vu* experience. Somewhere I had seen this face before. Then I remembered: at Berlin, in the Middle

Drawing of one of the extra-terrestrials from Holloman, by R Emenegger.

Eastern Department of the Pergamon Museum, on a 2,800 year-old relief. It originated from Kalchu, a city of the Assyrian ruler Assurnasirpal II (883–859BC) in today's northern Iraq. It shows a 'genius', as it says in the museum's catalogue, actually an Anunnaki, one of those 'who came from Heaven to Earth', who created humankind in their image. The same face with hooked nose (here however adorned with a full beard), the same sceptre, the same ear-ring, the same 'helmet' – although here only decorated with three 'bands'. The Egyptians depicted these gods, which they called *neteru*, or 'Watchers', with greyish-blue skin colour and an extended back of the head, a characteristic which we – whether they are artificial or genetically-formed – also find in the representations of pharaoh families (and likewise the eagle nose) – who describe themselves as direct descendants of the gods.

Have the gods of ancient times returned? A further detail: twenty-four hours before the Holloman contact a small, oval object landed in the vicinity of Socorro, New Mexico. A witness, patrol policeman Deputy Marshall Lonnie Zamora, saw two 'small, slim beings' getting into a spacecraft, and then it took off. The UFO left behind four circular imprints in the ground which originated from the landing legs.

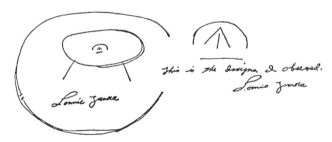

This is how Deputy Marshall Lonnie Zamora drew the UFO which landed on 24th April 1964 at Socorro, New Mexico. The symbol on its back corresponds to the Sumerian DIN-GIR and appeared in similar form in 1992 as part of a crop formation.

The US air force investigated and confirmed the incident. Astonishingly, the object had a red shining symbol on its back – an arrow on a base, surrounded by a semicircle. It resembles the Sumerian cuneiform script symbol for DIN-GIR, which the orientalist Zecharia Sitchin translates as 'the Righteous Ones' with the fiery, pointed objects' or 'the Nobles with the fiery rocket ships' – one of the names for the Anunnaki.

The same symbol appeared – and here the circle closes – at the end of July 1992 as part of a pictogram at East Meon in Hampshire. Much indicates that the return of the Anunnaki has actually already started, and that since 1964 (or even earlier) they have made secret contact with the 'kings' of our time, the government of the 'greatest empire on earth', USA. Holloman wasn't the only case of an apparently official UFO landing at a US air force base.

In March 1992, I interviewed a young ex-sergeant of the US air force Larry Warren, in San Diego. In 1980 Warren had been stationed as security officer at NATO Bentwaters AFB in Suffolk, England. One night, on 30th December 1980, he was driven together with other security officers in the direction of the nearby Rendlesham Forest. When they left the base, Warren noticed that rabbits and deer were running out of the forest as if in panic. The car drove into the forest on a forest track, until the engine suddenly failed. The group continued along the path by foot, while Warren noticed a convoy had just left the base, likewise in direction of the forest. The young soldier wondered whether this was a night exercise. Or an accident? Had something gone wrong? From some distance away, he heard voices and the sounds of radio sets, soon drowned out by the noise of an approaching helicopter. Then his group bumped into some British officers, as well as soldiers from the neighbouring US air force base at Woodbridge. A man in the group started to shout hysterically, and ran away. The situation was weird. Warren swallowed hard. He wondered if the Third World War had broken out.

Then he saw a mysterious object in a clearing. It had the shape of a gigantic aspirin, about 45ft (15m) in diameter, and hovered, pulsing lightly, above the ground. Warren noticed that many cameras were directed at the disc and that – at a respectable distance – security officers stood around it. He heard a voice – probably from a helicopter pilot – announcing over the radio: *"Here it comes!"*.

Drawing of the Bentwaters landing, by L Warren.

Everybody looked up and saw a reddish object flying directly towards them. The bright red light hovered for a short time above the 'aspirin', then it exploded in a rain of colours. For a moment, everyone was dazzled. When they could see clearly again, a large dome-shaped spacecraft stood in front of them. Warren and some of his colleagues decided to come closer to the object. But when they could almost have touched it, a green ray of light shot out of the UFO – and Warren lost consciousness.

He woke up back at the barracks. The mud still stuck to his boots and trousers from the night-time expedition.

On the next afternoon, Warren and his comrades were called to the base commander. They were told that they must not under any circumstances inform the public about what they had seen the previous night – it was a top security matter. All the same, or precisely for that reason, over the following days the rumour kitchen at Bentwaters AFB almost boiled over. Comrades who had stood on the opposite side of the spacecraft swore to have seen small extra-terrestrials, who had left the craft. One year later, Larry Warren was honourably discharged from the air force, and returned to the USA. But he could not forget Bentwaters. He dreamed at night of the encounter with the UFO and woke up screaming.

So he began to busy himself with UFO research. He read of Betty Andreasson, who lived nearby, and had to meet her. He followed Betty's advice, and let himself be hypnotised. The psychoanalyst Fred Max carried out the sessions, recording them on tape. Under hypnosis, Larry described precisely what had happened that night, and gave the names of the others who had sat with him in the jeep. Then he recounted how he had seen the extra-terrestrials: small beings, about 3ft (1m) tall, with large heads, clothed in silvery overalls. They slid to the ground in a beam which came out of the UFO, and seemed to communicate with the base commander General Gordon Williams. Then one of the aliens hovered in the direction of Larry's group. *"My God, he's coming over to us!"*, shouted Warren – then even under hypnosis he experienced a black-out, and found himself back again at the barracks.

As unbelievable as Warren's story sounds, it is only a partial aspect of the hitherto best-documented case of a UFO landing. In January 1981 the British UFO researcher Brenda Butler had learned from a US security officer, a good friend of hers, about the UFO landing at Rendlesham Forest, and managed to seek out and interview, with her colleagues Dot Street and Jenny Randles, a full dozen further witnesses in the course of her investigations, among them high-ranking officers. Also a young sergeant who had sat with Larry Warren in the same jeep confirmed his story.

But the most surprising proof of the Rendlesham incident is the official report by the US air force Colonel Charles I Halt, commander of US Woodbridge AFB, which is located only a few miles from Bentwaters. This document is authentic – it was officially released by the US Department of Defence following a request.

It says that in the early morning hours of 27th December 1980, a UFO landed at Rendlesham Forest, described by a search party as *"being metallic in appearance and triangular in shape, approximately 6–9ft (2–3m) across the base and approximately 6ft (2m) high. It illuminated the entire forest with a white light. The object itself had a pulsing red light on top and a bank of blue lights underneath. The object was hovering or on legs. As the patrolmen approached the object, it manoeuvered through the trees and disappeared. At this time the animals on a nearby farm went into a frenzy."*

Halt further describes how, on the next day *"three depressions 1¹/₂in (4cm) deep and 7in (16cm) in diameter were found where the object had been sighted on the ground"*, and that in the area of the landing place heightened radioactivity was detected. On the night of 29th December there was a second UFO landing, which Halt describes as follows: *"A red, sun-like light was seen through the trees. It moved about and pulsed. At one point it appeared to throw off glowing particles, and then broke into five separate white objects and then disappeared. Immediately thereafter, three star-like objects were noticed in the sky, visible for two or three hours and beamed down a stream of light from time to time. Numerous individuals, including the undersigned, witnessed the activities."*

Col. Halt's report was confirmed by an official audio tape released to the US news station CNN, on which Halt recorded the landing of the UFO. At the moment when the *"bright light exploded"*, Halt shouts out excitedly: *"My God, it is a machine!"* Then the tape is quiet for minutes – it seems as if Halt, similar to Warren, also experienced a black-out.

Eleven years later, a film turned up which could almost serve to illustrate the Rendlesham incident. But the film had nothing at all to do with the British UFO landing. It was made in Canada, in the province of Ontario, on 18th August 1991. The parallel: here also a UFO landing took place in the immediate vicinity of military exercise grounds, near the Carp Canadian Forces Station and the Carp NATO listening post, not far from the subterranean command-centre for Canada, near Ottawa. The film reached Bob Oechsler by mail in a brown A4 envelope without sender's address, with a postmark from Ottawa, Canada. Oechsler, a former mission specialist for NASA, is today a committed UFO researcher.

With the video cassette, the envelope contained several photocopies, drawings, a map and a large-format photo. One of the documents seemed to refer to the video. It carried the heading *"Ministry of National Defence. Blue Secret. Information concerns national security"*. Furthermore it says: *"Video tape 'A' – discovery of an extra-terrestrial disc – copy no. 1, 18th August 91. Military test area Old Almonte marsh, 11.00pm"*. Photocopies of three polaroid photos were added, allegedly 'picture three' and 'picture ten of sixty', which show a bell-shaped flying object in the foreground illuminated by the camera flash, and grass and undergrowth. The video-tape was signed 'Guardian' – the Watcher.

Curious, Oechsler put it into his video recorder. What he then saw took his breath away. For here, clearly recognisable, was a flat white disc, with a blue-white, strongly flashing light at the top, and next to it a group of flares, whose smoke slowly ascended into the night sky. All this happened noiselessly, and only the chirping of crickets and one call of a wild duck were to be heard. Then this scene ends, and steps are heard tramping through the undergrowth, with bushes seeming to cover the scene – and the blinking light continues to send out further flashes. When the film-maker approaches the object, details can be made out: a large, bell-shaped disc hovers there above the ground, surrounded by coloured lights. From the underside blazing light emanates, shrouding three smaller spheres and, in the middle, a larger hemisphere on the undercarriage. In the background, dogs bark. When the witness still comes closer to the object, he is hit by a blue light ray. Then the film ends.

At once Oechsler realised what he held in his hands: never before in the 45-year long history of UFO research had there been such a clear, detailed film of a landed spacecraft. This brilliance, these colours, the sharpness of the pictures: evidently, the anonymous witness had used a high-quality camera. But under what circumstances was this film made, and who had shot it?

The enclosed documents provided only partial information. A map declares the area around Carp as a 'zone for extra-terrestrial operations 1970 to 1991' within a triangle of 'magnetic navigational patterns'. Apparently two extra-terrestrial groups operate here, the human 'blonds' and the small, humanoid 'greys'. Apparently *"extra-terrestrial blond ground troops have lit up the flares, to give the signal for landing"*.

A Freemasonry symbol (a pair of compasses and protractor, and in the middle God's all-seeing eye) is given as the symbol of an organisation which works with extra-terrestrials in Canada, while the Sumerian 'Anu' (heaven) sign is used as the *"symbol of the extra-terrestrial confederation"*. The *"origin of the extra-terrestrials"*, says the document, is a planet named 'Eden' with a *"comet-like orbit, beyond Pluto"*, which *"takes 3,600 years to orbit our sun"* – obviously Zecharia Sitchin's 'Twelfth Planet' *Nibiru*. *"The silvery-grey disc (stood) on an open field for hours"*, said an enclosed, three page long, heavily-censored document. *"It was fully visible to Cessnas, military and commercial flights... A controlled landing"*. And further: *"All information about the extra-terrestrial contacts is systematically released by the Brotherhood. This group is responsible for the building of the New World, North America... It has members at every level of modern society. Their conviction is based on secret knowledge about the creation of man and relations with heavenly forces."*

Fascinating as this information sounded, Bob Oechsler wasn't sure anymore with whom he was dealing: with a nutter, a secret lodge or with deliberate disinformation from secret service circles. Also a large-format photo enclosed with the documents didn't contribute much to the riddle's solution. It showed a being in an overall with a hood, with a mask-like, snow-white face, behind dense bushes, obviously taken through a telephoto lens. The picture was labelled "Carp, Ontario, 15th August 1991", taken three days before the filmed landing. Fascinating material, that much is certain!

Oechsler decided to get at the case's roots by all available means. The first step was an analysis of the photo and film material. Oechsler handed the video film to experts for analysis, who on the basis of the reflective characteristics of its surface identified the filmed object as a circular, metallic body, about 24ft (8m) wide. The flashing light on its surface flashed faster than any known signal lights – such as from police or fire vehicles – and furthermore in irregular sequences. The photocopied polaroids admittedly showed very much less detail than the film, but instead it showed the foreground illuminated by a camera flash: high buffalo grass, as is also seen on the large-format picture of the extra-terrestrial. The flash of a polaroid camera reaches but several yards, and the object is definitely located outside its range. It doesn't reflect any camera flash light, and is evidently some distance away and thus quite big. But this was all that could be extracted from the picture material. Bob Oechsler was certain that only an investigation of the place of the incident would give more conclusive information.

On 5th May 1992, he flew to Ottawa, and drove on to Carp. Using the detailed maps in the film's enclosed papers, he easily managed to make out the alleged landing place, a slightly marshy meadow, surrounded by some woods, invisible from any road. He found a small elevation from which 'Guardian' must have shot the starting scene, and the undergrowth through which he pushed forward to the landing place, and finally the landing place itself, a circular area of 17yds, now scorched and infertile. Here bushes and grass were wilted and dried out, brittle and blackened, lying flat on the ground, while outside the circle the grass remained hip-high and healthy. What had caused the plants to die?

Samples which Oechsler took and later had had analysed in a laboratory showed a strong titanium contamination. Oechsler found individual traces of burns where the flares must have stood. About 700yds away from the landing place stood a lonely house, the home of a local veterinary surgeon. Inside a shed lived the dogs whose barking could be heard on the video. And the vet's wife – her husband was away at work – had observed the UFO landing from her bedroom window during the night in question.

"It had a small dome from which radiated a blue light, which shot into the sky", she explained to Bob Oechsler when he interviewed her in front of his video camera. Then he played her the video he had been sent. The witness was overwhelmed. *"This is exactly what I saw"*, she said with a steady voice, *"only from a different perspective"*. Seen from her place, the UFO stood in front of the flares, while in the film it was to the right of them. *"Yes, the dogs barked all the way through. Finally the object ascended to a height of perhaps 25yds before it suddenly, like, turned off, disappeared. Thereafter, black helicopters turned up, which flew over our house at such low altitude that tiles fell off our roof. They flew so low that I could make out the pilots"*.

The witness gave permission to do a lie-detector test. The inhabitants of the neighbouring house, located quite a distance away and inhabited by a doctor and his wife, confirmed the statement, and a fourth witness as well. But when she had inspected the area the next morning, all traces of the nightly activities had disappeared. The commanding officer of the Carp Canadian Forces Station of course didn't want to comment on the incident on 18th August 1991. But even he conceded: *"We've had quite a lot of UFO activity in the last 3–4 years"*.

Why do these UFO landings take place? According to the information from 'Guardian' it is because the extra-terrestrials are preparing for open contact with the people of Earth. *"There isn't much time anymore. Archaeological proof for the existence of the 'Eden' planet in our solar system piles up. The rulers of Heaven are worried about our military technology… we are already managing to stop the biological aging process. Man becomes God."* It is of secondary importance who 'Guardian' really is: is he, as he claims, a member of a secret lodge which, since the last 'visit of the gods' 2,500 years ago, guards the extra-terrestrials' legacy? Is he member of an intelligence service, who leaks information like this to the public? Or has he himself had contacts with extra-terrestrials, or been abducted on board a UFO, like Betty Andreasson and thousands of other Americans?

The government documents, shown to journalist Linda Moulton Howe in 1983 in the office of AFOSI on Kirtland AFB in New Mexico, also report an agreement, a contract between the extra-terrestrials and the US government. Therein they offered the Americans technology – in exchange for land and the possibility of carrying out genetic experiments with livestock and humans. At the same time they would reveal their existence slowly, step by step and in cooperation with the governments, to the public.

On 7th September 1967, the rancher Harry King found his three years-old Appaloosa mare 'Lady' dead, after a long search, between some chico bushes. It lay on its side and was, from neck up, but a skeleton of white, faded bones, which looked as if they had been exposed for days to relentless sun. This was incomprehensible for King, who had been on his favourite mare only two days before, galloping. Still more mysterious was the fact that her body was totally untouched from the neck downwards. What had happened to 'Lady'? Had she been a victim of carrion eaters?

Yet there were no traces of bites – the flesh was clean at the neck, *"as if cut off with a sharp hunting-knife"*. When

One of the sensational UFO photos taken by Ed Walters in Gulf Breeze, Florida – at the high point of a UFO sighting wave, during which the first crop circles in the USA turned up. The picture was taken on 12th January 1988 and shows one of the 20ft (6m) wide UFOs, as it hovered over a street. Experts believe the bright light on its underside to be plasma – it is so bright that it reflects on the street's tarmac.

A UFO picture by the Swiss Eduard 'Billy' Meier, taken on 3rd March 1975.

A further UFO photo by Eduard 'Billy' Meier, taken on 29th March 1976. The spacecraft left behind circles of flattened grass.

Spacecraft during landing approach. These two photos were taken by Paul Villa on 16th June 1963 near Albuquerque, New Mexico – in the vicinity of the Holloman air force base, where the first official UFO landing took place on 25th April 1964.

A further photo taken by Paul Villa on 18th April 1965, showing three retracted landing legs on the underside of a spacecraft. Villa likened the spacecraft's shape to a Navaho shield, and 'coincidentally' there appeared a cloud formation above the object in the form of an Indian with head decoration, lying on his back.
Telepathically, Villa then received the information that 'they' had been in contact with the Indians since time immemorial, and that especially the Hopi and Navaho had an important function for the new age.

A football-sized, strongly-reflecting telemeter sphere accompanies a spacecraft. Photo by Paul Villa, taken near Albuquerque, New Mexico, on 19th June 1966.

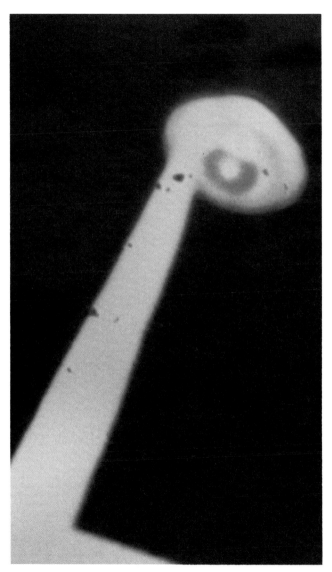

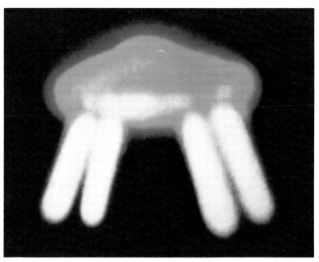

'Short rays' – for us a physically inexplicable phenomenon – sent out by a UFO. Photo: Dr Anon, Albiose, France, 23rd March 1974.

A red shining UFO sends a beam to earth. Photo by the Japanese secondary school pupil Ninacto Hi from Hokkaido, August 1973. It is possible that similar rays are used to produce the crop circles.

A light sphere projects a human face, photographed in summer 1989 near Moscow.

A UFO over Bristol, England, photographed in March 1991. After a similar sighting in June crop circles appeared locally.

A ring of lights, photographed in June 1972 over Australia. A similar phenomenon was observed by the CSETI group around Dr Steven Greer in July 1992 at Alton Barnes, Wiltshire.

UFO over Charleston, South Carolina, taken on 22nd January 1978 by Bill Herrmann, who several times was 'abducted' on board the spacecraft.

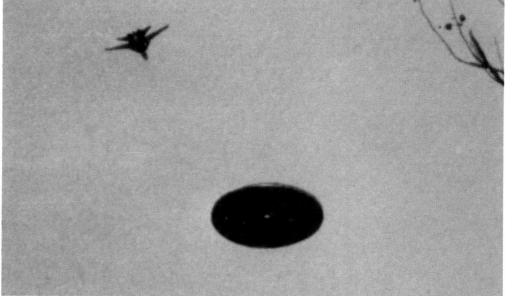

Two pictures from a sensational series of photographs which Amaury Rivery took on 9th May 1988 in the south-west of Puerto Rico. The spacecraft is being chased by a F-14 Tomcat interceptor of the US Navy. On the previous night, Rivery was abducted aboard such a craft, in which he – together with 14 other Puerto Ricans – was instructed about the future of mankind by a human-like extra-terrestrial and two small humanoids.

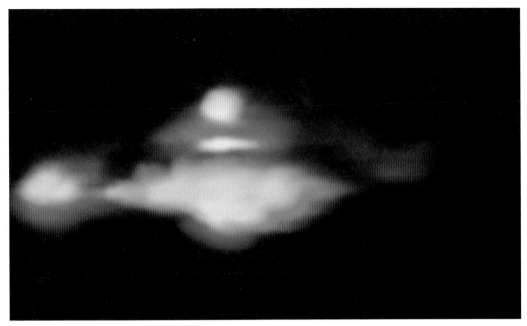

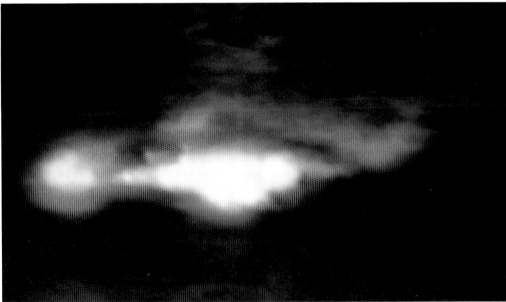

Two pictures from the ten minute video film handed to the ex-NASA mission specialist Bob Oechsler at the beginning of 1992. It shows the landing of a space ship at Carp, Ontario, in Canada on 18th August 1991. One can clearly recognise the dome-shaped, black object, surrounded by coloured lights.

Photo of an extra-terrestrial, photographed at Carp, Ontario on 15th August 1991. Zecharia Sitchin believes these small beings to be bio-robots, the Malachim of the biblical scriptures.

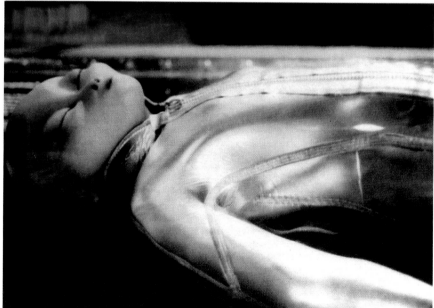

Model of one of the four extra-terrestrials who, according to American government documents, crashed in July 1947 near Roswell, New Mexico. The model was exhibited in 1982 in Montreal and is based on original pictures.

In summer 1992, this 'UFO landing place' was created near Budapest. In the following weeks the first Hungarian crop circles appeared in the Puszta. An experimental contact by earthlings! Possibly the 'White Horses' in southern England fulfilled a similar function?

A formation of 47 perfect circles was found by a local farmer on 27th December 1975 at Meeker County, Minnesota, in the immediate vicinity of a mutilated calf.

Inti, the sun god of the Inca, descended to Earth as Huiracocha. The sacrificial knife shows the winged sun logos during its descent to Earth (lower semi-circle).

Two 'Watchers' or Anunnaki in front of a tree of life. Relief from the palace of Assurbanipal at Nineveh, today exhibited in the British Museum in London.

Relief from Kalchu, North Iraq, 9th Century BC, Far Eastern Museum, Berlin. It shows an Anunnaki with sceptre and 'band helmet'. Similar beings landed in 1964 at the Holloman air force base in New Mexico (see drawing p. 115).

UFO (bottom left) and the moon, a scene from a video film which J. Holman from Yorkshire shot on 22nd June 1991, around 10.26pm, near Silbury Hill. After few seconds, the disc literally blinked out.

This stone at Ickfield Moor, Yorkshire, is covered with 'cup and ring' marks which resemble crop circles.

Spiral cut into a rock by forebears of the Hopi Indians.

he looked around at the place of the death, King came across further strange things. He found that the last hoof-prints ended 30yds away from the dead mare. In between he found, about 15yds away from the carcass, a flattened chico bush, surrounded by a 3ft (90cm) wide circle of holes pushed 6–8cm (3in) deep into the ground, each 10cm (4in) wide. Traces of burns were also found.

Harry King called the sheriff, and the press reported the mysterious incident. In response to the article dozens of witnesses claimed to have observed mysterious luminous objects over the San Luis valley during the night in question. Finally a scientist came into the case: Dr John Henry Altshuler from McGill University, later a pathologist and haematologist at the Rose Medical Center at Denver, Colorado. *"The cut in the mare's neck was extraordinarily cleanly carried out"*, Dr Altshuler asserted, *"and at the cutting edge I noticed a slight darkening, which looked as if the flesh had been cut through with a surgical laser-knife. I have taken samples from the hard, dark-cut edge, which I later examined microscopically. I came upon a change of colour and destruction of the cells typical for burns."* Still one more fact bewildered the doctor: he didn't find the slightest trace of blood – and this although all organs had been taken out of the horse's trunk. When the journalist Linda Moulton Howe interviewed Dr Altshuler in 1988, he was of the opinion that such 'operations' could only be carried out with a modern surgical laser – and this didn't exist in 1967.

But 'Lady' was only the beginning of a phenomenon which, as 'cattle mutilations', would hit the headlines across the USA over the following years – especially in the Mid-West. Up to today – 1994 – the US FBI knows of about 24,000 cases in which ranchers found carcasses of cattle and horses mysteriously mutilated in their pastures. All of these cases followed the same pattern, according to FBI statistics:

1. Mysterious, unidentified flying objects are observed. Sometimes they are lights which stand out due to strange flying manoeuvres, and at other times dark, black discs, and now and then black, unmarked helicopters are associated;

2. Cattle and horses are found mutilated. Various organs have been taken. Most often it has been sexual organs, testicles and rectum, but also heart, liver, kidneys, udder, muscle fibres, womb, brain, eyes, tongue, nostrils, lips, and in some cases even the complete lower jaw. The cuts are carried out precisely and show traces of burns, which suggest the use of lasers;

3. Sometimes all the mutilated animals' bones are broken, as if they had crashed onto the ground from some height;

4. Near the place of discovery, circular imprints as if from UFO landing legs were found. All around are inexplicable burns which often show increased radioactivity;

5. Often the mutilated animals were marked on one side with a powder of potassium and magnesium, which becomes visible only under ultra-violet radiation.

One of the most interesting cases happened on 27th December 1975 in Meeker County, Minnesota: a rancher found on his meadow, in the midst of a circle of flatly-pressed, freshly snow-covered grass, a dead calf. The eyes, the left ear, the tongue and part of the mouth were cut out. 500yds away the cattle breeder came upon further such circles. When Terrance Mitchell of the University of Minnesota examined the circles, he noticed extreme magnetism. Then one of his colleagues flew over the area – and found a whole formation of 47 equal-sized, perfect circles, which together formed a pattern.

"A number of experts are convinced that the cause of this strange 'harvest' is extra-terrestrials who carry out genetic experiments with our DNA, and that the chromosome material which they take from the animals and from abduction victims is used to create a new, perhaps different life form", Linda Howe explained to me in summer 1992, when I – by chance –

met her in crop circle country in Wiltshire. I invited her to join me in a flight over circle country, and when she booked a room in our hotel, the 'Merlin' in Marlborough, I interviewed her the next morning.

Linda is convinced that behind all this – crop circles, UFO abductions and cattle mutilations – is a 'big picture', a common denominator, which has a lot to do with the cosmic future of humankind. *"Michael, have you heard about the new book by David Jacobs?"*, she asked me. I had to say "No". *"'Secret Life' is the book's title. It immediately caused a stir in the USA after publication."*

Jacobs, professor of history at Temple University, has investigated over 300 cases of 'abductions' or UFO-kidnappings between 1986 and 1991. People, who only could remember 'missing time' which they could not account for, but who since then suffered nightmares which usually involve encounters with strange beings with large heads and narrow bodies, were later hypnotised. Under hypnosis they were able to describe in detail what they had experienced.

His result: all reports follow the same fundamental pattern. The persons are taken out of their daily routine, whether they are just lying in bed, are on duty at work or are driving a car on a lonely country road. They are taken on board a space craft by small humanoids, and first are thoroughly medically examined. Then sperm or egg cells are taken from them. Finally they receive a short teaching or explanation of what has happened to them – and the instruction to forget everything. During later abductions, they are sometimes shown embryos in retorts, or babies. Jacobs concludes from this that *"the central focus of all abduction cases is the reproduction of children, the creation of a new race"*.

Over a dozen further titles address the 'abduction' phenomenon. I have material about identical cases in Russia and Georgia. Alone in Tbilisi, capital of Georgia, in 1989–90 there were over 2,000 cases of 'abduction', among them around fifty cases with artificial pregnancy, all of which ended under mysterious circumstances in the fourth month – through removal of the foetus during a further abduction.

A survey by the Ropers Institute in USA from 1992 showed that 2% of 6,000 people polled from all sociological groupings had possibly experienced an 'abduction'. Every person who could answer four of the following five questions with a 'yes' was taken to have been abducted:

1. Have you ever felt paralysed when you have woken up in the middle of the night, and did you experience being surrounded by strange beings?
2. Have you ever in your life had a 'time gap' of more than one hour which you cannot account for?
3. Have you experienced gliding through the air?
4. Have you seen unusual light spheres in your room?
5. Have you had any scars of unknown origin?

Two percent of all adults means 3.7 million Americans. This however comes quite close to a number which the British UFO researcher Timothy Good heard from secret service circles: one in forty, or 2.5%. Also the American 'UFO-pope' and ex-CIA adviser Prof J Allen Hynek explained shortly before his death that 'one in forty' had been on board a UFO.

Unbelievable as this may sound, everything indicates that something is being prepared which the Bible and other sacred scriptures have prophesied for our time: the 'return of the gods', the creation of a New Heaven and a New Earth, a New Humanity. The next step in our evolution is possibly already pre-programmed.

12. Messages from the Cosmos

"The tendency to preoccupy ourselves more with the medium than with the message is typical for our time", wrote John Michell. *"Instead of devoting our attention primarily to the phenomenon's possible meaning, many crop circle researchers have devoted themselves to the investigation of the physical influences producing the circles. It is as if the assembled guests at Balthazar's banquet table – when the notorious finger appeared to them and drew the fateful writing on the wall – were more interested in the anatomical composition of that finger than in what it clearly wanted to bring over... There are no known precedents that messages from the gods of Heaven or Earth ever consisted of good news or of congratulations on the happy course of things. Almost always they appear as warnings and omens of approaching difficulties. As a consequence it is hardly surprising that many people associate crop circles with ecological crisis and comprehend them as a spontaneous expression of protest on the part of our mishandled Earth."* Yet how many brave Daniels are there amongst us who will interpret these mystery symbols?

Attempts at more or less sensible interpretations do already exist, and I shall present some of the more interesting ones below, together with some studies of my own. It is reasonably certain that most of the crop symbols have their parallels on antique temple walls and in prehistoric cave-paintings and petroglyphs. They resemble symbols from the world of saints, gods and myths, and also glyphs representing transformation and change.

Native American Symbols

The most important symbol is the circle itself. In the handed-down texts of the Hopi Indians it is stated that in very ancient times the Great Spirit foresaw the arrival of the 'White Brother'. It was said that if his symbol was the circle, representing unity and completeness, then his development will have gone well and would bode no ill. If he came bearing the sign of the cross, it would mean great suffering for the people of the Hopi.

"To us, the circle symbolises wholeness", the Aztec Xokonoshtletl confirmed. *"The circle is sacred to us, for all life is circular. When we talk or learn, we sit in a circle, and the energy flows through it. It always flows in a clockwise manner. The circle is for us the symbol of all things, containing everything and at the same time symbolising the One. Behind this is the idea that all phenomena in space are contained in Unity. Everything is round: the stars, the planets, the galaxies. Everything moves in circles: the moon, the planets, the planetary systems."*

We find a number of Native American-like symbols in the pictograms. The sacred sweat lodge, for example, consists of a dome-shaped structure with a round place in the middle in which red-hot stones are put, taken from a round fireplace outside the hut. The Indians believe that these two circles inside and outside the lodge are connected via an energy flow, a straight line. Doesn't this suggest the form of the 'dumb-bell' structures? The Indian medicine wheel is none other than a stone circle inside which four stone-lines form a cross, coming together in a central circle.

Such a pattern appeared in 1989 at Winterbourne Stoke, usually identified as a swastika. The classic quintuplet formations, for the Maya, represent the Universe itself.

During a visit to one of the Indian reservations north of Las Vegas, Nevada, I came upon a book by an Indian called LaVan Martineau with the title *The Rocks Begin to Speak*. It is a key to the understanding of numerous petroglyphs found on rocks in the American South West.

One of these symbols resembles a dumbbell and stands for 'speaking, communication'. The right-turning (clockwise) spiral means 'ascent', the left-turning one (counter-clockwise) 'descent', and a feather means 'healing'.

I was greatly surprised when I discovered the Indian counterpart of the 'insectogram': it symbolises the 'hunchbacked flute-player' of the Hopi, who led the ancestors of the Indians from the fourth into the fifth world and symbolises the transition into a new age.

He is also depicted as a grasshopper, which carried seeds in its hump and made the land fertile. The two 'antennae' of an insectogram would then be the flute-player's legs (or the grasshopper's antennae), the 'ladder' being the flute itself.

But the most classic Native American-style formation was the second pictogram of 1990, discovered on 2nd June at Cheesefoot Head.

The four streamers or 'beaver's tails', which seem to hang off a 'shield', represent for the Hopi the four quarters of the world, or alternatively thunder, wind, the morning star and the summer, and the 'four spirits', which in the end are one spirit.

In the fundamental pattern of most pictograms of 1990 it was possible to identify a symbol of Indian culture: Inti, the Peruvian sun god, descended to earth as Huiracocha. A sacrificial knife shows the winged sun logos (a circle, surrounded by two or three semi-circles as a 'radiating wreath') descending to Earth (circle without rays). Two parallel lines each side symbolise his arms and wings. We find similarly stylised shapes to the crop circles on the mysterious tableland of Nazca, which is covered with straight lines, animal figures and astronomical symbols. It originated around

A 'Solar Logos' formation, which appeared on 16th June 1990 on Telegraph Hill at Cheesefoot Head.

600BC, and was the cause of numerous speculations. Erich von Däniken thought the landscape glyphs to be a collection of 'signals for the gods', created to persuade them to return.

'Solar Logos', a fundamental pattern of many corn pictograms, on a rock engraving at Bidston Hill, Cheshire.

The above resembles a pattern on the tableland of Nazca in Peru.

Symbols of the ancient Celts and Germans

Other symbols seem rather to originate from the Celtic-Germanic culture-zone. In *The Goddess of the Stones* George Terence Meaden points out a number of parallels with the Neolithic art of the megalith culture.

Here the spirals stand for the cosmos and evolution in general, but also for life's path, for birth (clockwise) and death (counter-clockwise), and their unification in the 'sacred marriage' of Heaven and Earth. It especially refers to the ritual circle and spiral dances of the Neolithic mysteries. We find spirals and concentric circles on numerous stones and mound stones from this time, the most beautiful being on the megalithic stone at Ickfield Moor in Yorkshire and on the chambered long-barrow at Newgrange in Ireland. Their meaning is unknown – astronomical symbolism is likely.

Engraved stone at Old Bewick, Northumberland.

*A stele from
Gallarus, Co Kerry,
Ireland.*

Others describe these inscriptions as symbols of a very ancient Goddess religion. Archeologist Michael Dames believes Silbury Hill to be a symbol of the belly of a pregnant Earth Mother, bearer of all life, and of the mountain at the centre of the world which rose up from the primeval flood. Avebury, a massive circle, originally with two smaller circles inside it, represents to him the all-seeing eyes of the Earth, a symbol which we commonly find in megalithic sites. Interestingly enough, a pictogram found on 11th July at Ogbourne corresponds to the ground-plan of the stone circle at Avebury.

  Also, the medium in which the circles appear – wheat – suggests Mother Earth. In ancient times, the corn of Demeter, goddess of nature and Earth, was regarded as holy and embodied her daughter Ceres or Persephone, who was taken off into the underworld by Hades, before she could marry Dionysos. Although Demeter and Dionysos freed her, Zeus decided that Ceres had to go down into the underworld to Hades every year for four months. In this way she became the symbol of harvest and the cycle of the year, but – especially in the Elysian

Spiral at the entrance of the chambered mound of Newgrange, Ireland.

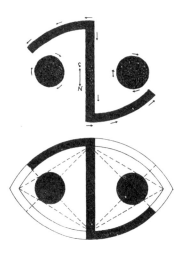

Mysteries – of the cycle of death and reincarnation also. A 1990 pictogram near Colchester, Essex, 'oZo' shaped, is believed by John Michell to be the 'sign of Ceres' or the 'halo of the Virgin Mary', or a vessel similar to the Grail, symbol of the fertile unification of opposites.

The cross surrounded by a circle is identified as a 'sun wheel'.

And a Germanic Tree of Life, an 'Irminsul', we find in a series of patterns of 1991, one being a threefold circle, which could stand for the three worlds of Teutonic cosmology, the underworld, Middle Earth and Asgård, the world of the gods.

Oskar von Zaborsky wrote a book in German (*Urvätererbe in deutscher Volkskunst*), in which the ornaments of rural carving are interpreted as symbols and relics of the old, heathen religion. In 1991 I was surprised to find symbols amongst the crop circles resembling some that he mentioned:

The six-pointed star and wheel: sign of the Sun, but also of the solar wagon of Baldur, Krishna, Elias or Apollo.

The spiral: the Cosmos.

The two Suns and the oval: the dumb-bell, as cereologists would call it, means 'the inheritance of the ancestors'.

The Tree of Life: the tree as symbol for life and its cycles.

The two mountains: understood to be the circle makers' 'signature', and interpreted by cereologists as 'eyebrows'. Doug and Dave declared this signature, like two 'C's, which were found on many 'insectograms', to represent their initials D & D. The 'two mountains' are symbolically related to Mother Earth. In the forest of Bohemia they are called 'Matky Bozi', the 'breasts of the god-mother', successor to the Earth Mother.

The serpent: bringer of life, new birth, the paradise.

The toad: this appeared on 15th August 1991 at Clatford and suggests 'the transformation of the person concerned'.

Oriental Symbols

Other symbols seem to originate from the religions of the East. The dumb-bell, a fundamental pattern in many pictograms, can be perceived in its ground structure as a Vajra sceptre. The *Vajra* represents the inseparable Absolute of the Universe, to Buddhists. One end stands for the world of form (*samsara*), the other for the limitless void (*nirvana*). It is a ritual instrument of immense power, which takes its energy from the diamond of ultimate truth (*Dharma*). The *Vajra* (Sanskrit) or *Dorje* (Tibetan), the 'diamond sceptre' is used in initiations and healings. It usually consists of bronze. Its counterpart is the *Ghanta* or

Tilbu, the bell, as John Haddington observed. *"In his book 'A History of Paganism in Caledonia', T A Wise mentions a number of Hindu and Buddhist symbols which he found on Scotland's sacred standing stones. He believed that Buddhist missionaries once visited this country."*

There is an interesting counterpart to the form of the basic circle pattern in Buddhism, in the mandala. A mandala is a circular shape which encloses a quadratic sacred pattern or representational realm of a deity. It serves as a visualisation guide in meditation or initiation. Each circle represents a level of consciousness or a dimension which is to be passed through on the way to realisation of the godhead. *"The Mandala is a gate to the Otherworld, in which*

every world seems to interpenetrate all others. Its only universal constant is the principle of the centre. The centre symbolises the beginning of time, space, creation itself. Here at the centre lies the origin of all things, the spirit of creation, the kingdom of eternity, from which all things manifest."

One detail which especially interests me is the three-fingered 'hands' or 'claws' which emerged especially from the large long pictograms of 1990. The most interesting parallel I found in the Hindu trident symbol, the *Trishula* of the god Shiva, the transformer, who destroys the old and transforms it into the new. The three prongs represent the 'transformation of the world and destruction of illusion' – destruc-

tion of three fundamental patterns in our thinking, lethargy, passion and delusion, through realisation of the true nature of existence. Hermann Wirth on the other hand interprets the trident in his *Heiligen Urschrift der Menschheit (Ancient Holy Scripture of Mankind)* as a symbol of the god-man.

Symbols of Unification of Heaven and Earth

One of the most remarkable experiments in deciphering the crop patterns was undertaken by archeologist Michael

Green, chairman and co-founder of the Centre for Crop Circle Studies (CCCS) and retired inspector of prehistoric sites for English Heritage.

Green detected seven fundamental patterns in the early, simple circles and identified them as old Celtic symbols of the seven astrological planets, as they are depicted on the mosaic floor of a Roman villa at Chilgrove – as well as an 'esoteric' eighth planet, which Green calls 'Ceres'. In the formations of 1988 and 1989, Green saw:

- Cosmic symbols: the planets, the Sun, or the large Central Sun of esoteric science;
- the cosmic spiral, symbol for Creation, from the cell to the galaxy;
- the cosmic egg, the awakening of the primeval centre, from which the physical cosmos emanated;
- the cross (especially in the quintuplet formations): the Christos energy, but also the four points of the compass and the connection between heaven and earth.

Green divided the pictograms of 1990 into four groups:

I. The solar *logos* and its manifestation on Earth. A being whose head is the Sun, surrounded by two or three radiating wreaths, comes down – often at each place there are two 'wing symbols' – on a circle, which symbolises the

Earth. But it also stands for the Earth's evolution from a physical towards a 'radiating', 'sacred planet' and humankind's evolution towards the cosmic human. This was, for him, the strongest symbol of 1990;

II. The Earth *logos* or 'Mother Earth' with a round 'belly' symbolising her pregnancy, and four little boxes on her side, which stand for the four elements;

III. The 'sacred marriage', the unification of Heaven and Earth, depicted as a merging of Sun and Earth *logoi*;

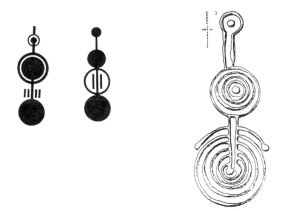

IV. The cosmic dragon. The symbol of the 'dragon paths', the evolution and the energy-streams between the planets. Often seven circles are interlinked, symbolic of seven chakras or the seven 'sacred planets' of the esoteric interpretation of our solar system. In other cases there are

four, which Green interprets as Neptune, Vulcan, Uranus and Pluto. *"The meaning of these four planetary principles in this arrangement symbolises great levels of initiation in mankind's evolutionary advancement, as well as in the individual's life"*, Green interpreted, in the light of Alice A Bailey's *Esoteric Astrology*. Neptune represents the ascent from the mire of dead matter to the threefold life-force of spirit (life), soul (wisdom) and personality (matter). Vulcan stands for growth, individuation. It ends with the dual development of natural man. The dual aspect of the new man begins with Uranus, which stands for spiritual transformation and service. Pluto, the last symbol, symbolises death and transformation to a new level of reality, according to Green's reading of the pictogram at Alton Barnes 1990. In this state, the individual leaves the Wheel of Life and carries a fully integrated threefold persona, depicted by the three-fingered hand or claw. The ever-decreasing circles behind Pluto hint at a quote by the Tibetan Dhjwal Khul, who revealed knowledge to Alice Bailey: *"The circle is complete. The serpent of matter, the serpent of wisdom and the serpent of life appear as a whole, and behind the three stands the eternal dragon, who always hatches out the threefold serpent, who forever says: 'Go forth and return'."*

For Green, the circles and pictograms are the work of the 'Devas', highly-developed spirit-beings: *"First of all I believe that these beings are desperately concerned about this planet's continually deteriorating ecological situation, and that they are trying to communicate with us not only to express this, but also to offer a kind of cooperative effort for our mutual benefit... They know the difficulties the scientific world has in accepting their simple existence, and for this reason they chose this means of regular communication, in a way which especially attracts the attention of those people who are open to these things."* And: *"The crop formations are a visible sign for mankind that the Kingdom of God is near"*. This is also hinted at in one of the most peculiar formations, which turned up in the middle of August 1991 at the foot of Milk Hill at Stanton St Bernard in Wiltshire: lettering in an unknown language, which Green identified as a mixture of Phoenician, Hebrew and Iberian and which he read as *"The Creator, wise and kind"*. Thus we return to the Sumerians.

by one or more rings are symbols for Nibiru, which according to the Sumerian texts was 'enclosed by a radiating wreath'. The 'trident', which emerged from some of the pictograms and circles of 1990, is an attribute of the god Marduk, personification of Nibiru, who killed the 'monster' Tiamat – which, according to Sitchin, was once the fifth planet of our solar system, which Nibiru collided with in ancient times. Also the cross is, according to Sitchin, an original symbol of the 'planet of the crossing', Anu, and is used in Sumerian cuneiform script to represent Heaven as well as 'God'.

AGRIGLYPH, MILK HILL
STANTON ST. BERNARD, WILTSHIRE

E. CH.- CH.   E.- A. E.   I. TH.- H. E. PH

PH.EH.TH.I   EA-E.CH-CH.E.
Phehthi   Ea-cheche
Ptah   Ea/Enki
Egyptian Creator-god   Sumerian Wisdom-god,
                        Friend of Man]

Sumerian Symbols

The American philologist Steve Canada interpreted the pictograms as signs of the Anunnaki, who announce their approaching return through the circles. For Canada, the large circles surrounded

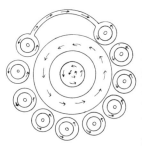

For the Sumerians, the pictogram's 'horns' were attributes and signs of the gods, the Anunnaki, while the F-shaped flag-extensions were the Egyptian hieroglyph for the 'neteru', the 'Watchers' or gods. What makes Canada's interpretation probable was a crop pattern which turned up in 1990 at Hopton, Norfolk, consisting of a large, ringed circle surrounded by ten satellites, of which two were linked with each other by an arch. Is this a depiction of the solar system with ten planets, of the visit of Nibiru's inhabitants to Earth?

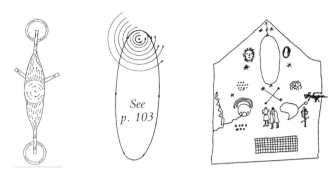

See
p. 103

Canada's most interesting interpretation is of one of the 'delphinograms', especially the one of the large 'whale' from Lockeridge. Here, the elongated oval sketches Nibiru's orbit, the ring at either end representing its perihelion and aphelion (closest approach to and furthest reach from the Sun), the two 'fins' representing Pluto's orbit, or the outer rim of the known solar system. A circle of flatly laid corn of the width of the rings at the oval's centre signals the present position of Nibiru 'half-way', where it is possibly located at present! A depiction from the sun temple at Cuzco, Peru, reproduced by Sitchin, shows an elongated oval between the five outer (Pluto, Uranus, Neptune, Saturn, Jupiter) and the four inner (Mars, Earth, Venus, Mercury) planets as well as Sun and Moon – and seems like a counterpart to the 'Delphinogram'.

We also find the ladder and the half-moon of the delphinograms on the Sumerian roll-seals. The ladder stands for the descent of the Anunnaki down 'Heaven's ladder'. Other crop symbols Canada interprets as sperms and

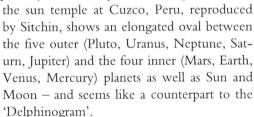

Old Babylonian 'Trees of Life' in comparison to crop patterns.

ovaries, which to him symbolise man's genetic ennoblement through the intercession of the 'Watchers'. I remember a small circle and a circle with coiled 'tail' next to a 'delphinogram' above the Avenue at Avebury, which fits well into Canada's scheme.

Beyond Euclidian Geometry

A totally different approach was pursued by Emeritus Professor of Astronomy Gerald S Hawkins – the same

Hawkins who caused a stir in the sixties with his interpretation of Stonehenge as *"gigantic computer for calculating important Sun, Moon and star positions"*. At the beginning of 1990, a colleague of Hawkins' sent him *Crop Circle Enigma* (Gateway Books, 1989) edited by Ralph Noyes, with the proposition that there might be a geometric-mathematical link with Stonehenge. Fascinated, Hawkins leafed through the book, and spent days playing with complicated calculations of all formations which consisted of more than one simple circle. No, he couldn't find any connections to Stonehenge, but instead Hawkins made a totally different discovery. In eleven out of eighteen structures, he found ratios of low integer numbers, which precisely corresponded to the ratios of the diatonic scale. These ratios embodied the eight notes of the octave. *"This was surprise number one"*, Hawkins later wrote, and he continued his search for geometrical keys to the crop circle riddle.

He gave special attention to a threefold formation which had turned up on 4th June 1988 at Cheesefoot Head. Hawkins noticed that he needed only to draw three straight lines or tangents to connect all three circles with each other. The three tangents formed an equilateral triangle with a new centre between all three circles. When he drew a circle touching the ends of the triangle, he came upon an unknown mathematical equation, which he described as the First Theorem: the ratio of 4:3 between the intersecting tangents inside the large circle and the diameters of the three small circles.

Diagrams: Hawkins

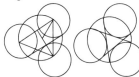

Theorem IV

However, 4:3 is a perfect interval in the diatonic scale. Furthermore, each of the circles of the crop formation had 48 spokes, of which 24 were enclosed by the

Theorem II

Theorem III

Theorem IV

triangle. 24 is the smallest common denominator of the fractions which form the seven intervals of the diatonic scale. *"This wouldn't leave me in peace"*, said Hawkins, *"I thought about it under the shower and while driving my car. Then, Eureka, I found it!"* Hawkins discovered three further theorems, all of them with connections to the diatonic scale. In the case of the triangle which had appeared in 1990 at Beckhampton, the astronomer calculated that the areas of the outer and inner circles stood in the ratio of 4:1, and the circumference of the two stood in a ratio of 3:1. The 'Swastika' of 12th August he enclosed with a square, and the square with a circle.

The result: the ratio of the outer circle to the inner one is 2:1. If a second square S2m is formed within the inner circle, the ratio of areas is C1:Im; if the ration is 2m:1, the ratio of the areas (C1:Im):Im is (2m−1):1. When m=4, the ratio of these squares is 16:1 resp 15:1 − perfect intervals in the diatonic scale.

In the case of the great 'single ringers' from Beckhampton in 1990, Hawkins drew a hexagon between the circle and the ring and calculated a ratio of 4:3 between the area of the outer and the inner circles. These four examples, Hawkins found, are four different theorems and at the same time special contributory elements of a fifth, more general theorem, the 'common denominator' of all corn patterns.

A look at geometry's classic textbook, the work of the Greek thinker Euclid, reveals that none of the above theorems goes back to Euclid. Also in mathematical textbooks they are missing. The result: the crop circles reach way beyond ordinary known geometry. Hawkins concluded *"Whoever created the circles must have understood a lot about geometry".* And they invest importance in the diatonic scale.

When the two pensioners Bower & Chorley appeared in public, Hawkins wrote to them: *"How did you manage to develop a number of ingenious and until now unknown geometrical theorems? Obviously the media have omitted to give you recognition for your great designs."* An answer never arrived. Hawkins doubted the Doug and Dave 'explanation' of the phenomenon. *"The use of trigonometry in a corn field could prove to be extremely difficult, if not impossible. The circle-makers had to split an angle into equal parts – and this in the dark."*

Further Interpretations

The mysterious and unique corn message of 1991, the 'Milk Hill inscription', turned up in August in Wiltshire, only few days after the American John Erik Beckjord had cut the words "Talk to us!" into a corn field, seeking to elicit response. While Michael Green interpreted the Milk Hill inscription as *Senzar* – an ancient script from the time of Atlantis – and read it as 'Ptah Enki', 'the Creator, wise and kind', Gerald Hawkins offered another interpretation. He observed, as a starting point, that it consists of six different signs in the arrangement oII 122131 II 45615 IIo. He then tried out all possibilities with a team of twelve linguists and a linguistic computer: 18,000 variations in forty-two languages. Three alternatives emerged. The only one which really made sense translates the inscription as the Latin (and grammatically correct) OPPONO ASTOS, literally 'I am against (oppono) works of craftiness and cunning', or 'I am against trickery' – which certainly is a very sensible comment in the circles debate (and possibly even refers to Beckjord's experiment).

Perhaps the most beautiful pictogram of the year 1992 was the 'Dharma Wheel' at Silbury Hill, which appeared on 17th August and was harvested but two days later. Michael Green interpreted it as an Indo-Germanic initiation mandala, with reference to the 'eightfold path' of

Buddhism, and also full of Celtic symbolism. Green's interpretation is now confirmed by an excursus by John Earl of Haddington, honorary president of the CCCS. He compared the pattern with the 'eight paths between the worlds', which John Matthews describes in his book *The Celtic Shaman*. A comparison between the Celtic 'medicine wheel' and the 'Dharma Wheel' leads to amazing similarities – even the eight directions of the formation correspond to the Celtic Mandala:

The Celtic Eight Paths		The Wheel of the Dharma
North	The short trident	The path of Wisdom search of the Sun
Northeast	The crescent moon	The path of Inspiration (the unconscious)
East	The keyhole	The path of Opening the Ways
Southeast	The heart of Bos, the bull	The path of Strength
South	Cernunnos (nature)	The path of Coming into Being
Southwest	The Cosmos (consciousness)	The path of Insight
West	The key of Mercury	The path of Passing Within
Northwest	The cattle water trough	The path of Cleansing (integration), water
Centre	The Mabrysithe double-axe (or sun-wheel)	The Creative Principle (godhead/self)

The directions lying opposite each other demonstrate clear polarities:

The heart and the water (blood and water)
The key and the keyhole (male and female)
The Sun and the Earth (as above so below)
The Moon and the stars (the unconscious and the superconscious)

We thus have a valuable eightfold 'Gate to the Other Worlds'

Sacred Geometry

John Michell discovered definite signs of sophisticated sacred geometry in the triangle at Barbury Castle. Michell, who has written at length about sacred measuring

systems, spent years researching ancient number symbolism and its cosmological meaning. *"This is a new and interesting lesson in geometry"*, Michell believed. *"It embodies the principle of 'Three in One', in which the central circle exactly contains the sum of the areas of the three surrounding circles. In addition, the sum of all four circle areas of the diagram comes to 31,680 square feet. This is a number after which I have searched for my whole life"*, he confided during an interview, and he handed me a working sheet which later would be publicised in the specialist journal *The Cereologist*. It is the number of God. *"Traditional cosmology assumed that the circumference of the sublunary world measured 31,680 miles, and the first Christian scholars calculated the number 3168 as a numerical symbol for Jesus Christ. The same number was assigned in past heathen religions to the name of the highest principle... The construct reveals that neither in a physical nor in an intellectual respect were any formations created by human hand... Reason shrinks from the conclusion that this*

arrangement presents a godly revelation... Its content is... a cosmic law, a canon or a collection of numeric, musical and geometrical harmonies which founded the prevailing order in every old civilisation."

The historian and antiquarian Brian Grist observed surprising parallels to the symbolism of the alchemists. In this case the triangle of linked circles stands for the threefold nature of God (which we also find as the

Trimurti of Brahma, Vishnu and Shiva in Hinduism), and the central circle, connected with all three outer circles, for the Creator's throne – or, as in the scripts of Basilius Valentinus from the 16th Century, for the *Tria Prima Materia*, primeval matter which consisted of the three primeval elements salt, sulphur and mercury, the Philosopher's Stone (see *Ciphers in the Crops*, ed by Beth Davis, Gateway Books).

Manly P Hall, in his encyclopaedic master work *The Secret Teachings of all Ages* (1928), reproduced a Rosicrucian diagram whose centre depicts an almost

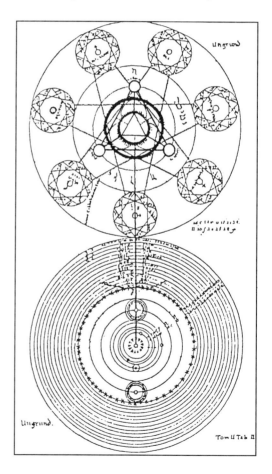

exact image of the Barbury Castle pictogram. According to Hall it is a symbol for the realm of the Godly.

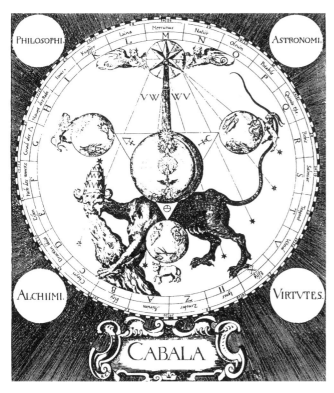

The rays of the primeval centre represent *"the first godly manifestation, symbolised by the equilateral triangle. The eternal world of the inner circle is manifested in the water (salt), light (mercury) and fire (sulphur) of the archetypical world, represented by the three outer circles, which are connected with each other by the triangle of complete equality, which partially is surrounded by the circle of the High Throne."* Opposite this world of the Godly stands the worldly sphere, the Sun, surrounded by the seven astrological planets, and these by the sphere of the fixed stars and finally by the spheres of the angels.

Another alchemical diagram, corresponding to the triangle at Barbury Castle in an amazing way, originates from the work *Cabala in Alchymia* (1654) by the Alchemist Steffan Michelspacher from Augsburg, depicting primeval matter: the world of matter is brought to life by a flash from the world of the Godly; the energy flows through the circles, which, once activated, together start the process of creation.

Each circle or *Sephira* has different complimentary functions: one serves as the point of energy-conduction, another as the resonating 'repeater', one as the 'absorber' – and the fourth, at the centre, is a place of stabilisation and convergence, which harmonises the energies, conducted from the 'heavenly star' to Earth. This corresponds to the three different outer rings of the Barbury Castle pictogram: the plain ring is the absorber which grounds the energy, the 'sun wheel' is the 'repeater' or radiator, and the interrupted spiral serves as an energy feed-through, as a transmission. Grist: *"In this way, the Barbury formation can be read as a graphic representation of the 'Philosopher's Stone' or 'cosmic egg', from which all life emanated at the time of the transmutation of matter, which preceded the completion. The end state is the fall in creation."*

From this point of view, the Barbury Castle pictogram is none other than an alchemical counterpart to the Mandelbrot Set which appeared on 12th August 1991 at Ickleton near Cambridge. *"According to the alchemical and hermetic texts, the process of Creation signals the transition from primeval chaos to cosmic order. Both stand for the transition from one dimension of matter into another, with similarly changeable qualities."*

For Isabelle Kingston, the psychic, the triangle at Barbury Castle shows *"the different dimensions, the path through the dimensions, which becomes possible through the energy of the pyramid."* The three corner circles seem to correspond to the three dimensions of physicality: the 'empty' circle to the first dimension (length), the circle with the curvy spokes to the second (breadth), the circle with the jagged spiral to the third (depth); and the central circle inside the tetrahedron to the fourth integral dimension, which cosmologically is the next phase in our evolution.

ARCHETYPICAL SYMBOLS

Programs for the Unconscious?

Sacred geometry supplies us with the last and most complex key. It goes beyond superficial understanding of a pictogram as a glyph in the sense of a symbol language and leads us into the field of the human unconscious. For perhaps the symbols of the circles were taken from the 'collective unconscious' of humanity or the 'morphogenetic fields' of our planet, and perhaps their meaning and purpose represents a psychological re-programming of humankind. John Michell is convinced: *"The regular geometrical patterns which form the crop circles show archetypical symbols which are inherent in the structure of the universe as well as in man's mind..."*. Archetypical symbols – primeval images – speak directly to our subconscious by by-passing pure reason, to communicate with us by purely looking at it.

In his book *Flying Saucers – A Modern Myth of Things Seen in the Skies* (1958), the great Swiss psychologist Carl Gustav Jung investigated the circle archetype in respect of the UFO phenomenon. He diagnosed parallels to Buddhist mandalas: the mandala is a path of initiation into the core of our psyche, and mandala *thangkas* act upon our subconscious through form and colour, without our needing to understand their symbolism intellectually.

Jung saw the UFO phenomenon – and the crop circles would confirm this – as sign of *"great forthcoming changes, comparable with the end of an era"*, and as *"agents and omens of change in the thinking patterns and psychic structures of mankind"*. The more people reacted to these signals, the closer this change was. Or, in C G Jung's words: *"It is not presumption that drives me, but my conscience as a psychiatrist that bids me to fulfil my duty and prepare those few who will hear me for coming events which are in accord with the end of an era. As we know from ancient Egyptian history, they are manifestations of psychic changes which always appear at the end of one Platonic month and at the beginning of another. Apparently they are changes in the constellation of psychic dominants, of the archetypes, or 'gods' as they used to be called, which bring about or accompany long-lasting transformations in the collective psyche. This transformation started in the historical era and has left behind its traces…"*

"Today's world situation is suited more than any time to the awakening of an expectation of an all-resolving, celestial event. If such an expectation isn't fulfilled clearly, then this is merely for the reason that nowadays no one is deeply enough rooted in the world-view of past centuries to be able to view an intervention from heaven as completely natural… Faith in this world and in the power of man has, in spite of intimations to the opposite, become the practical and for the time being the irreversible truth. This attitude, held by an overwhelming majority, is the most suitable foundation for a projection to come into being – for a manifestation of unconscious origins which, in spite of rationalistic critique, pushes through in the form of symbolic hints, accompanied and supported by corresponding visions, and which in the process take the shape of an archetype which has always expressed regulating, relieving, healing and completing. It is certainly a characteristic of our time that the archetype, in contrast to its earlier forms, takes up a factual… form, to bypass the offensiveness of a mythological personification.

"The psychological experience which is connected with the UFO phenomenon consists in the image or legend of

circularity, of the symbol of wholeness and of the archetype which expresses itself in mandala form. In my experience, the latter usually appear in situations which are marked by confusion and perplexity. The thus constellated archetype presents a scheme of order, which is laid as psychological cross-threads or as four-part circles over psychic chaos, in which every detail finds its place, and the whole, tending to disperse into the indeterminate, is held together by the caring and protective circle. Correspondingly, the Eastern mandalas in the field of Mahayana Buddhism represent a cosmic, timely and psychological order. At the same time they form Yantras, the tools with whose help this order is achieved…"

The division into four, the quadrature of the circle, about which Jung talks, is a very ancient alchemical symbol which he examined in his book *Psychology and Alchemy* (1943). *"The circle in the middle is called… 'the mediator, which brings about peace between the enemies or (the four) elements'"*, wrote Jung, quoting an old hermetic text.

The most important circle symbol for Jung was another 'quadrature of the circle', a five-fold unit which he called a 'quincunx': a circle at the centre surrounded by four smaller circles, in quadratic arrangement, one of them 'very different'. This symbol, Jung was certain, was an unequivocal omen of coming change: *"This is a symbol of the Quinta Essentia, which is identical with the Lapis, the Philosopher's Stone. It is the four-part circle with a centre, the godhead unfolded in the four directions or the uniform foundation of consciousness characterised by four functions… The number four as a natural division of the circle is a symbol of wholeness in alchemical philosophy, which extends over 17 centuries. One shouldn't forget that the central Christian symbol likewise presents a 'quadrature' (unit of four), and as a long cross even the 3+1 structure… The fourth function is that of the first or main function, which characterises the personality's shadow side."*

The Anthropos with four elements, the Quinta Essentia of the alchemists. From a Russian manuscript of the 18th century (from: C G Jung: Psychology and Alchemy).

This 3+1, the Trinity and the Devil, also represents, as 4+1, the four elements and the fifth element, aether. Jung would have been enthused to see the first 'quintuplets' appear in British corn fields, the most beautiful of them in 1988 in the area around Silbury Hill. They have a large, clockwise-turning central circle surrounded by three clockwise satellites – and a fourth in which the corn lies anti-clockwise.

What is the message of the crop circles? What do they mean? I asked George Wingfield: *"Many of them are mystical symbols, which act on the subconscious rather than on the viewer's mind"*, was his answer. *"Why? I think it is connected with a rise in human consciousness. Who is behind this? I believe, non-human forms of consciousness, something which comes from outside, from a very much higher level of existence, and it acts upon the planetary consciousness. I think it will change all of us."*

The spiral, the primeval image of creation in the microcosm as in the macrocosm, in a galaxy (above left) and in a crop circle (above right).

13. A COSMIC MESSAGE?

In May 1991, during a conference at Potsdam, I met the Chippewa medicine man Sun Bear. We were old friends – though this turned out to be our last meeting, since he was to die in June 1992. I first met him in 1987, when I interviewed him for *MAGAZIN 2000* and introduced him to our readers as a 'Prophet for the Earth', for Sun Bear was a man with a strong vision. The Earth, so the spirits of his people had told him, stood before a great change, and it was his task to collect people from all countries in a 'medicine wheel' and to teach him to live again in harmony with Mother Earth, for now the time for the return of the medicine wheels had come, the time for healing of the Earth. I took the opportunity to ask him about the crop circles' meaning. Could he help me to solve the riddle?

"When I had my vision of the medicine wheel in 1979", Sun Bear answered, *"the spirit explained to me: if they don't listen to you, they will have to listen to us. I didn't know then what this was to mean. But then I heard that these crop circles turned up in all parts of the world and that their symbols are the sacred circles of the Old. For this reason these circles say the same as I tell people: they must return into the sacred circle, to learn that the whole of Creation has the same right to life as they have themselves. We must begin again to honour the energies of the Earth, to carry out ceremonies for it. At first people thought the crop circles were but a natural phenomenon, but then they appeared in such complex patterns that this explanation became* more and more improbable. Now they have to admit that something is happening here.

"What is that? The spirit beings urge us to return to the sacred teachings. The crop circles are symbols for the ceremonial circles of the Old Ones, and the sacred circles which one finds on the walls of caves and old graves in Europe and throughout the world are the circles of the old Mother religions, in which the Earth Mother was worshipped. We must again return to honour the Earth. The reason for her now so desolate state is that your priests preach that you are only a few years on Earth, and that until death you may by all means destroy her as you like, since you will all go to Heaven. They say: 'Don't worry about the Earth, worry instead about your soul getting to Heaven'. They don't bother whether we destroy our Earth."

In connection with the crop circles, strange lights and UFOs are seen again and again. What do you think about the UFO phenomenon?

"For hundreds or thousands of years my people said that once upon a time a large, white shell descended from the heavens and opened. Out of it climbed beings who were teachers and who taught us many things. They shared their knowledge with us. It was those teachers who brought us our spiritual knowledge, which is preserved by us since ancient times. I believe that today we are experiencing the same: they are teachers from outer space who bring knowledge to us."

Have they something to do with the crop circles? Or do they originate from the spirits of the Earth?

"I don't know — both are possible. We had some circles in Indian reservations in the North West of the USA, at places where these UFOs, as you call them, visit us every year. It is possible that a connection exists."

It seems as if *somebody* is forming their own 'medicine wheels' to enable us to come into contact with the energies of Heaven and the Earth. And everybody who gets involved with the circles for any length of time goes through an inner transformation.

What is the message of the crop circles? What do they want to teach us? I asked the psychic, Isabelle Kingston. *"Their message, I think, is received in an extremely subtle way by anybody who sees these pictures"*, she answered. *"The subconscious receives these impulses, whether we are aware of the changes which they cause in us, or not. I believe that people's consciousness and spirituality are awakened through them."*

The more I thought about the crop circle phenomenon, the clearer it became that its relevance doesn't lie in its mysterious nature or origin, nor in its hidden meaning. The true mystery of the crop circles was their *effect* on people, especially on those who became more intensively involved with them, who exposed themselves repeatedly to their energy. They teach us so much: in the first instance a sense of wonderment, of amazement. Everybody with whom I spoke had experienced it: first he or she was smitten by the 'circle-effect' — that unfathomable fascination which radiates from the phenomenon. Then people experienced things which expanded their outlook on the world: they discovered unknown abilities, experienced that the circle-makers seemed to react to their intimate thoughts, saw mysterious lights or heard mysterious buzzing sounds, and slowly they began to integrate these new experiences into their lives. People went through an inner transformation, each one becoming a new person.

Two people who experienced this are Colin Andrews and Pat Delgado. I interviewed them about this outside a conference in Berlin in August 1991 and was so impressed by the deep seriousness of their replies that I gave them the last word in our film. *"Although I still investigate the phenomenon with scientifically meticulous precision, after one decade of thorough research I understand that an intelligence is behind this"*, explained Colin. *"And if one becomes aware of this deep down inside, it has to change one. I certainly became more aware and sensitive to the unbelievable implications, potentials and possibilities of what is happening at present here on Earth. I am very much aware of the implications this phenomenon has for religious and politics, and I am certain — this I repeat again and again — that this is the beginning, the beginning of something great."*

Colin told me how one day he went into the 'delphinogram' at Lockeridge with a psychic. After a short meditation, the medium suddenly said: *"They speak now. They say: 'Go, Colin, and find your stone.'"* Colin stood up, looked around and asked: *"What do they mean by 'my' stone?"* *"They just said, 'Find your stone'"*, the channel repeated. Colin rooted around in the corn, to discover a stone which stuck out of the ground. He dug it out and finally held it in his hands. When he looked at it more carefully, he discovered that it carried on its underside the pattern of a stone circle, similar to Stonehenge. *"How did they know I was going to find precisely this stone?"*, and the answer came through the psychic: *"They say they knew because they have programmed you."*

Also Pat Delgado confessed: *"It has deeply changed me since I introduced the public to the crop circle phenomenon in 1981. I was an engineer, who stood with both feet on the ground, and I examined them asking whether it would be possible to reproduce these circles artificially. I soon became aware that this was something totally separate from our material world. At the beginning of the 1980s I had a presentiment that they are a spiritual phenomenon. There is no other word for this. We need a new vocabulary to express our innermost feelings. For this we have to use stereotypes such as 'paranormal', 'channelled', 'spiritual', if we want to describe things beyond our material world. It is beyond our material world, and we have to cross the membrane which separates the worlds. We must begin to think spiritually. For the phenomenon of the crop circles is completely spiritual, it is totally intelligently controlled, possibly by the same intelligence which controls everything, even us."*

Busty Taylor also admits that the crop circles have changed his life. He had never been bothered with subjects such as psychics or telepathy, but suddenly he experienced these things himself. When the first ringed circles turned up in 1986 at the Punch Bowl at Cheesefoot Head, Busty said to Colin Andrews while he flew over the formation: *"All we now need is the circles of this and last year together".* In the previous year the *'quintuplets'* had caused a stir. On the next morning the first quintuplet of the year was found at Cheesefoot Head, one of the very special kind: its central circle was surrounded by a ring!

This was the combination of that year's and the previous year's formations together. At the beginning of 1991 Busty stated that there would be larger formations that year, and around 10th July something 'spectacular' would happen. The pictograms were larger then ever before that year, and on 17th July the triangle at Barbury Castle appeared. *"I have a kind of intuition, which seems to hit the nail on the head",* he confided in an interview, *"I myself don't know why. But many people seem to have such inputs, and this happens throughout the country. I alone received eight telephone calls in the last ten days from people who had said to themselves that they would like to have a circle on this or that field in their vicinity – and in the morning it was there. I am not the only one, certainly not."*

Something similar had happened to George Wingfield. Once – on 26th June 1988, to be exact – he wrote to his brother, a geologist who lives in Leicestershire, about his circle research. He concluded his letter with the remark that if he wanted to know what this was about, he should come with him to Wiltshire or Hampshire, for he couldn't send a circle to him in the Midlands. George's brother was surprised when he heard on local television about a new circle which had turned up close to him, at Oadby in Leicestershire, only one day after he had received the letter. It was the first circle ever found north of Oxfordshire.

In June 1989, Wingfield was driving from Bristol via Bath, to a concert at Longleat near Warminster. When he passed Newton St Loe, west of Bath, he saw a wide, green wheat field, which stretched up a hill. *"What a wonderful place for crop circles",* thought George fancifully. Some days later, a gigantic pictogram turned up on exactly that field, and hundreds came to marvel at it – visible as it was from a main road. His friend and IBM colleague Nigel Foster, infected by George's enthusiasm, used to drive regularly over a hill above the city of Bristol and said, when close to a prehistoric burial mound: *"Come on, give us at least a couple of circles."* When he told George his anecdote, George showed him a few aerial photos from the area in question – and circles had actually turned up on the other side of the hill, though nobody had given them much attention.

Another friend of George's, Mike Carrie, who had taken part in 'Project Chameleon' and who had been one of the first to discover a dumbbell-shaped pictogram after a foggy night, didn't believe his eyes when he returned home to Nottinghamshire. In front of his office windows were corn fields, and in one of them he found the perfect counterpart to 'his' dumb-bell from Wiltshire. It had the same size and was even the same distance from his office as the 'Chameleon' dumb-bell had been from the observation camp. *"Do these circles follow people back home?"* asked Wingfield...

When I visited the British-Japanese observational station at Adams Grave, Alton Barnes, I talked with the four young Englishmen who were there on watch. One of them, Paul Randall, told me that they and two other friends had carried out a meditation one night inside a newly-formed circle at Cheesfoot Head. They lay down inside the circle, with feet towards the centre of the circle, where one of them, John Martineau whose main interest is sacred geometry, placed a six-sided crystal. At first the idea was to come into contact with the circle energy, and then John suggested they could ask the circle-makers for a new formation – and since there were six of them and they had laid down to form a hexagon, they asked for a six-pointed star. Nothing happened, and after some time they went to sleep. Next morning, they discovered a new formation, on a neighbouring field, separated only by a hedge from 'their' field: a six-petalled flower, enclosed by a ring. Aptly, it symbolised the sought-after star, the group of six people and their concerted striving (the ring). One week later I came to England, and wished for a ringed Star of David – and a further six-pedalled flower appeared, this time surrounded by two rings, on Telegraph Hill, not far from the first.

Others communicated more physically with the circle-makers. *"Talk to us"*, was what the American John Erik Beckjord cut into the corn, with the farmer's permission, in July 1991. One week later, thirteen miles (20km) away, that hieroglyphic lettering which Michael Green translated as 'The Creator, wise and kind' appeared. And more than once (not only in North Germany) it seemed that the circle-makers understood a hoaxed circle as a communication to them by humans – or competition? When the 'Wessex Skeptics' hoaxed a rather bent 'Celtic Cross' at the beginning of August 1991, on a field belonging to the bio-farmer Martin Pitt near Marlborough, there appeared on a neighbouring field, exactly one week later, one of the most beautiful and largest pictograms of the summer, and Pitt was simply *"completely over the moon"* about it.

There was much discussion about whether deliberate 'imitations' should be attempted the following summer, to encourage the real circle-makers. It would be worth a try – although only under controlled conditions and with permission of farmers concerned! No great effort has yet been made in this direction. However, to everyone who visits circle-country in England I would recommend to try a communication with the energy behind the circle phenomenon, to each person in his or her very own way. True wonders will be revealed, if only we open ourselves to it!

"This is perhaps the simplest and most obvious message of the circles", George Wingfield wrote. *"They tell us that the most important thing is our consciousness, and if we manage to expand it, by opening ourselves to these events, we can draw an almost unlimited potential from our innermost being. If such an interpretation is correct – and I am not the only one who thinks about this matter in this way – it opens a view to a future which could be filled with hope."*

Happy and fulfilled – with 18 hours of interviews, inside shots and aerial views of the circles – we returned to Germany at the end of August 1991 from our filming expedition on the trail of the crop circles of southern England. Our last date had been with a man who, from the beginning, had understood the crop circle phenomenon in the context of the whole mental-spiritual paradigm-shift towards a holistic and integral world-view. John Michell, a modern follower of the teachings of Plato and Pythagoras, a student of sacred geometry and collector of unusual stories in the tradition of Charles Fort, fascinates me repeatedly with his intellectual brilliance. As a philosopher he views things from a higher perspective. John lives, in an appropriately white, Victorian house in West London, surrounded by avant-garde style galleries and antique shops. Past a gigantic marble statue of Homer we went upstairs to the fourth floor, John's living and working room, where stacks of books, letters and magazines testify to his creative chaos. After the camera was set up, John leant back and answered my questions in his calm, mindful and deliberate way. I asked what his interest was in the crop circles.

"The crop circles are the most interesting matter happening today", John replied. "They are something which challenge science, which science can't explain. They endanger the scientific world-view, and this I observe with great satisfaction. I think that the rationalistic, materialistic world-view is responsible for many of today's crises, and that it is time to replace it. It is only too evident that the crop circles disprove our materialistic approach, and this is a very contemporary and creative development. For it is quite extraordinary what we observe here. Something starts to draw symbols on corn fields, and this in a very beautiful way, without shocking people, without threatening them and suddenly it begins to quickly change people's view of the world. It is a wonderful and beautiful phenomenon, and it originates from a very high source."

I reminded him of an article in *The Cereologist*, in which a hard-hitting art critic wrote about the circles. "Yes, I asked John McEwen, a well-known London art critic, to write an article about the crop circles from his point of view. He had already reviewed artists like Richard Long or Hamish Fulton, who are specialists in landscape art, artists who depict imagery in the landscape. He compared the crop circles with their works and passed a clear judgment in favour of the circle-makers. One must have seen the crop circles to be able to judge them. They are of such beauty, in every way and kind: their position, the corn's placement, the wonderful effect they have on people — they are great works of art! And McEwen thought whoever had created them is a genius, and one of the greatest artists of our time."

What is the source of this phenomenon, in your opinion?

"It is only too evident that it can't be a creation of man, and if it isn't human and has sense and intelligence, then it can only originate from a non-human intelligence — that means from the world of spirit beings. Not lower spirit beings, not of a ghostly manifestation with séances and mediums, but something higher. You can recognise this in their beauty and skillfulness and the symbolism used. For this reason it must originate from the world of higher spiritual beings — in other words, the world of the gods. And if we take a look into the world of the gods, if we try to identify the originator of this phenomenon, then most possible of all is Mercurius, the messenger of the gods, the inventor of writing, of the first letters. When ever Creation wanted to tell us something, Mercurius, the Hermes of the Greeks, was the medium. The originator of these circles is a very high intelligence, of the world of the gods. And what do they want to tell us? I think we already have a presentiment, for the consequence is that people begin to change their consciousness, to think anew about the nature of our world, our place in it and our understanding of it. It changes our complete perception."

An age comes to an end, a circle closes. The gods return. The mystery of the crop circles teaches us that some sort of new age, a new step in man's evolution, is likely to happen. It makes its beginning, as Blake prophesied, all around England's prehistoric temples. Only, what is the warning sign that is written by invisible fingers into the corn? Have we again been 'weighed and found too light'? We only can surmise. For this reason it is more than important for every one of use to try to understand the language of the circles.

14. 1992: The First Contact?

If things had happened the way the British press made out, the summer of 1992 passed without any crop circles. Not a single headline was given to circles and pictograms, and those who omitted to visit 'circle country' were given to believe that the riddle had been solved when the two pensioners Doug & Dave made their 'confession'. Was it an order 'from the top' which imposed this curtain of silence over circle phenomena? Or was it simply journalists' laziness and disinterest, once they had filed away the theme once and for all after the sensational Doug & Dave reports of September 1991? The fact is: in 1992 there were dozens of circles and pictograms. I travelled back to southern England in July 1992, on the tracks of the circle-makers.

"Tell us where the circles are!", I was asked repeatedly by other German visitors in circle country, when we crossed paths at Stonehenge, Avebury or Marlborough. Circle-tourism had noticeably declined, but there was still a little going on. The circles and formations, lying in majestic beauty in the golden corn – ripened early thanks to the heat of this summer – often remained undiscovered, unnoticed, for quite a long time. What had happened in Wiltshire and Hampshire in the year after Doug & Dave?

A depression lay like a dense layer of fog over the realm of the circles and 'croppies', and it seemed as if this shroud only rarely let through that mysterious 'unknown energy' which, according to leading circle researchers, draws the mysterious figures down from above into the corn. Were this year's circles being made by those sprightly pensioners Doug Bower and Dave Chorley, who had officially retired from their alleged circle-making work after their big bombshell of September 1991? Or was Barbara Davies, a sensitive and secretary of CCCS, correct in saying that there was a resonance phenomenon at work, in which we receive back only as much as we put in? Had the annoyance of farmers affected the mood; had the scepticism of the public and the mutual mistrust of researchers caused the cereological crisis?

Mercifully, this was only one side of the saga that year. The other side saw refreshingly new approaches towards insight into the mystery, a number of spectacular formations and phenomena, and towards the end, two outlandish 130yds long special gifts – two gigantic snails, one in the valley of Alton Barnes, the other on a military prohibited area at Pewsey along the road to Everleigh. Snails! A symbol for the slowing down of energy and the snail's pace at which humankind's consciousness is adjusting to the new circumstances? A hint to take things slowly?

When we flew over the circle country in a two-engined Cessna, we made out around thirty circles and pictograms. We had been in England for two weeks by then, and had been waiting for something yet to happen. There were eight recognisable hoaxed circles, easily distinguishable from genuine pictograms by their irregularity, coarseness and simplistic styles. The centre for the hoaxing gangs this year was the otherwise circle-rich area around Silbury Hill, from which we could see a crooked ring, a bent circle and a clumsy long pictogram in the direction of Avebury. They lay conspicuously, as if somebody had put them there to frighten off circle fans. But there were also real circles around this magic hill, not very spectacular, but captivating in their simple beauty: near West Kennett there was an impressive group of three, a threefold formation on the grounds of Firs Farm at Beckhampton and a simpler formation in the shape of a fish (which turned out to be a popular theme that year, resembling the ICHTOS symbol used by the first Christians).

The Firs Farm trio was apparently new and 'unexamined' – the farmer Stephen Horton guarded his fields this year like a watchdog, so that neither circle researchers nor hoaxers could spend time on his land. He had given a very definite signal to all circle-makers on camera: *"Please look for another farm next year"*. It almost looked as if they had respected his wish, but later on circles still turned up: three perfectly round circles with the corn bent over half-way up the stalks, one of them exactly between the tram-lines: a hoax was impossible. No human could have crossed the corn unnoticed and without making tracks.

On the fields at Alton Barnes, among the gigantic snails, visible to everybody, there was another circle with a ring, and a simple circle with a beautiful swirl. A thin, crooked, trampled hoax and a fake pictogram nearby, made by a few Germans, paled in comparison. At Upton Scudamore near Warminster there were two antenna constructions, another pictogram at Lichfield resembled the symbol of Circle Phenomenon Research, and a formation at Petersfield, judging by its style, had something of a 1990 flavour to it. At Woodhenge – the wooden neighbouring counterpart to Stonehenge – two simple circles with extensions shone out in the evening sun, and below the ramparts of Old Sarum – a geomantic point connected with Stonehenge, and a hillfort since the Iron Age – a long-pictogram pointed exactly at the site's centre.

The most beautiful of the all pictograms of the otherwise unspectacular summer of 1992 was discovered at East Meon near Southampton: a 'dumb-bell', one side enclosed by a semi-circle, and below it a corn-glyph reminiscent of the Sumerian symbol for the gods, the *Din-Gir* ('the Righteous Ones with the fiery heaven ships'). Quite a good example, at least a perfect imitation of the real phenomenon: in the upper circle the corn at the centre was swirled clockwise, and around that it was counterclockwise.

It was a short season. Although the first events in oilseed rape and winter-barley fields had already arrived in April and May, the circles hesitated until July – then it really started, after having kept everyone guessing. When we left England on 4th August, 50% of all fields had been harvested. The heat which ripened the corn early reminded people about a Sumerologist of the University of London who had interpreted a 1990 pictogram as Sumerian cuneiform, saying: '*Build wells. A drought is coming.*'

While a number of pictograms resembled formations from 1989 and 1990, there were also individual – and energetic – reminders of the mega-circle year of 1991. One of the early pictograms comprised three circles in a triangle arrangement, with the same proportions as the 'Mother of all Pictograms' at Barbury Castle. And at Lockeridge, where the first large 'delphinogram' had appeared, came the overnight arrival of a whole group of small 'grapeshot' circles, as if the energy was still in the ground.

Such was the circle year of 1992. Smaller, less spectacular and mostly remote events: at one stage it cost me a pair of torn trousers to get to a pictogram! Because of remoteness, only serious researchers reached the circles – and they weren't disappointed. The circles were tidy and perfect as in previous years, and they showed a number of highly interesting anomalies. Their unique energy remained much longer as a result of the decline in visiting.

In Germany there were crop circles too. I received reports of three pictograms, and heard rumours of at least half a dozen others. But the press kept quiet about them or ridiculed them, so it was hard to get information early enough to make an investigation possible. At the beginning of June, there was an event at Ahaus on the German-Dutch border. During the night of 1st–2nd July there appeared a triangle pictogram, three circles linked with each other via lines, at Eschen on the road to Nendeln on the Swiss border. According to statements by the Swissair pilot Ferdinand Schmidt, who visited the formation shortly after its appearance, it was a real formation: the circles showed the characteristic whirl.

Two pictograms turned up during the night of 26th–27th July on a wheat field at Ettlingenweir, south of Karlsruhe: a 'double dumb-bell' 32yds (30m) in length, with a clockwise-turning circle of 11yds (10m) diameter and a counter-clockwise circle enclosed by a ring of 17yds (16m) width, plus a by a ringed circle, the ring 22yds (20m) wide, from which a three-armed 'key' emanated. A detail photograph of one of these circles sent

by my friend Dr Jens M Müller, convinced me of the genuineness of this formation: a wonderful swirl with a clean centre, which almost certainly excluded a hoax. Muller, author of the excellent book *Geomantie in Mitteleuropa* ('*Geomancy in Central Europe*', Aurum Verlag) indicated that the pictograms lay in the immediate vicinity of the ancient sun-oracle site of Malsch, a prehistoric sanctuary. Unfortunately, the Ettlingenweir formations were harvested only few days after their appearance, such that we couldn't take aerial photographs. They were hushed up by the national press. It almost seemed as if somebody wanted them to be kept quiet, to leave the public in the belief that the enigma had indeed been solved with Doug & Dave.

Three big events were intended to get to the riddle's roots in the summer of 1992. The first was the crop circle hoaxing competition at West Wycombe in Buckinghamshire, on 12th July, sponsored by the German popular science magazine *PM*, by *The Guardian* and *The Cereologist* . After *PM* publisher Peter Moosleitner had dismissed the crop circles in 1991, implying they were just a 'silly season' phenomenon, he now seemed to have had a Pauline conversion. In their July edition, *PM* brought out the first more or less objective report on the phenomenon, admitting that Doug & Dave had not put all salient questions to rest. So the magazine offered a reward of £3000 and invited hoaxer teams to meet and do their work, to prove once and for all that everything was either simply a deception, or not. Were the clever crop circle mafiosi really capable of imitating all those details which had long been declared as 'characteristics of genuine pictograms'? Here they would be able to prove the validity of hoaxes, and additionally win a nice lump of money.

But the result disappointed the hoax-theorists. Half a dozen hoaxer teams formed just as many pictograms over the hours of that night, under controlled circumstances, but none of the efforts were convincing: the edges were untidy, the circles asymmetrical, the corn was broken, damaged and visibly rolled down, and key swirl characteristics were missing. Moreover, pictogram 'corridors' were simple trample-tracks, and the 'semi-circles' irregular, bent and crooked. Not one of the hoaxed pictograms convinced us, and none was worth that £3000 handed over to the pathetic 'winning team'. Meanwhile, the true circle-makers had their own cosmic joke: only a few miles away from the hoax-olympiad, on the same night, they miraculously created a long pictogram of recognisable quality – and they generously abstained from their (well-deserved) fee.

'Operation Argus' was organised that year as an attempt to prove that many circles were not hoaxed. 'Argus' was an American-British co-operative project, sponsored by the US research group MUFON and the British CCCS, headed by the American physicist Michael Chorost and the British agricultural scientist Montague Keen, with the aim of examining circles closely with several physical and chemical measuring techniques, immediately after their appearance. They first of all had to check whether anomalies found in 1991 in spot checks were general characteristics of crop circles, or just chance results – genetic changes in the plants, traces of short-term exposure to heat, radioactive irregularities and short-lived radio-nuclides or isotopes otherwise unknown in nature. If they could be measured repeatedly, then not only would they constitute evidence against the hoax hypothesis, but also in future they could help us objectivise criteria in distinguishing real from fake crop circles. After all, radioactive isotopes can't be deposited by hoaxer teams trampling down the corn, *"no more than coal can be thus transformed into a diamond"*, as Keen put it.

For this reason, Chorost and his colleagues planned to undertake investigations in as many circles as possible in 1992. In cooperation with the University of Nevada and

with Canadian scientists, samples were collected, brought to a laboratory at High Wycombe and evaluated there. Additionally, measurements were carried out on the spot with highly sensitive geiger-counters and magnetometers. The initial result: radioactive and magnetic anomalies *could* really be measured, and unknown short-lived isotopes *were* found, though many results were inconclusive, and the project was not overwhelmingly successful, because unscrupulous hoaxers destroyed real formations, created fakes to mislead the Argus team and contaminated their results. Only this this much is certain: everything we know thus far hints at neither human nor natural causes of circle-formation, and thus more and more researchers favour – at least secretly, for nobody really wants to commit themselves in public – the 'extra-terrestrial hypothesis' that the crop circles are the work of non-terrestrial intelligences, who seem to draw their messages in the corn with a narrow, inches-wide scanner-beam from great altitude.

This hypothesis brought to life the third large project of the summer of 1992, called the 'CE5 Initiative'. CE5 stands for 'Close Encounter of the Fifth Kind'. In an 'encounter of the third kind' (CE3) one meets an ET face-to-face, the 'fourth kind' (CE4) is an abduction on board a UFO, and the 'fifth kind' constitutes a mutual intentional communication, a deliberate contact. This is aim of a group of scientists and others from USA – ex-astronaut Dr Brian O'Leary is involved – called CSETI, Centre for the Study of Extra-terrestrial Intelligence, headed by a hospital surgeon Dr Stephen M Greer.

CSETI was quite a new project, about two years old. At that time, Dr Greer, himself a 'victim' of a UFO abduction, had the inspiration that maybe abductions could have totally different purposes than commonly suspected, and that perhaps UFO pilots had not come into open contact with us because no one had ever asked them to do so. When UFOs show up, people tend to stand there in awe and stare into the sky. Only in very few cases has anybody tried to communicate with the lights in the sky – and they have always received an answer. Greer tried this on several occasions – for example, in front of thirty-three witnesses on 14th March 1992 in Gulf Breeze, Florida, the Mecca for US UFOlogists, where there are UFO sightings almost weekly.

In his UFO seminars Greer talked about his ideas on initiating CE5 contact, and now it was a matter of putting them into practice. Equipped with UFO sound samples – original sounds from a UFO sighting – and searchlights of the brightness of one million candles, the group tried meditations to create telepathic contact. At the same time, Greer drew triangles with light beams in the night sky. It took only thirty minutes for the first UFOs to appear. There were four of them, standing majestically in the sky, pulsing with cherry-red light. Greer grabbed the searchlights and flashed three times into the night sky. To the surprise of the whole group, the ship at the very front answered by blinking three times. If Greer flashed twice, the UFO answered with a double flash, and if he blinked five times, it answered fivefold. This 'light dialog' lasted some minutes, until the first UFO 'blinked out'. Then Dr Greer drew triangles in the sky again. Immediately the remaining three objects went into position and formed an equilateral triangle in the sky, before they finally disappeared. His efforts thus found success: in front of thirty-three witnesses, direct communication with the UFOs had been achieved, and five participants had recorded the event on video.

A further experiment was to take place in England. From 16th–28th July, Dr Greer was in circle country together with four close colleagues. Every night they took up position inside the circle/ring pictogram at Alton Priors, on the grounds of the Carson farm, whose owners proved to be cooperative. Greer was helped by a group around Colin Andrews, who observed events at some

distance – from Woodborough Hill – while he and his core group practised what he calls 'CE5-initiative protocol' – a combination of light, sound and consciousness techniques. For one week they waited in vain, apart from individual observations of unusual lights, and then things developed quickly.

On Friday 24th July, contact started. Exactly at 10.30pm, the sun just had set, and an object appeared in the sky, surrounded by a ring of coloured lights which rotated counter-clockwise. A little later, around half past midnight, Andrews and his 20-strong group observed a golden light sphere, in the direction of Warminster. While one member of the group (Reg Presley, once pop singer in the rock group 'The Troggs') filmed the object with his video camera, Andrews observed through his telescope how a military helicopter took up the chase. Presley flashed with his torch, and the UFO flashed back. When the helicopter approached the object disappeared, to turn up again suddenly in the north-west – whence it flew towards the hill on which the UFO-watchers stood. At the very moment Greer directed his searchlight at the UFO, it disappeared. Some of the witnesses report to have seen how it divided into two red lights, which shot away in different directions.

But this was only a start. Sunday 26th July 1992 was a very special day. Thousands of 'New Age' followers throughout the world celebrated it as the beginning of a new cycle in the Mayan calender, a completion of a five year period of 'reorganising the Earth', which had begun with the legendary 'Harmonic Convergence', the world meditation on 16th–17th August 1987. Two hundred people meditated on 26th July at dawn on Glastonbury Tor and around 1.20pm in the grounds of Glastonbury Abbey to greet the new cycle. But 26th July also was the second day of the annual crop circle symposium in Glastonbury. Here Stephen Greer met the British air and spacecraft engineer Roy Dutton.

Dutton has not only put forward a scientific model of how the crop circles form, but also he has investigated the timeframes in which UFO observations take place. After he had entered the data from hundreds of UFO sightings into his computer, Dutton realised that they turned up at certain distinct times which correspond to the hypothetical cycles of ET satellite orbits above the Earth. His thesis was that there are up to six parent ships stationed in regular earth orbit. They send out their reconnaissance ships when they cross a certain region, and in this way, UFO sightings can be predicted in time. A daring thesis. For the period around 26th July, Dutton gave two times as being favourable: 10.30–11.30pm and 0.30–1.30am. At that moment, Dutton didn't know that the UFO sightings of 24th July had happened at 10.30pm and 0.30am.

We interviewed Dutton on the afternoon of 26th July, and nobody had any warning of what was about to happen that memorable night. It was a rainy night. Around 10.30pm, four strange lights were observed above the horizon, minutes after the majority of Andrew's UFO research group had departed because of a cloudburst. Only Greer remained with his team, sheltering inside a car, with equipment packed away. A woman and a man from his group waited outside, and he was with another woman inside the car, where they practised the visualisation exercise of their 'CE5 initiative protocol'. Suddenly, Christian, one of the outside observers, ran to the car, knocking excitedly at the window: *"A space ship! A space ship is coming!"* Greer rushed out into the rain. It was exactly 00.25am. At only 400yds distance, in front of a wood, something hovered towards the west at tree-top height, some 30ft above the ground. Greer later described it as an 'illuminated Christmas tree': a 90ft wide conical object, enclosed on its underside by a ring of counter-clockwise rotating coloured lights, with about four golden lights on its top.

Between the ring of lights, which shone white, blue, red and golden, the four witnesses could clearly identify a metallic structure.

Quick-witted, Greer grabbed one of his lights from inside the car, and began to signal, blinking twice. The UFO, which in the meantime had hovered in the direction of a wood to the west, reacted with a twofold flash. Greer repeated, and the UFO signalled back. Then it released a small amber-coloured light-sphere which disappeared with a clearly audible buzzing noise towards north-west. Greer's body hair was standing on end with excitement – his dream had come true, close enough to grasp it. The whole sighting lasted ten minutes. Then the spacecraft glided slowly over a valley south-westwards and finally disappeared over the horizon.

The whole group was more than excited, and slowly they became aware that they had forgotten many of their planned routines. Since the cameras had been packed into the car because of the rain, there were no pictures. One hour later, at 1.20am, an amber-coloured light appeared south-south-east, about one mile distant. Again Greer flashed twice, and again the UFO answered with a twofold blinking. Greer repeated, and the UFO flashed back, before it disappeared behind a group of trees. A further phenomenon: between the two sightings, the needle on Greer's compass rotated a full 360°, counter-clockwise.

Dr Greer is convinced that this might have solved the mystery of the crop circles, and that he had communicated with their originators. *"The interim result which we are taking back home from this project is that definitively structured space ships are observed in connection with these circles, that a well-motivated and prepared group can interact with them and that the circle-makers are non-terrestrial visitors which produce these circles by using an advanced technology"*, he explained in an interview. *"We have collected very good data which supports this thesis and we will soon offer a model to explain how this happens."*

Dr Stephen Greer describes his close encounter on 26th–27th July 1992 to Colin Andrews.

This incident from 26th July wasn't the only one which convinced Greer's group of the circle-makers' intelligence. On the night of 24th July, the group visualised a symbol, three circles in a triangular arrangement, connected with each other by lines. In their minds they drew it in the sky, and with lines of light into the corn. Two days later they heard that on this very night the symbol in question had actually turned up in a corn field – northwest of Devizes, at the feet of the Iron Age hillfort of Oliver's Castle.

We stayed at the same hotel as Greer, and liked him and his work, and since he had asked us to search for the pictogram from the air, we set off, together with our friend Dr Chet B Snow, who we had met 'by chance' in the midst of circle country. We climbed Oliver's Castle, from which we had a perfect view over the area – and discovered the pictogram. Two hours later – after a climb down the hill, over hedges, ditches and rivulets to the field, and after finding the farmer to get permission – we stood in a tram-line in front of the formation. I was breathless with

joy: such perfection, such harmony, stem lying next to stem...

Nobody had entered the field before us. There was no doubt about its authenticity. We took the opportunity to sit down, to meditate. As subjective as 'inner experiences' are, I felt a very strong energy which, I was certain, didn't originate from this Earth. This was only a feeling, an intuition, and didn't need to mean anything. Yet, at least for me, it was certain that the circles are a real phenomenon, and that they are the work of a superior, non-terrestrial intelligence: messages of the gods, preparing us for a new age.

On the next day I heard that exactly where Stephen Greer had seen the first UFO, a new circle had turned up. On 29th July Dr Greer said goodbye, and we once again arranged a meeting with Colin Andrews in Alton Barnes, when we heard of a new event. The previous night, ten people had once again kept a night watch on Woodborough Hill and had observed UFOs.

Around 1.20am in the morning they saw two parallel lights which descended from the sky and hovered over a field. Smaller lights came out of the objects and seemed to circle them. Then the right-hand light intensified and became as bright as the sun, while a small red object emerged out of the left-hand UFO. The whole manoeuvre lasted for one hour, until a ground fog arose, making the lights disappear. A group of Australians documented the incident on video. And, lo behold, when we flew over the field later that day, we discovered two newly-formed circles at exactly the place above which the ten witnesses had seen the UFOs.

There thus exists no doubt about the nature of the 'circle-makers'. And it is probably only a question of time until we are able to come openly in contact with them. This however would really be the beginning of an utterly new era.

15. 1993: A NEW PHASE?

The birth of a phenomenon

The crop circle summer of 1993 was like none before – characterised by mistrust and depression. While the bad weather played its part and the circle-makers had also apparently lost a degree of enthusiasm, the main reason for these doldrums was the 'hoax-virus', also known as 'ADDS' (Acquired Doug & Dave Syndrome), which had clearly deeply damaged the mental immune system of many circle researchers. BBC film-maker John MacNish, producer of the documentary film *Crop Circle Communique* glorified the pensioner duo in the second episode of his series, and the German journalist Jürgen Krönig, until now an enthusiastic cereologist, was converted to scepticism.

Ken Brown, a businessman from Yorkshire, made himself manager and spokesman for Doug Bower (of the infamous 'Doug & Dave' team), whom he presented in an arrogantly-chaired live TV talk-show. There sat Doug Bower, the self-announced 'father of all crop circles', cynical and insolent – and he couldn't answer even the simplest questions from the audience. Sometime around 1978 (Ken Brown tried desperately to make it 1975, but Doug was honest enough to not go along with that) he and his boozing partner Dave had decided to make fun of UFO fans and to fake circles. Why? Because Doug had been interested in UFOs since his youth, and had been living in Australia when the 'UFO-nests' had appeared there and caused a media flap – he wanted to get his foot in the door.

The hoaxing was allegedly concealed from their wives – *"Women talk too much, as is well known"*, explained Doug – so the two intrepid companions went out into the fields only on Fridays. Apparently they had felt no frustration that it had taken a full 24 hoaxes, until 1981, before the first circle was discovered by Pat Delgado and reported to the press. What perseverance!

As 'proof' of these early faking activities Brown then proudly presented photos of circles from 1980 onwards. None of these photos showed how Doug & Dave had made these circles – also some of the photos had been shot by other people. But, however it may be... spurred on by the 'enormous success' of 1981, their efforts continued over subsequent years. Apparently Doug's wife got wind of her husband's nightly activities in 1984, since she noticed his car's high mileage (six years of dirty boots and trousers had seemingly passed her unnoticed), and Doug had confessed to her. He was thereafter permitted to go out more regularly, and their 'works' increased to twenty per year.

Then in 1987, they averred that they noticed that 'someone else' seemed to be faking circles too. The best example was the Charity Downs formation of 1988, which made cover picture of the Andrews-Delgado book *Circular Evidence*. An untidy double-ringer from 25th June 1988 unquestionably originated from D & D, and the perfect 'Celtic Cross' of 10th August was claimed to have been made by an imitator or 'copycat'. However, the 'imitation' was perfect, symmetrical and tidy, and it showed details which Colin Andrews was absolutely certain were not wrought by human hand. For in some places in the ring the corn wasn't brushed in the 'direction of flow' – which would be the case if it had been flattened with a garden roller or a metal rod – but towards the outside. Interestingly, D & D had claimed in 1991 that they had created that formation.

When Colin Andrews asked Doug Bower how he had made it, the latter admitted, subdued: *"That one didn't come from us"*. But how had he felt, when he, after claiming ten years' experience in faking circles, managed to make such a lousy, cheap double-ringer, while a plagiarist was able to make this perfect Celtic Cross? On the talk-show I asked Doug Bower whether this had been frustrating for him, or if it had caused him to consider giving up, to which he laconically answered that there had been other circles as well. *"Why then were the others so much better than yours?"*, I kept on. *"Do you find that they were better?"*, Doug replied. *"Well, your circles are crooked and bent, while those by the 'copycat' are perfect, graceful and beautiful. Isn't it at least possible that there is a real phenomenon which could have reacted to your attempts at communication?"* *"Everything is possible"*, was Doug Bower's evasive answer.

Doug and Dave *claimed* to have faked around two hundred crop circles, and in 1992 the 'crop circle spy' and disinformation expert Jim Schnabel claimed to have made around thirty, with his friend Robert Irwin doing *"at most twenty"*. Perhaps another fifty go on the account of the 'Wessex Sceptics' and the mysterious UBI group (active since 1991). This makes three hundred, at the outside. There were around 3,000 crop circles up to 1993 in England alone. Thus 10% were hoaxed, *at the most*. And the other 90%?

And if there truly is a real phenomenon, Bower at least thought it possible that he, who since childhood had been interested in UFOs, had been inspired from 'somewhere' to make the circles. *"I too have often asked myself where the ideas and the energy to get through all of this over the last fifteen years came from."*

"The Watchers explained to me in 1988 that they would also use humans to form the circles", Isabelle Kingston explained to me a few days later. She too had witnessed the Doug Bower PR spectacle. In any case, the message is more important than the medium. The fact is that even hoaxers don't really know what they draw there in the corn. Jim Schnabel claims to have created the 'Dharma-Wheel' or 'Charm-Bracelet' at Silbury Hill in August 1993, but believes that the symbols – interpreted by Michael Green as initiation paths of Indo-European and Celtic tradition – had sprung from his 'imagination'. He interpreted the 'horns of Cernunnos' on this complex formation as 'fractals'.

Doug and Dave claimed – without proof – to have drawn the 'Din-Gir' at East Meon – but where did the precise knowledge about the planet Nibiru come from, depicted correctly at East Meon with three moons and the remainder of the fourth moon which collided with Tiamat? Where did the depiction of the heavenly ship come from, with the Sumerian Din-Gir symbol? I asked Bower whether he had read any of the Zecharia Sitchin books. Answer: No. Had he ever gone into orientalism, Egyptology, or ancient symbolism? No. How then had he been able to use these symbols? *"Chance"*, said Bower. Or inspiration? *"Everything is possible"*.

From this the following can be concluded: even if a percentage of the crop circles – realistically, no more than 10% of all circles, and perhaps 30% in 1992–93 – were made by human hand, then the symbolism used still brings one to the conclusion that these are not just a meaningless 'public nuisance'. Rather, hoaxers must have unconsciously acted on behalf of true circle-makers and 'channelled' their symbolism through a form of 'automatic writing' in the corn – at least in some cases. Many hoaxes contain symbolism most hoaxers cannot know and which they are not aware of – according to Schnabel, if he speaks the truth. He only feels a drive, an inspiration, to draw something in the corn. His pictograms can be of proportional harmony and can go way beyond his artistic understanding and ability. Like a medium he has become a tool of a higher intelligence. However, let's not forget that the hoaxes are only a small percentage of the crop circles, and that the hoax thesis is intentionally over-stressed as part of a campaign of disinformation, with the aim of thoroughly discrediting the phenomenon and its researchers.

Use of any tricks is permissible for the 'debunkers'. This was demonstrated clearly in Jim Schnabel's revelatory book *Round in Circles*, an entertaining, though cynical read. He follows the best tradition of American boulevard journalism, of the 'unauthorised biographies' which sell copies of 'sensational revelations', unproven claims and fact-fiction collages. The book was less about the circles than about 'Physicists, Poltergeists, Tricksters and the secret history of the crop watchers' – as the subtitle puts it. Or, using the words of the US reviewer Peter Sorensen: *"In a disarmingly light style, Schnabel portrays everybody (with the exception of his hoaxing friends) as erroneous, quarrelsome and eccentric mystics – with the exception of the scientists, who are only erroneous, quarrelsome and eccentric. He digs deeply, to bring to light everyone's dirty washing, so that the public may see it and be delighted by the philosophical and legal disputes between researchers. One of his aims obviously seems to be to widen the gulf between different 'factions' by rubbing salt into old wounds and by opening a few new wounds as a precaution"*. Much was twisted or simply invented, a common disinformation practice, mixing broad revelations of real information with completely incorrect, misleading statements and bare lies. Thereby, people's ideas are controlled.

Only after 236 pages of circle-gossip and tittle-tattle, anecdotes and dirty washing does Schnabel 'let the cat out of the bag' and tell us why he curses circle-researchers with the eagerness of a Zealot. The circles, for him, are an expression of a satanic conspiracy, behind which are the 'friends of Hecate', practising black magic, who are setting out to bring about *"the preparation for the arrival of the Anti-Christ"*. Moreover, the Centre for Crop Circle Studies (CCCS), with physics professors, agricultural scientists, systems analysts and top civil servants for members, is *"clearly a religious organisation with definite heathen overtones…"* and *"…apparently one of the front organisations"* of the black magic lodge of the 'Friends of Hecate'. Yes, even a scientific symbol such as the Mandelbrot represents not chaos theory, but Crowleyan chaos magic – all of this with the aim *"…of undermining the orthodox religions"*. All that he left out was a call for a new Inquisition.

Of course he takes all this back in his book's epilogue, and rehabilitates CCCS members and croppies as 'obliging fools' – possibly on the advice of his publisher's lawyer – but the seeds of mistrust are already sown. The epilogue offers yet another 'new age conspiracy theory'. It isn't the Hecate witches this time, but a group of young UFO enthusiasts who call themselves UBI – United Bureau of Investigation: They believe *"that the circles were a sign, a sign of the end. The more an individual could do to hasten this end – by producing chaos, disorder, cosmological confusion, signs upon the earth – the more he would earn his place among the chosen"*, who would be evacuated by extra-terrestrials to observe the Apocalypse from a safe cosmic seat. Apparently this thought fascinated Schnabel so much that he himself began to fake crop circles – allegedly virtually everything which appeared in 1992. Of course he doesn't have any proof for this, apart from the fact that he took second place at the hoaxing competition at West Wycombe in July 1992. (Incidentally, UBI also took part and came a pitiful sixth place!).

Schnabel's 'revelations' poisoned the atmosphere in circle country – so much so that many farmers asked the police for help, should new circles appear on their land. For the first time, farmers got the police to get 'croppies' out of newly-formed pictograms, while others mowed the formations before they could be examined, and one of them even threatened to run over crop circle researchers with his combine harvester. The pattern which appeared on his field – opposite Silbury Hill – on 13th August, was not lost: only five days later, on 18th August, the same pictogram turned up on a field at East Kennett.

But the 'croppies' themselves also regarded each other more mistrustfully, almost suspiciously, and it seemed as if those 'active measures' against the phenomenon, which Schnabel had announced in August 1992, had been quite successful. After the eventual failure of the unsophisticated Doug & Dave campaign, Schnabel admitted he not only disturbed the scientific Project Argus so that it could not achieve definite results – which would have disproven much of the hoax hypothesis – but also he significantly determined the character of the circle debate in the summer 1993, stirred up mistrust, and deprived the phenomenon of its virginity – and hence its beauty.

But does the hoax hypothesis solve the riddle around the crop circles? By no means! For it does not explain many phenomena observed in real crop circles:

- UFO appearances preceding the arrival of circles;
- genetic and molecular changes in the wheat;
- radioactive anomalies;
- traces of rapid heating from within, cracks in the cell walls inside the plants;
- the 'flow' of the real circles (up to now unhoaxed), the 'bent not broken' stems;
- electromagnetic noises, disturbances in recording machines, and repeated rapid discharges of batteries and accumulators inside circles;
- the white spheres observed and filmed inside or near to real pictograms.

Thus we again return to the *real* phenomenon. For even if 30% of the crop circles closely inspected in 1993 are clear and uninspired hoaxes – they differ qualitatively from the inspired genuine circles – a large number of 1993 pictograms show anomalies which are characteristic of the 'actual phenomenon'. Even if we grew cautious in 1993, there were still plenty of valuable instances of genuine circles. The Cherhill pictogram, which turned up during the night of 31st July below the White Horse at Calne, 120 yards long, was approved with 'a high degree of probability of authenticity'. This I demonstrated when my geiger-counter measured radioactivity of up to 0.38 microsievert/hour in the largest circle, while all values in the surrounding corn field were between 0.08 and 0.13Sv/h. This means a value roughly 300% above normal.

I spoke with two members of the London UFO study group who, on the night in question, had filmed a light sphere from the 315ft (100m) high Adams Grave hill. The sphere descended for some seconds in a north-westerly direction out of the sky – exactly in the direction of Cherhill. A farm worker from Cherhill claims to have seen a light object hovering above a field around the same time – at about 1.20am. Radioactive anomalies were also measured in another formation, the 'Spermium' – which seems to symbolise the 'genetic programme' of the extraterrestrials – which appeared above the Avebury avenue and showed values in the circle centre of only 60% of the average, while at the circle's edge it was 180% above the average.

There were also observations of how genuine crop circles are formed. Diverse witnesses – among them Colette Dowell, a geometry buff, and the Canadian Chad Deetken – experienced before their very eyes the interweaving of standing stems, as if directed by an invisible force, in the centre of the long pictogram at East Kennett.

The real circle-makers, as usual, operated mainly in Wiltshire, even if they did pull back somewhat and shift their field of operation – in the face of so much human misunderstanding and offensive behaviour by hoaxers, who had hijacked the public's attention and made a laughing-stock of the whole phenomenon. Highly interesting pictograms turned up also in Sussex, Kent and Nottinghamshire. The most beautiful of them was a mandala in form of a ten-petalled lotus, with a pentagram inside a pentagon in the centre, enclosed by three rings. It was also the last pictogram, appearing on 30th August at Bythorn, Northamptonshire, maintaining a by now established tradition of ending the season with a masterpiece.

Germany had its share of crop circles too. A pictogram 66yds (60m) long and 44yds (40m) wide appeared during the night of 4th July on the 'Drudacker', near Geisslingen in Baden Württemburg. Two rings were connected, one with a circle at the centre and an extension in the form of a '4' (representing Mars, the fourth planet?), the second resembling a 'peace-sign' with an 'F' or 'neteru' hieroglyph. While the farmer, Peter Hartmann, reckoned it was

a childish prank, at least at the beginning, the local newspaper *Sudkurier* pointed out that at the time of its discovery by a private pilot there was no beaten path leading to the pictogram. Additionally, the 'Drudacker' (Druid-field) was, up to the last century, regarded as a haunted area. It was said that the prehistoric Druids had got involved in some 'ghostly subversive intrigues', and had bewitched the whole region. Archaeological findings indicated that there had been a neolithic sacrificial place here, and in the immediate vicinity of the pictogram the remains of a levelled stone circle or burial mound are located.

On the same night as the Geisslingen pictogram appeared, the second German formation of the year, a 14yds (13m) wide ring and a 8.2yds (7.5m) wide circle at Otterfing in Oberbayern (Bavaria) appeared. A further

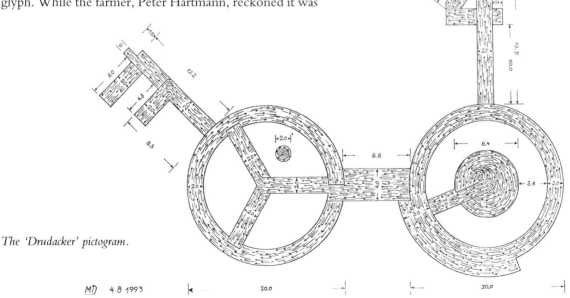

The 'Drudacker' pictogram.

pictogram was discovered in the beginning of July near the A1 Bremen-Cologne autobahn, then a plain, 24yds (22m) wide ring at Arnsberg-Herdingen, Westphalia, a fifth at Munster in Westphalia, and a sixth one near Pulheim in the Eifel. A 26yds (24m) long 'dumb-bell' – one of the circles enclosed by a simple ring, of great precision – was reported 30 miles (50km) away from the Externsteine, a Stone Age sanctuary, Germany's Stonehenge. Finally, in the middle of July came the most impressive German pictogram, at Halle, at the Saale in Saxony-Anhalt, not far from Bitterfeld. It attracted hundreds of visitors. It was an 'appleman' or Mandelbrot fractal, similar to but simpler than the 1991 Mandelbrot near Cambridge – the small outside circles were missing – though it was still 50yds (45m) long. Agricultural engineer Erhard Grass examined three circles and was convinced that *"Something like this can only have been left behind by a UFO: exact geometrical shapes, no stem broken, no human traces"*. The same applied to the last German circle, surrounded by a wide ring: it appeared in the middle of August near Halle – not in corn, but in a sunflower field.

In Wiltshire, by comparison, in the neighbourhood of the sacred sites of Stonehenge and Avebury, it seemed that the phenomenon's next phase was being prepared. A dozen videos of UFOs were made in summer 1993 in Wiltshire, the best of them – shot on 30th July by Foeke Kootje and Connie de Bruyn from Holland at Alton Priors – shows four lights – the one in the middle flashing – and remarkably resembles the triangular UFO filmed in 1990 over Belgium. *"It flew totally noiselessly"*, the couple told me. Warminster experienced its own 'revival'. Since late 1992, mysterious light objects were regularly turning up above the mysterious prehistoric Cley Hill – reason enough for a local UFO enthusiast, Ken Rogers, to take an initiative and found the 'Warminster Centre for UFO Studies', to organise regular night-watches on the hills around Warminster.

Dr Steven Greer, with his CSETI team, was also active for ten days in the area around Alton Barnes, this time less successfully than in 1992. Nevertheless his group reported a number of spectacular UFO observations, and once, when the cassette tape playing their sound signals ended (Colin Andrews' recording of trilling, recorded inside a crop circle), the sound continued, emanating from an invisible separate source. But the centre of UFO activities this year was the harbour city of Bristol, located only half an hour west of circle country.

The wave began on 30th March 1993 when, according to the *Western Daily Press*, forty people observed a 'large catamaran-shaped object' over Bristol. According to witnesses the UFO was about 185yds (170m) wide and 75yds (70m) long, gliding noiselessly in the sky and sending out light rays from time to time. Half a dozen policemen witnessed it, chasing the object 'from a wide area'. The UFOs came again on the night of the 27th–28th June 1993. Around 1.15am inhabitants of the Pewsey Road in Bristol's suburb of Hartcliffe observed the approach of a cigar-shaped flying object in the eastern sky. *"It all began with a number of light flashes, which came closer and closer"*, explained one of the witnesses, Paul Hudson, *"and finally, around 3.00am a large object flew towards us, cigar-shaped, with a large, white-shining light in the middle and a small light at each of the two ends. A whole four hours the UFO stood in the sky, before it flew away at great speed."* Hudson first raised the alarm in the neighbourhood, then contacted the police and finally the press. Around twenty witnesses, among them two policemen and three journalists, observed the mysterious UFO, while Hudson's brother-in-law Andrew MacDonald filmed the event.

Two days later the UFOs returned, this time at 0.30am. *"I saw five lights above Hartcliffe"*, reported *Evening Post* reporter Robin Edwards on the next day, *"two of them flickered red and green and seemed to hover over the roofs. Three further ones were larger and shot at unbelievable speed right across the sky. Then they stopped – and seemed to hover. They all appeared out of nowhere and disappeared equally mysteriously."* Another journalist, Michael Bimpson from the *Western Daily Press*, described his sighting as follows: *"Through my telescope I recognised an elongated object, blue and orange in colour, shimmering in appearance. It definitively wasn't a star. Around 1.55am I saw – with the naked eye – a white object, which shot across the sky – too fast to catch it with my telescope."*

In both newspapers the local UFO researcher Lee Winterson asked further witnesses to contact him – and received 160 telephone calls. Excited Bristoleans reported more and more frequent sightings in July, of dark, cigar-shaped objects with orange lights at both ends – and finally Lee himself was in the position to observe such an object. Also the police from Bristol looked into the UFO reports. Police spokesman Ian Gibson: *"The tower of Bristol Airport wasn't able to locate anything unusual on radar in the night in question. There thus seems to exist no terrestrial explanation for what people from the south of the city of Bristol have observed."* When I rang Gibson, he confirmed the correctness of this quote. Also the Ministry of Defence was interested in the incidents and sent an official letter to a witness quoted in the press asking for her report and a copy of her video.

Crop circles turned up at the end of June in the area of Dundry, south of Bristol, and at Bath, east of Bristol – exactly in the direction in which the UFOs were seen. Coincidence? A similar interrelation between UFO observations and new crop circles was observed in June-August 1993 in West Sussex, in the area around Brighton, and in Kent. A coincidence? *"In our databanks we have over 200 reports of UFO observations in immediate connection with crop circles"*, Colin Andrews explained in an interview. *"Seventy entries describe the making of a crop circle by a luminous sphere, a beam of light, a cylinder, a fog or a 'force'".* But what convinced him most of the UFO connection was the reaction of an elder and prophecy-keeper of the Hopi Indians, when Colin showed him photos of a 1992 formation of a crescent inside a ring. *"This symbol announces the return of the Star People"*, stammered the deeply touched old Indian. *"We have known this symbol for millennia – it is part of our prophecy. They have therefore returned…"*

Since the number of crop formations no longer grows in an 'exponential curve' (Andrews), as it did up to 1991, but instead UFO observations are on the increase, many are convinced that the phenomenon is now entering its 'second phase': this phase implies direct encounters with the circle-makers, behind which hides a superior, non-terrestrial intelligence…

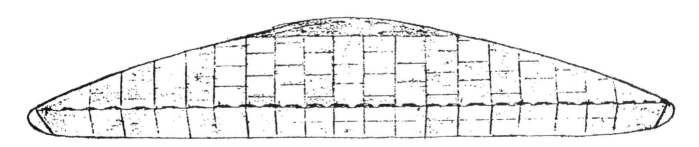

This is how eye-witnesses drew the UFOs from Bristol. (Drawing Lee Winterson)

16. 1994: The Resurrection of Circles

People who omitted to take the time to visit Wiltshire during the long and lovely summer of 1994 will mostly have gained the impression that the age of the circles indeed was over. Not a single bit of information concerning crop events reached the rest of the planet, and many people were obliged to believe that the circle-makers, like Doug and Dave, had retired one year earlier. This impression was unquestionably wrong! Silenced by local, national and international media and ignored by the world public, the circles continued to appear in 1994.

More than this, they were larger, more impressive and more complicated than in any preceding year, continuing the 'exponential curve' (to use Colin Andrews' expression) of the crop-circle super-summer of 1991. But this time the biggest mystery was that they were ignored. Too great was the insecurity of many leading researchers, many of them losing their enthusiasm – since they learned there were hoaxed circles appearing during July in circle-country – and being overwhelmed by what they saw. Money was also a problem for many of them, such that only a few went up regularly by plane to monitor the Wiltshire farmlands.

Thanks to this, many formations remained undiscovered for days, thus allowing them to be meticulously investigated in an undamaged state. Indeed, everyone who held out and stayed faithful to the circles was rewarded. *"The circles of 1994 are larger, more beautiful and more impressive than ever before"*, John Michell, former publisher of *The Cereologist* confirmed. *"It seems as if they want to show us that they got through the last ten years without any damage."*

Wiltshire, year three after Doug and Dave. *"And yet they swirl"* seemed to be the catch-phrase of the hour. With every day it became harder for the organised hoaxer gangs around the dubious Adrian Dexter and the sinister Robert Irving to keep up with the constantly rising standards of the real phenomenon. Out of the original twenty or so theories of their origin, from the crying of Mother Earth to mating hedgehogs, from intelligent plasma vortices or Star Wars experiments to creative fairies, only two alternatives remained: aliens or hoaxers. Every new formation challenged us to decide in favour of one of the two alternatives.

Since the hoaxers had been training themselves well, three men were able to produce a beautiful flower in just four hours, in bright daylight, before TV cameras. But what about the 600ft long Scorpion which appeared on July 15th, directly visible from the A361 above Devizes, on a field belonging to an unfriendly farmer who now was threatening visitors with guns and dogs? Or the 2,500ft long giant pictogram with a 475ft wide ring which appeared north-east of Swindon?

"We have to admit that hoaxing has become a part of the phenomenon", Colin Andrews acknowledged at the

'Glastonbury Symposium on Crop Formations and Signs of our Time', *"and I have inside information from a young man who infiltrated one of the hoaxing groups that they receive great amounts of money for what they are doing…"*. Indeed, they contaminate the real phenomenon, discouraging researchers and destroying the results of scientific investigations – comparable to an archaeological excavation in which hoaxers bury modern-day ceramics secretly by night. But just as a professional archaeologist is able to distinguish between an original and a copy which every layman might believe to be antique and genuine, so there are unfakable characteristics which we again discovered in the 1994 pictograms. One example is radioactive anomalies, found in the 'Avebury Avenue Maze', the 'West Overton Infinity-symbol' and the

'Wilsford Scorpion', in which it was either the case that the radiation at the edge of the circles was extremely low (up to 50% below average) and remarkably high at the centre (up to 150% above normal) or vice versa (higher at the edge and lower at the centre). Also there were burn-marks showing evidence of heat – as at the 'Wilsford Scorpion' – and deformation of seeds, a widening of cellular knots in the stalks and bending and twisting of stalks.

Still, it is indisputable that hoaxing gangs were responsible for around 30% of the crop formations of 1994. They gained additional publicity through *Crop Circle Apocalypse*, a badly-edited book by the BBC co-worker John McNish, who had made the remarkable video film *Crop Circle Communique* when it was still fashionable to see Doug and Dave as agents of a disinformation campaign. With his follow-up video *Crop Circles: Case Closed*, McNish proved to be a professional bandwagon-jumper who ignored nearly everything he documented two years before, just because he had more recently convinced himself that Doug and Dave indeed were able to successfully trample down a circle in a cornfield. Then McNish met

up with the dubious Jim Schnabel, who had earlier disclosed himself in a telephone conversation with researcher Armen Victorian (alias 'Dr Ntumba') as someone *"taking active measures… with support from the highest levels… so that people will no longer take notice of it…"*. McNish not only joined Schnabel when the latter was out hoaxing, but also he helped him launch red-orange and green helium balloons with fluorescent tubes to mislead people out looking for UFOs.

These clandestine activities neither explain the Bristol wave of sightings in 1993 nor the triangular UFO filmed by a Dutch couple in the same year, nor the luminous balls filmed by two German students and Steve Alexander in Wiltshire in broad daylight. Indeed, even Schnabel himself – quoted in John McNish's video – admitted *"I actually believe there is a genuine phenomenon that is beneath all the hoaxing. I do not see what the nature of it is. Unfortunately it's probably too rare for people to notice if they just go out in the countryside waiting for something to happen"*. And Doug Bower revealed: *"Why we did it I cannot explain"*, to which Dave Chorley added: *"It may sound crazy"*, but sometimes he had the impression *"…we were being told to go out and do them"*. Does this confirm my suspicion that some of the hoaxing might actually be a form of 'automatic writing' or 'channelling' from a higher intelligence? The interesting symbolism of even some of the hoaxes makes this assumption at least plausible. Might it be that Doug and Dave triggered and 'vectored in' the real phenomenon, establishing communication?

But isn't the role of hoaxers exaggerated? Doug and Dave finally retired in 1992, Schnabel spent most of the summer of 1994 in USA, Irving, who married a German woman, doesn't go to circle-country very often nowadays, and if Dexter is responsible for the more than 220 pictograms of 1994 then there is a lot of eating of hats to be done! *"Isn't it simpler to **claim** that you made a pictogram than to go out and create it on a cold rainy night?"*, Chet

Deetken, the Canadian cereologist, said at the Glastonbury Symposium. *"60% of all pictograms appeared on rainy nights, and yet we found no footprints in the mud. In spite of dozens of crop-watches in circle-country no hoaxer was ever caught 'in the act'. We call them 'jolly hoaxers', and some even call them 'landscape artists'. But that's not what they are. They are criminals. They enter farmland illegally, destroying crops and many days' work to cheat and deceive hundreds and thousands of honourable people. I honour the British tolerance, and maybe as a 'colonial' I might sound quite rude, but I think we shouldn't allow them to walk into our pubs, grinning proudly and cynically, knowing that everyone hates them and enjoying the attention. They are sociopaths, criminals, frauds and cynics, suffering from an attention disorder syndrome. And we should take serious measures to stop them!"* The audience applauded.

"There are spies everywhere, working for every kind of institution, and there are also freelance spies, merging with madmen and mischief-makers", wrote John Michell in the Summer 1994 issue of *The Cereologist*. *"All these types have been attracted to the crop circles, and their involvement in the subject has confused and repelled many honest and innocent researchers. This has a familiar pattern, repeated throughout the history of psychic research. We are left with a continuing phenomenon, just as mysterious now as in the beginning. Nothing has changed except ourselves, and we have been constantly changing and reacting."* So let's get to the facts!

The beautiful and, for England, dry circle summer was actually foreshadowed in early March when two rings appeared in winter barley at the Avebury Avenue and opposite Silbury Hill. The season itself started on the night of April 23rd, when a 'Celtic Cross' appeared in a rape field near the Avebury Sanctuary beside the A4 highway. Two nights later it was followed by a crescent in the same field, and two nights later still, by a circle with a corridor. One month and eleven pictograms later came the first sensation: on May 22nd the first 'Scorpion' was discovered in a barley field opposite Silbury Hill, with a Celtic Cross with a crescent on one side, and eight circles plus a small crescent on the other.

Shortly before this pictogram was reported to him on the phone, Colin Andrews was visited by an Aztec shaman from Mexico who described a vision of his to him: he had dreamt of 'the site of the last ceremonial dance' and saw a symbol which he drew – a Celtic Cross, a crescent on one side and eight circles on the other. Then Andrews discovered a similar symbol on Palaeolithic petroglyphs, illustrating the lunar cycle. Indeed, the 'Scorpion' had appeared three nights after the previous half moon and ten nights after the May full moon. According to the farmer his dog barked between 4am and 6am. On 28th May a visitor observed small white lights gliding along the long axis of the pictogram.

Sixty-six pictograms appeared before July 1st, when the phenomenon performed its next 'quantum jump'. At the Avebury Avenue, exactly where a ring had appeared four months earlier, a pattern in the form of a galaxy was formed, with groups of stalks standing upright inside it, like stars, planets and a moon. After talking to Adrian Dexter – who did not hoax this pictogram – the farmer destroyed the inside of this formation with his harvester. This sad example of anti-circle vandalism shone brightly in the summer sunshine until the middle of August, drawing much attention.

One week and twelve pictograms later the next mystery, a 150ft long Bee, appeared on a field at Barbury Castle at the same site as the famous 1991 Tetrahedron. In the same night a triangular UFO was seen. Eight days and twenty-five pictograms later, on 15th July, came the 'night of the scorpions': three giant pictograms at Wilsford (480ft, a ring, twelve circles and a small crescent), at Devizes (600ft, a crescent, two circles, a circle with ring, a crescent, then eleven circles, a crescent and three small circles) and at Cholsey in Oxfordshire (480ft long, a ring, crescent and eight circles). The gigantic work of a hoaxing team – which incidentally would need at least two hours just driving from one site to another? Or the 'real phenomenon'?

Another week and fifteen pictograms later there came a giant 'Eye' at the Alton Barnes East Field, right where the spectacular long pictogram of 1990 had appeared, and two nights later came another 'Galaxy' – replacing the one destroyed at Avebury Avenue – at the foot of Golden Ball Hill, where UFOs are frequently seen. Next night, 23rd–24th July, six pictograms appeared around Wiltshire, and, after a sighting of 'luminous balls' by an American visitor at the Avebury Avenue, there appeared at that location a giant maze, 420ft long and 100ft wide, including a Hopi sun symbol and other Hopi petroglyphs.

On July 27th, a night when five pictograms appeared, a giant 150ft wide 'Triple Crescent' formed at the foot of Oliver's Castle near Devizes, where a three-circle pattern had appeared in 1992 in answer to Dr Steven Greer's 'CE5 initiative'. For John Michell this triple crescent was a 'symbol for the restoration of kingship' – the crescent being an attribute of the king in Celtic times – and for Julia Zimmermann from Germany it was a 'reminder of the significance of Islam in our times'. One day later an 'infinity symbol' – an eight within a ring – formed near West Overton by the A4 between Marlborough and Silbury Hill. On August 1st I discovered an alignment of seven circles and three satellites – immaculately placed between tram-lines – and another circle inside a triple crescent at Berwick Bassett north of Avebury. On August 5th a 240ft wide 'Rosetta' was found near Froxfield, followed by a circle surrounded by a ring, with seven small rings of standing crop inside the opposite field. After learning about a strange 'web' near Avebury, I finally left England on 11th August, when 75% of the cornfields had already been harvested.

When I arrived home at Düsseldorf I found reports from all over the world on my desk. In USA three pic-tograms received publicity, two of them near Portland, Oregon. In the Netherlands my colleague Hermann Heffe investigated fifteen formations. In one of them, a woman found a lot of extremely light metallic fragments, some of them with dozens of little holes in them, which are under scientific analysis as I write these words. According to *The Cereologist* of Winter 93/94, pictograms are appearing regularly around Krasnoyarsk in Siberia.

My Czech publisher Eva Tothova informed me about the first Czech crop circles discovered in early August 1994, near the village of Kolinec, not far from the city of Klatovy. The first one, 70ft in diameter and formed like a Celtic Cross, appeared on 30th July after people had observed a red ball of light. It was followed five days later by a smaller Celtic Cross, and by the middle of August there came an 'infinity symbol'. Researchers measured an increase of radioactivity in the formation, while measurements outside it were normal. *"It is absolutely regular, and the crop is combed in a counter-clockwise direction"*, Mr Tothova wrote. *"The stalks are bent but not broken. The formations appeared near to an ancient burial ground."* Indeed, the formations caused tremendous interest in the Czech media.

In Germany at least two pictograms were found in Westphalia and Lower Saxony. The most interesting one was reported by the *Neue Westfalische Zeitung* of July 19th 1994. It was found in Hullhorst-Huchzen near Bröderhausen, and it had the form of a circle with two satellites and two 'F' appendages as well as a crescent – a formation 135ft in diameter and *"of great mathematical precision"*, according to the newspaper. At the same location UFOs were seen... which brings us back to where we started...

The summer of 1994 again brought some spectacular UFO incidents around Avebury and Silbury Hill and the surrounds in Wiltshire. The American CSETI (Center for the Study of Extraterrestrial Intelligence) performed its CE5 project in the area around Marlborough, though without Dr Greer this time. At two nighttime UFO watches near Alton Barnes and West Kennett Long Barrow opposite Silbury Hill strange reddish lights were observed, hovering 5–10° above the horizon, moving horizontally, coming closer and fading again, reacting to blinking signals – and they were definitely no helium balloons!

After several group meditations on and around Silbury Hill, Avebury and Windmill Hill some young participants stayed atop Silbury Hill together with a group of pagan enthusiasts. When a mist arose around 1.30am the UFO watchers left their stations, just three staying behind. At 2.00am the mist lay swathing Silbury Hill, and the pagans fell asleep. Suddenly the three young UFO watchers observed a giant, luminous, colourful triangular object appear in the sky. It hovered above the hill and, both fascinated and paralysed, they observed how three little beings glided out of the UFO on beams of light down to a meadow next to Silbury Hill, where the fog lifted. The visiting beings seemed to trace a network of light on the ground with luminous sticks. When a car passed on the nearby A4 they ducked behind a hedge and remained unseen by the driver. Minutes later the beings glided back in their spaceship. When the UFO shot away, the dense mist around the hill dissolved slowly. A contact? Indeed it was an experience which changed the lives of the three, shaking them deeply.

A similar reaction was shown by two young Germans who held a nocturnal UFO watch on August 4th at the 'Galaxy' pictogram at the foot of Golden Ball Hill. Three times, a bluish luminous object appeared directly above them which finally was also seen by a young German couple who found their friends shaken and trembling.

One of the most spectacular cases indicating contact of the fourth kind (CE4) – a possible alien abduction – was described to me by Colin Andrews. A scientist working for the British government was driving along the Avebury Avenue – accompanied by his wife and mother-in-law – when he lost track of time. When he looked at his car clock again it was forty minutes later and he was still driving just a little distance further along the same road. Next morning, when he awoke, his nose was bleeding. Then he dreamt of lying naked on an operating table. His wife and mother-in-law had similar memories from sleep, confirming even specific details. His wife remembered how her mother was still wearing her chain, dreaming of her lying on the operating table naked except for this chain.

Colin himself was a witness to a strange incident. Together with some friends he set up a crop-watch station in a caravan on Adam's Grave on July 27th, high above the East Field at Alton Barnes, where five formations had already appeared. It was about 5pm, when they heard the roaring of two army helicopters, flying directly towards the hill. When they headed directly towards the station, Andrews and his friends had an eerie feeling. *"One of us grabbed his video camera and filmed how one of the helicopters was roaring about us in a kind of low-level attack, such that it nearly collided with the tumulus on top of the hill. Obviously it wanted to chase us away. The second helicopter, full of recording equipment, hovered a few feet in front of us, and we could see one of its occupants filming us. Minutes later they turned around, heading towards the pictograms, where one researcher was taking overhead pole-shots with his camera. He had to duck. Then the second helicopter shot toward a neighbouring field, seeming to have traced something, which we now saw and took film of: a luminous ball, about one foot in diameter, gliding through the cornfield. The helicopter went into a tilting position, seeming to be filming the object. before the object shot away. Then the helicopters turned around, leaving the area. We could now relax."*

Do these reports indicate a connection between crop formations and the UFO phenomenon? Are they 'their' method – or one of 'their' methods – to communicate with us, to prepare us for their return, cosmic messages like the 'menetekel' written by a fiery finger on the palace wall of the Babylonian king Balthazar? Do they belong to the 'signs in heaven and on earth' predicted in the Bible, announcing the return of the gods and the beginning of a new age?

In the Summer 1994 issue of *The Cereologist* the two Berlin physicians Joachim Koch and Hans-Jürgen Kybord reported their attempts to establish communication with the 'circle-makers' in summer 1991. Indeed, the two Germans interpreted many important pictograms as coded star maps of an extraterrestrial civilisation which *"highly emphasised the principle of 'strong connection' between two suns, planetary systems or beings: yes, contact has been achieved"*.

Whether or not we agree with their interpretation, I can resonate with their conclusion: *"When we are talking about communication with the phenomenon, we must stress that we don't think the phenomenon needs the circles to communicate with humans. 'They' surely could use other tools than circles in wheat fields if it were their only intention to talk with us. The circles are here to help us in a gentle way to reorientate ourselves with our natural environment on this planet and in space, and to open our eyes so that we can look around and see who and where we are. They are a challenge to our spirit, a reminder that there is a larger reality than the one we are accustomed to living in. And if we can accept this, we help the phenomenon to reach us. This is the way we can all bring things back into balance, to help evolve planet Earth towards a better future"*. There is nothing I need to add to this enlightening statement.

BIBLIOGRAPHY

Argüelles, Jose: *Das große Mandala-Buch*, Freiburg 1974.
Andrews, Delgado/Colin, Pat: *Circular Evidence*, London 1989.
   . . . : *The Latest Evidence*, London 1990.
Ashe, Geoffrey: *The Quest for Arthur's Britain*, London 1988.

Bartholomew, Alick (ed.): *Crop Circles – Harbingers of World Change*, Bath 1991.
Bauer, W./Dümotz, I./Golowin, S.: *Lexikon der Symbole*, Wiesbaden 1980.
Bord, Janet & Colin: *Mysterious Britain*, London 1974.
Buttlar, Johannes von: *Supernova*, München 1988.
   . . . : *Zeitriß*, München 1989.
   . . . : *Drachenwege*, München 1990.
   . . . : *Adams Planet*, München 1991.
   . . . : *Gottes Würfel*, München 1992.

Canada, Steve: *Crop Circle Language*, Morro Bay/CA 1991.
Chapman, Robert: UFO – *Flying Saucers over Britain?* London 1969.
Chorost, Michael: *The Summer 1991 Crop Circles: The Data Emerges*, Fund for UFO Research Publication, Washington D.C. 1991.
Dames, Michael: *The Silbury Treasure*, London 1976.
Däniken, Erich von: *Der Götterschock*, München 1992.
Delgado, Pat: *Crop Circles – Conclusive Evidence?* London 1992.
Delgado, Andrews/Pat, Colin: *Circular Evidence*, London 1989.
   . . . : *The Latest Evidence*, London 1990.
Devereux, Paul: *Earth Light Revelation*, London 1989.
Durrant, Henry: *Les dossiers des O.V.N.I.* Paris 1973.

Edwards, Frank: *Fliegende Untertassen – eine Realität,* Wiesbaden 1967.

Fowler, Raymond E.: *The Watchers*, New York 1990

Good, Timothy (ed): *The UFO Report 1990*, London 1989.
   . . . (ed.): *The UFO Report 1991*, London 1990.
   . . . (ed.): *The UFO Report 1992*, London 1991.
   . . . *(ed.): Abore Top Secret*, London 1990.

Hamkens, Frerk-Haya: *Das nordische Jahr und seine Sinnbilder,* Berlin 1937.
Hawkins, Gerald S.: *Stonehenge Decoded*, London 1966.
Hesemann, Michael: *UFOs: Die Beweise*, München 1989/1991.
   . . . : *UFOs: Die Kontakte,* München 1990.
Howe, Linda Moulton: *Alien Harvest*, Littleton/Co. 1989.

Jacobs, David M.: *Secret Life*, New York 1992.
Jung, Carl Gustav: *A Modern Myth*, London 1960.
   . . . : *Psychology and Alchemy*, London 1973.

Krönig, Jürgen (ed.): *Das Rätsel geht weiter*, Frankfurt 1991.
   . . . : *Spuren im Korn*, Frankfurt 1992.

Malone, Caroline: *Avebury,* London 1989.
Martineau, LaVan: *The Rocks Begin to Speak*, Las Vegas 1973.
Meaden, Terence (ed.): *Circles from the Sky*, London 1991.
   . . . : *The Goddess of the Stones*, London 1991.
Michell, John: *View Over Atlantis*, London.
   . . . : *New Light on the Ancient Mysteries of Glastonbury*, Glastonbury 1990.
   . . . : *Dowsing the Crop Circles*, Glastonbury 1991.

Miller, Hamish/Broadhurst, Paul: *The Sun and the Serpent*, Launceston/Cornwall 1989.

Moosbrugger, Guido: *Und sie fliegen doch!* München 1991.

Noyes, Ralph (ed.): *The Crop Circle Enigma*, Bath 1990.

North American Inst. for Crop Circle Res. (eds): *North American Crop Circles and Related Physical Traces in 1990*, Winnipeg, Manitoba 1991.

Page, Christian/O.C.I.P.E.: *Manitoba (Canada) Crop Circles 1990*, St.-Jean-Sur-Richelieu, QC, 1991.

Peiniger, Hans-Werner: *Kornkreise in Deutschland* 1991, Lüdenscheid 1992.

Pieper, Werner: *Starke Plätze*, Lörbach o.J. (ca. 1986).

Purce, Jill: *The Mystic Spiral*, London 1974.

Randles, Jenny, Street, Dot & Butler, Brenda: *Sky Crash*. Sudbury 1984.

Randles, Jenny & Fuller, Paul: *Crop Circles – A Mystery Solved*, London 1990.

Ross, Allan C. *Mitakuye Oyasin*, Kyle/South Dakota 1989.

Shuttlewood, Arthur: *UFOs – Key to the New Age*, London 1971.

Sitchin, Zecharia: *The Twelfth Planet*, New York 1976.

. . . : *The Stairway to Heaven*, New York 1988.

. . . : *The Wars of Gods and Men*, New York 1990.

. . . : *The Lost Realms*, New York 1990.

Spencer, John: *The UFO Encyclopedia*, London 1991.

Tobisch, Oswald: *Kult, Symbol, Schrift*, Baden-Baden 1963.

Waters, Frank: *The Book of the Hopi*.

Williams, Margo & Morgan, Carolyn: *The Answer*, Shanklin/Isle of Wight 1991.

Wirth, Herman: *Die heilige Urschrift der Menschheit*, Fulda 1979.

Zaborsky, Oskar von: *Urvätererbe in Deutscher Volkskunst*, Leipzig 1936.

Articles:

The Cereologist, Nr. 1-5, 1990-92, Hearne Ho, No. Wooton, Shepton Mallett, Somerset BA4 4HW.

Magazin 2000 Nr. 83-91, München 1990-92, Worringerstr, 1, 4000 Düsseldorf 1.

Anthony Dodd: "UFO Update", in *UFO – The Journal of UFO Investigation* Nr. 1, Leeds, Yorkshire 1991.

John Haddington: "The Year of the Vajra", in: *Global Link*, Blockerley/Glos, Nr. 44, Autumn 1990.

Nikolai Nowgorodow: "Magischeskije Krusi we Jigulja;" in: *Mir Neiswedannogo*, Nr. 2-3, Tomsk 1991.

Dr. Vladimir V. Rubtsov: "Soviet Ice Ring", in: *MUFON UFO Journal* Nr. 282, Seguin/Texas 1991.

Michael Strainic: "Once Upon a Time in the Wheat", in: *MUFON UFO Journal* Nr. 284, Seguin/Texas 1991.

Armen Victorian: "Crop Circle Phenomena: The Truth"; in: *UFO Magazine* Nr. 1, Leeds, Yorkshire 1992.

INDEX

abductions 122, 162
Adam's Grave 36, 72, 141, 154, 162
Afghanistan 62
Akkadian cylinder-seal 99
Alberta 66
alchemy 135
Alexander, Steve 73, 78
Alton Barnes 26, 144–5, 162
Alton Priors 34
ancient sites 90
Andrews, Colin 17, 22, 28, 31, 41, 43, 73, 79, 93, 140, 152, 157–8, 160, 162
Andrews, Richard 93
Andreasson, Betty 104–6
Angels' Hair 19
animals, mutilated 121
Anunnaki 100, 103, 105–6, 116, 130
Asclepios 98
Atkinson, Prof R.J. 9
Attwell, Rachel 15
Australia 61
Avalon 13
Avebury 9–11, 92, 95, 107, 110, 161

Bailey Alice 129
Barbury Castle 38, 71, 96, 111–2, 133, 135, 141
Beckhampton 21, 24
Beckjord, John Erik 133–4, 142
bee 160
Belgium 55
Bell, Dr.Fred 74
Bentwaters AFB 117
Besant, Leon 73
Blake, William 12, 14
Bond, Bryce 7

Bornheim 55
Boston 68
Bower, Doug 4, 39, 151–2
Bower/Chorley 4, 39, 41–3, 133, 144, 159
Branson, Richard 28
Bratton 20
Bratton Castle 27–8
Brazil 62
Bristol 157
British Airways 75
Broadhurst, Paul 12, 91
Brough, Graham 40, 43
Brown, Ken 151
Bulgaria 58
Butleigh Wootton 33
Butler, Brenda 117
buzzing noises 56
Buttlar, Johannes von 36, 54, 82

Canada 64
Canada, Steve 130
Carp, Ont. 120
Carrie, Mike 141
Carson, Tim 26
CE5 Initiative 147
Celtic Cross 22, 35–6, 152, 160
Celtic Symbolism 133
Centre for Crop Circle Studies 153
Chalice Well 13
Charity Downs 22
Cheesefoot Head 23, 25, 33, 79, 132, 141
Cherhill 154
Chilcomb Farm 25
Chorley, Dave 4, 39
Chorost, Michael 80, 83, 147

Churinga Stone 91
Circles Phenomenon research 23, 145
Circlegate 44
Circular Evidence 22
CIS 58
Clatford 127
Cley Hill 7, 14, 156
Concorde 75
Cornference 37
Crawley Down 26
Crop Circle Communique 29
crop circles, occurrence 4
CSETI 147, 161
Cydonia 107–110
Cydonia geometry 109, 111
Czech Republic 58, 161

D & M Pyramid 109–10, 112
Dames, Michael 126
Davies, Barbara 144
Day, Fred 30
Deetken, Chad 154, 160
Defence, Ministry of 29, 31
Delgado, Pat 18, 22, 31, 40, 44, 79, 140
delphinogram 42, 80, 131
DePalma, Bruce 108
Dexter, Adrian 158–9
Dharma Wheel 133, 152
diatonic scale 132
DiPietro, Vincent 107
Dodd, Anthony 32, 72, 106
Dowell, Colette 111, 154
Drudacker 155
Dudley, Marshall 83
Dutton, Roy 77, 86, 149

East Meon 145
EFODEN 53
Egypt 62
electromagnetism 24, 85
Elizabeth, Queen 31
Emenegger, Robert 114
energy, free 112
energy lines, centres 97
Estevan 66
extra-terrestrials, ... contact 115, 117, 119–20

Feng Shui 91
Firs Farm 37, 72, 84, 145
fish 145
Fowler, Omar 84
France 56
Freeman, Mary 22, 70

galaxy 160
Germany 50, 146, 161
Glastonbury 12–3, 33
golden mean 108
Good, Timothy 122
Goold, Rita 23
Gorbachev, Mikhail 102
Grasdorf 52
Great Circle Lines 90
Green, Michael 128–30, 132
Greer, Dr.Stephen M. 147, 149–50, 156
Grist, Brian 71, 134
Gulf Breeze 67, 148

Haddington, John, Earl of 25, 128, 133
Harmonic Convergence 148
Harris, Dave 32
Hartcliffe 156
Hawkins, Prof.Gerald S. 9, 131–3
Heerlen 49–50
Hildesheim 52
Hoagland, Richard C. 107–8, 110
hoax 28, 30, 32, 37, 55, 146, 151–2
hoax competition 146
hoax hypothesis 154
hoaxers 41–2, 142, 153, 158, 160
Holloman AFB 114–5
Hopi Indians 123
Horton, Stephen 21, 37, 145
Howe, Linda Moulton 115, 121–2

Hynek, J. Allen 122
Hullhorst-Huchzen 161
Hungary 56

ice circles 68
Ickfield Moor 125
Ickleton 38
Illinois 68
image-analysis 107
insectograms 33–4
Ireland 48
Irving, Robert 44, 46, 152, 158–9
Italy 56

Japan 61
Jigulja 59
Joseph of Arimathaea 12
Jung, Carl Gustav 136

Keen, Montague 147
Kennewick 68
Kingston, Isabelle 95, 112, 135, 140, 152
King, Harry 120
Koch, Joachim 163
Krasnodar 59
Krasnoyarsk 161
Krönig, Jürgen 30, 31, 151
Kybord, Hans-Jurgen 163
Kücück, Kemal 53

Lethbridge 65
Levengood, Prof.W.C. 81–2
Levett's Farm 37
ley lines 90
Lockeridge 80
Lovelock, James E. 93
Lyons, Dr Adrian 23

Macnish, John 35, 151
Malachim 104, 113
Maltwood, Katherina 13
mandala 128
Mandelbrot, Benoit 38
Mandelbrot Set, The 38, 135
Manitoba 66
Marburg 52, 73
Mars 102, 107
Mars face 107, 111

Mars Observer 113
Martineau, John 142
Mary Line 92
mathematical modelling 86
Matthews, John 133
MBF Services 43
Meaden, Dr.Terence 5, 21, 36, 38, 88, 125
mechanical failure 24, 26
Meier, Edward (Billy) 56
Merlin 8
Metepec 63
Mexico 63
Michell, John 38, 76, 92, 123, 127, 133–4, 136, 142, 158–60
microwave action 84
Milk Hill 25, 137
Miller, Hamish 12, 91
Minnesota 68
Molenaar, Gregory 107
Morcom, Stanley 80
Morgan's Hill 35
Morgenstern, David 35
MUFON 67

Nazca 124
Neptune 110
Netherlands 49
Netze 55
New Zealand 61
Newgrange 125
Nibiru 100–3, 110, 119, 130–1
North American Institute for Crop Circle Research 68
Nowgorodow, Dr. Nicolai 59

Oadby 22
Oechsler, Bob 118
official reactions 26, 30, 32, 47, 162
Ogawa, Mitchihito 36
Ogbourne Maizey 96
Ohtsuki, Prof.Yoshi-Hiko 62
oil-seed rape 19
Oliver's Castle 150
Operation Argus 147, 154
Operation Blackbird 26
Operation Blue Hill 36
Operation White Crow 26
Ozora 57

Pedley, George 61
Pennsylvania 68
Pepperbox Hill 18
Phobus 2 112
pictograms 25
Pinotti, Dr.Robert 6
Pitt, Martin 37, 77, 142
plasma vortex 21
porcupine 66
power places 14
prehistoric sites 76
Presley, Reg 148
Project Circle Study 49
Project SIGMA 115
Project Chameleon 35, 141
Puerto Rico 62
Pyramid City 108

radioactivity 53, 56, 83, 159
Randles, Jenny 21
Reagan, Ronald 102
Rendlesham Forest 116
Robertson Panel 32
Roermond 49
Romania 57
Roy, Prof.Archie 23

sacred geometry 133
sacred sites 55
Sala 48
Saskatchewan 66
Sayer, John 39
Schnabel, Jim 44, 152–3, 159
Scorpion 158–9
Sheldrake, Rupert 93

Shining Ones, The 97
Shuttlewood, Arthur 7
Siberia 161
Silbury Hill 10, 22, 37, 70, 95, 97, 110, 126, 145, 162
Sitchin, Zecharia 100–3, 110, 113, 116
Skyllberg 49
snails 144
snow circles 62
Socorro 116
soil analysis 83–4
Solar logos 124–5
Spain 56
Spagyric analysis 81
Star Hill 7
Stonehenge 8–9
Stukeley, William 11
St.Michael Line 13, 91
Sumerians 99, 130
Sumerian texts 105, 130
Sun Bear 139
Sweden 48
Switzerland 56
symbols 123–5, 127–31
synchroton 78

Taylor, Busty 18, 32, 73, 90, 141
Taylor, Teddy, M.P. 30
Telegraph Hill 26, 124, 142
Tenen, Stan 108, 110
Tennessee 68
tetrahedral metaphors 108
Tholus 110
Tickle, David 74
Tilt, David 93
trilling 23–4, 156

Trombly, Adam 110
Turkey 62

UBI (United Bureau of Investigations) 153
UFO connection 76, 105
UFO sightings 15–6, 19, 55–6, 63, 67, 70–2, 106, 120, 148–9, 150, 156, 160–2
UFO-nests 59, 76
Underwood, Guy 92
Upton Scudamore 20, 145
USA 67, 161

Victorian, Dr.Armen 45, 84
von Daniken, Erich 125

Waggon & Horses 90
Wansdyke Watch 73
Warminster 72, 14, 21
Warren, Larry 116
Watchers, The 95, 104, 116
Watkins, Alfred 90
Weiss, Dr.Robert 24
Wessex Sceptics 37, 42, 142, 152
Westbury 18, 19, 27
White Horses 106
Winchester 17
Wingfield, George 20, 23, 25, 29, 34, 43, 71, 79, 97, 137, 141–2
Winterbourne Stoke 25, 88, 124
Wintle, Richard 38
Woodborough Hill 150

Zamora, Lonnie 116
Zoser Pyramid 97
Zuckerman, Lord 31